Cambridge
IGCSE™ and O Level

····························

Literature
in English

····························

Geoff Case • Rose Forshaw
Series editor: Penny Yates

HODDER
EDUCATION
AN HACHETTE UK COMPANY

The Publishers would like to thank the following for permission to reproduce copyright material.

Cambridge International copyright material in this publication is reproduced under licence and remains the intellectual property of Cambridge Assessment International Education.

Every effort has been made to trace all copyright holders, but if any have been inadvertently overlooked, the Publishers will be pleased to make the necessary arrangements at the first opportunity.

The questions, example answers, marks awarded and / or comments that appear in this book were written by the authors. In examination, the way marks would be awarded to answers like these may be different.

Exam-style questions and sample answers have been written by the authors. In examinations, the way marks are awarded may be different. References to assessment and / or assessment preparation are the publisher's interpretation of the syllabus requirements and may not fully reflect the approach of Cambridge Assessment International Education.

Third-party websites, publications and resources referred to in this publication have not been endorsed by Cambridge Assessment International Education.

Although every effort has been made to ensure that website addresses are correct at time of going to press, Hodder Education cannot be held responsible for the content of any website mentioned in this book. It is sometimes possible to find a relocated web page by typing in the address of the home page for a website in the URL window of your browser.

Hachette UK's policy is to use papers that are natural, renewable and recyclable products and made from wood grown in well-managed forests and other controlled sources. The logging and manufacturing processes are expected to conform to the environmental regulations of the country of origin.

Orders: please contact Hachette UK Distribution, Hely Hutchinson Centre, Milton Road, Didcot, Oxfordshire, OX11 7HH. Telephone: +44 (0)1235 827827. Email education@hachette.co.uk Lines are open from 9 a.m. to 5 p.m., Monday to Friday. You can also order through our website: www.hoddereducation.com

ISBN: 978 1 3983 1751 2

© Rose Forshaw and Geoff Case 2021

First published in 2021 by
Hodder Education,
An Hachette UK Company
Carmelite House
50 Victoria Embankment
London EC4Y 0DZ

www.hoddereducation.com

Impression number   10 9 8 7 6 5 4 3 2 1

Year   2025 2024 2023 2022 2021

Cover photo © just2shutter – stock.adobe.com

Illustrations by Chris Bladon Design

Typeset by Chris Bladon Design

Printed in Italy

A catalogue record for this title is available from the British Library.

Contents

How to use this book

Organisation

This student's book, endorsed by Cambridge Assessment International Education, is organised in a way to make your study of Literature in English as rewarding and successful as possible.

The book begins with three units designed to introduce you to the study of Literature in English and help you familiarise yourself with the requirements of the course and the key skills you will need to develop.

Following this, there are sections dedicated to each of the three main forms of literature you will be studying: poetry, prose and drama. Every section is made up of seven units, each of which takes a poem, story or extract from a novel or play as its starting point and focuses on a different aspect of literature.

Ensure that you don't read the extract until directed to by an exercise, as some units contain exercises to complete *before* reading the extract.

The units are divided into several parts:
» **The text or extract:** A short poem, story or extract from a literary text. Difficult terms or phrases are defined in a glossary.
» **First impressions:** Exercises designed to foster an initial response to the text, or to introduce you to the unit focus.
» **Finding evidence:** Exercises to help you improve your understanding of the particular literary focus of the unit, using evidence from the text in question.
» **Writing practice:** Opportunities to develop your essay-writing skills using the evidence and ideas you have accumulated in the unit so far. There are also chances to assess the quality of other students' written work. (Please note: the example responses and teacher comments featured in this book have been written by the authors.)
» **Set-text focus:** A chance to apply the skills and knowledge you have developed throughout the unit to your set texts.

At the end of the book, there are two units that are designed to help you consolidate the writing skills you have developed throughout the course.

Features

The following features are included to support you throughout the course:

In this unit, you will...

A summary of the content to be covered in the unit. You will have a chance to check your understanding of these points in the unit summary at the end of each unit.

Glossary

Definitions of words from the literary extracts that may be unfamiliar.

Key terms

Definitions of important literary terms. These are collated in the glossary at the back of the book.

In this unit, you will:
- Identify quotations that demonstrate a poet's meaning and learn how to use them when writing essays.
- Explore the ways in which a poem creates meanings, beyond its surface meaning.
- Examine how writers use language and structure to create and shape meanings.
- Develop a personal understanding of a poet's intentions.

Key terms

Metaphor: A description of one thing as another thing that is mostly unrelated to make a comparison that highlights the similarity between the two things

Simile: A comparison of one thing to another, using the word 'as' or 'like' – 'They are *like* pale hair' is an example of a simile; the comparison gives emphasis to a description or makes it more vivid, but similes are generally thought of as less powerful than metaphors

Hyperbole: Exaggerated claims or statements, not meant to be taken literally

Personification: The description of an object or animal as if they have human characteristics

---

Glossary

Elegy: A sad poem, usually used to lament the death of a loved one

Cairn: A Scottish word, meaning a mound of stones built by people as a burial mound or memorial

Pipes: Bagpipes, a musical instrument associated with Scotland; they are often played ceremonially at funerals

Aaronsrod: A plant that naturally grows much taller than other plants: Aaron was a biblical figure and the brother of Moses, who led the Israelites out of Egypt and into the Promised Land; like Moses's rod, Aaron's rod had miraculous powers, demonstrated during the Plagues of Egypt – on one occasion, instructed by God, Aaron threw down his rod in front of the Egyptian Pharaoh and it turned into a serpent that ate all the other serpents conjured by Pharaoh's sorcerers; the rod is also a natural symbol of authority, as the tool used by a shepherd to correct and guide his flock, as well as being a plant that naturally grows much taller than other plants

Sods: Turf, pieces of grass attached to the soil

Burning-glass: A large lens used to catch the sun's rays to create fire in olden days

---

TIP

The title of a poem is often a good indicator of what the poem is about, the mood of the poem and / or the poet's intentions. Make sure you always read and think about the title of a poem before you read it.

MAKING CONNECTIONS

A poem in which the mood changes between the beginning and the end is 'Search for My Tongue' (Unit 7). Bhatt initially seems confused and unhappy but by the end feels triumphant and reassured. Are there mood changes in any of the other poems you have read?

Take your learning further

1 Derek Walcott was an admirer of another Caribbean poet, the Jamaican reggae singer / songwriter Bob Marley (1945 to 1981). In 1991, on a BBC Radio 4 programme called 'Desert Island Discs', Walcott described the 'haunting' nature, 'poignancy' and 'accuracy' of 'No Woman, No Cry', a song in which Marley depicts the life he used to live in the poor capital of Jamaica, Kingston, as a struggling poet and singer. The poem is a call to a woman in his life to be positive and not to grieve the bad times. Find the lyrics to 'No Woman, No Cry' and read them alongside an audio recording of the song. Consider why Walcott may have considered this poem / song so powerful. Does it have the same impact on you? Why? Or why not?
2 Choose a poem you have already read and worked on in this section of the book. Now that you have a more confident grasp of the skills you need to analyse a poem, can you see how your personal response to the poem could be improved? Make notes on how you could have written more effectively and demonstrated a more informed response to the poem.

Tips

Guidance and advice to help you with your studies.

Making connections

Interesting links with texts, concepts or skills discussed in other units.

Take your learning further

Extension exercises that give you the opportunity to explore a particular author, text or theme in more depth.

INTRODUCING LITERATURE IN ENGLISH

· ·

Units

1 Making the most of your course

The information in this section is based on the Cambridge IGCSE and IGCSE (9–1) Literature in English syllabuses (0475/0992) for examination from 2020, the Cambridge O Level Literature in English syllabus (2010) for examination from 2023 and the Cambridge IGCSE World Literature syllabus (0408) for examination from 2022. You should always refer to the appropriate syllabus document for the year of your examination to confirm the details and for more information. The syllabus document is available on the Cambridge International website at www.cambridgeinternational.org.

Why use this book?

This book aims greatly to enhance your enjoyment and appreciation of literature. You will read literary texts from different cultures and in the different **forms** of poetry, prose and drama. As the course progresses, and you work your way through the book, you will learn how to communicate your own personal response to literature appropriately and effectively through an appreciation of the many different methods that authors use to achieve their effects. Finally, it is hoped that this book, and your course as a whole, will contribute to your own personal growth as a human being – emotionally, intellectually, imaginatively and aesthetically – and that your experience and exploration of literature will deepen your appreciation of areas of human concern.

This student's book supports three different Cambridge International syllabuses:
» Cambridge IGCSE and IGCSE (9–1) Literature in English (0475/0992) for examination from 2020
» Cambridge O Level Literature in English (2010) for examination from 2023
» Cambridge IGCSE World Literature (0408) for examination from 2022.

Your teacher will be able to tell you which syllabus you are following.

Key term

Form: The text type a writer chooses to communicate in; the three main forms in English literature are poetry, prose and drama – within those main forms are other forms; for example, a sonnet is a poetic form and a short story is a prose form

Cambridge IGCSE and IGCSE (9–1) Literature in English (0475/0992) and Cambridge O Level Literature in English (2010): assessment overview

Assessment varies according to syllabus, although the literary analysis skills that you need to develop are the same for each one, and are detailed in the Assessment Objectives. You can read more about these in Unit 2 'Key skills'.

All the texts in the exams (and any texts you choose for coursework) will have been originally written in English.

The Cambridge IGCSE Literature in English (0475) and Cambridge O Level Literature in English (2010) syllabuses are graded from A* to G.

The Cambridge IGCSE Literature in English syllabus (0992) is graded from 9 to 1.

For the Cambridge O Level Literature in English (2010) syllabus, all students take Paper 1 – Poetry and Prose and Paper 2 – Drama. For Cambridge IGCSE Literature in English (0475/0992), there are three different assessment routes. Your teacher will be able to tell you which route you are following:

Cambridge O Level Literature in English (2010)	Cambridge IGCSE Literature in English (0475/0992)		
All candidates take: ↓	**Route 1** ↓	**Route 2** ↓	**Route 3** ↓
Paper 1 – Poetry and Prose Two questions: one on a poetry set text and one on a prose set text 1 hour 30 minutes 50 marks (50%)			
Paper 2 – Drama Two questions on two set texts 1 hour 30 minutes 50 marks (50%)	**Paper 3 – Drama (open text)** One question on one set text 45 minutes 25 marks (25%)		
		Paper 4 – Unseen One question on a new extract (either poetry or prose) requiring critical commentary 1 hour 15 minutes 25 marks (25%)	**Component 5 – Coursework** Portfolio of two assignments, each on a different text 25 marks (25%)

Cambridge IGCSE World Literature (0408): assessment overview

The texts in the exams (and any texts you choose for coursework) can have been written in any language and translated into English.

All students are graded from A* to G.

There are three parts to the assessment:

Component 1 – Coursework

Two written assignments: one on a drama text and one on a prose text

One must be a critical essay and one must be an empathic response

50 marks (40%)

Paper 2 – Unseen Poetry

Two questions on one unseen poem

1 hour 15 minutes

30 marks (20%)

Paper 3 – Set Text

Two questions: one extract-based and one general essay question

1 hour 30 minutes

50 marks (40%)

Assessment Objectives

Every subject at IGCSE or O Level has its own Assessment Objectives (AOs) that specify the skills it is important for students to develop. As you learn to appreciate literature critically and become an active reader, you will practise several key skills. By the end of the course, your aim is to show that you can:

AO1	Show detailed knowledge of the content of literary texts in the three main forms (drama, poetry and prose), supported by reference to the text.
AO2	Understand the meanings of literary texts and their contexts, and explore texts beyond surface meanings to show deeper awareness of ideas and attitudes.
AO3	Recognise and appreciate ways in which writers use language, structure and form to create and shape meanings and effects.
AO4	Communicate a sensitive and informed personal response to literary texts.

The skills in this table all depend on each other, and you will often find that when you write about literary texts you are showing more than one skill at a time. However, it is useful to know and understand the different AOs, so that you can measure your own growth and progress as you work through your course.

Question types

The questions you are asked to answer in written exercises in this book and on your literature course as a whole will usually invite you critically to evaluate the methods that the writers use to convey ideas and attitudes. There are a number of situations in which you might be asked to do this:

» Questions based on your whole set text
» Questions based on passages from your set text
» Questions about texts you've never seen before ('unseens')
» Critical essays for coursework.

You should recognise how the questions you are asked to answer enable you to show your skills of critical evaluation.

Command words and question stems

You will begin to recognise certain 'command words' and question stems that invite you to answer in a particular way. 'Explore' has a specific meaning in literature questions: when it is used, you should write in detail about the particular aspects the question mentions.

Command word	What it means
Explore	Write in detail about particular aspects
Question stems	
What do you think?	
What are your feelings about [...]?	
Explore the ways in which [...].	
How does the writer convey [...]?	
In what ways does the writer [...]?	
What do you find particularly memorable [...]?	

In this student's book you will learn how to tackle these types of questions and have opportunities to practise your skills in answering them.

Key words

The key words in the question are the important words on which your essay response will focus.

For example, take this question stem and command word for a question based on a prose text:
'Explore the ways in which...'
↓
Then comes the author's name:
'... [author's name]...'
↓
Then come the key words:
'presents **poverty** and **injustice**...'
↓
Then, depending on whether you are answering a passage-based question or a question based on a whole text, either:
'... at this moment in the novel.' (extract)
OR
'in [text's name].' (whole text)

Looking at this question as a whole, 'poverty' and 'injustice' are the key words, which tell you what your essay focus is. The question stem 'Explore the ways in which' tells you what approach you should take. The word 'ways' is an important word, asking you to look in detail at the methods the author uses. You will learn more about this in the pages of this book, and there is detailed essay-writing practice in Unit 25.

Coursework essays and empathic responses

Coursework essays have different requirements from timed essays. You can learn more about how to write these – and empathic responses – in Unit 26.

Applying your skills to your set texts

As you have seen in the assessment overview, there are a number of assessments for which you will be asked to write in detail about your **set texts**. These are texts that you and / or your teacher will decide upon ahead of time and that you will need to study in detail. This book provides you with regular opportunities – in the 'Set-text focus' exercises – to apply the skills that you have learned to your set texts, but you must also take responsibility for ensuring that you know and understand your set texts, and feel confident in answering questions on them.

Your teacher will give you guidance on how to read and revise your set texts. However, there are some strategies you can use by yourself when reading and revising to maximise your learning and help you prepare for the essays you will be asked to write. Here are some strategies that will help you to study and learn independently:

> Key terms
>
> **Theme:** A key idea or subject that is repeated throughout a text
>
> **Context:** The circumstances around a text; for example, the writer's life or the historical background

» After reading a poem, or a section of a drama or prose text in class, reread it at home, thinking about the skills and ideas you covered in class.
» Make notes about **themes**, characters, **contexts**, language and other literary devices while you are reading and rereading.
» Discuss your reading and your ideas with a friend in your class to see if they have made the same notes or have noticed anything different that it would be useful for you to make a note of too.
» Test yourself or your friend on important quotations. You can test yourself by looking at the quotation for a minute, then covering it up and trying to write it down. If you don't get it right the first time, do it again until you do.
» Read the next chapter or scene of your prose or drama set text ahead of your lesson, thinking about how it builds on what you have already read.
» When you have completely finished the text, take the old notes you made during the course of reading and put them in a central file under headings:
  – Key characters (write down the name of each key character as a heading)
  – Themes
  – Contexts.
» Under each of these three headings, collect important quotations and what they mean, as well as comments on language and literary devices they incorporate.

If you organise your notes like this, you will be well prepared for a question on a character or theme in your set text.

Unit summary

In this unit, you have:
● Considered the reasons for studying literature as a subject.
● Discovered the structure of the exam papers and coursework in the Cambridge IGCSE and IGCSE (9–1) Literature in English (0475/0992), Cambridge O Level Literature in English (2010) or Cambridge IGCSE World Literature (0408) syllabuses.
● Found out the key skills you should aim to develop.
● Learned about the types of questions you may be asked to address.
● Thought about how to apply the skills taught in this book to your set texts.

You may want to refer back to this unit throughout your studies.

2 Key skills

- Think about the importance of active and independent learning.
- Practise some of the skills covered by the Assessment Objectives.
- Begin thinking about some of the aspects of literature – language, structure and form – that you will need to consider throughout your course.

Active learning

One of the most important skills you can develop is to be an active learner, rather than a passive one. This means you need to think about what you are aiming to learn, and work out the ways you can achieve it. When you are reading, you should think about what you understand and be prepared to find out more about what you don't – perhaps by referring to a dictionary, or considering the problem from another angle. Many of the exercises in this book are designed to help you develop your active learning skills, by inviting you to discuss and explain your thoughts; think about texts in unusual or creative ways; or to think about what you have learned so far and whether you are confident or need more practice. The more you understand how you best learn, the more active a learner you are.

This unit takes the Assessment Objectives that you met in Unit 1 as a starting point and introduces some of the key skills you will need to develop as part of your literature course. A good understanding of the skills that you need will help you focus your attention on what is important while working through the remainder of the book and when studying your set texts.

Knowing your texts

AO1	Show detailed knowledge of the content of literary texts in the three main forms (drama, poetry and prose), supported by reference to the text.

Key term

Literary aspect: An essential element within a text: the structure, the language, the themes and ideas, the character and perspective, the setting and the mood

To demonstrate a detailed knowledge of your set texts in drama, poetry and prose, you need to read and reread them carefully over the duration of your course. Reading may take place in your classroom, but you will also need to do as much reading as possible independently or at home. You need to make notes on your reading and also seek help with any **aspects** of your texts that you find difficult. This book has a number of exercises that will help you to develop your skills and will answer many of your questions about how to read your set text.

CHOOSING AND USING EVIDENCE FROM THE TEXT

One essential skill you will need to master very quickly is the effective use of quotations to support your notes. Where quotations are concerned, 'less is more' is the best advice you can heed. Quotations are intended to support your points and so you need to look carefully at the words of the text and work out how much you actually need as evidence. You also need to be able to analyse and explain the relevance to your argument of the quotations you have chosen, or to the question you are answering.

Exercise 1

Read the following passage from *Wuthering Heights,* a novel by the English writer Emily Brontë (1818 to 1848). At this point, the child Heathcliff is speaking about how he and Catherine have run across the moors from their own house to look through the windows to find out about the privileged lives of Edgar and Isabella Linton.

> Both of us were able to look in by standing on the basement, and clinging to the ledge, and we saw – ah! it was beautiful – a splendid place carpeted with crimson, and crimson-covered chairs and tables, and a pure white ceiling bordered by gold, a shower of glass-drops hanging in silver chains from the centre, and shimmering with little soft tapers. Old Mr. and Mrs. Linton were not there; Edgar and his sisters had it entirely to themselves. Shouldn't they have been happy? We should have thought ourselves in heaven! And now, guess what your good children were doing? Isabella – I believe she is eleven, a year younger than Cathy – lay screaming at the farther end of the room, shrieking as if witches were running red-hot needles into her. Edgar stood on the hearth weeping silently, and in the middle of the table sat a little dog, shaking its paw and yelping...
>
> Emily Brontë, from *Wuthering Heights*

A student has copied some quotations to illustrate Edgar and Isabella's lifestyle. The student's teacher had a look at the notes and made the improvements to the notes on 'Where Edgar and Isabella' live, as shown below.

> **Key term**
>
> **Perspective:** Like a lens through which readers view characters and events in a text; the perspective of a text is created by the speaker: we interpret the characters and events based on what the speaker shows and tells us

From Heathcliff's **perspective**: 'ah! it was beautiful'

Lavish lifestyle in beautiful house: 'splendid place', 'carpeted with crimson', 'crimson-covered chairs and tables', 'pure white ceiling bordered by gold', 'shower of glass-drops hanging in silver chains… shimmering with little soft tapers'

Where Edgar and Isabella live:

'Both of us were able to look in by standing on the basement, and clinging to the ledge, and we saw – ah! it was beautiful – a splendid place carpeted with crimson, and crimson-covered chairs and tables, and a pure white ceiling bordered by gold, a shower of glass-drops hanging in silver chains from the centre, and shimmering with little soft tapers.'

What Edgar and Isabella are like:

'Shouldn't they have been happy? We should have thought ourselves in heaven! And now, guess what your good children were doing? Isabella – I believe she is eleven, a year younger than Cathy – lay screaming at the farther end of the room, shrieking as if witches were running red-hot needles into her. Edgar stood on the hearth weeping silently.'

The teacher has improved these notes by:
» making a point
» only selecting relevant evidence
» considering the perspective from which these quotations are spoken.

a Improve the student's notes under the heading 'What Edgar and Isabella are like'. Write down your improved notes by following the teacher's model.

The student took the teacher's improved notes and used some of the evidence in a paragraph as part of an essay:

> **Student's paragraph**
>
> Brontë emphasises the contrast between Heathcliff and the Lintons by having Heathcliff describe the Lintons' house. He describes their **drawing room** as 'beautiful' and 'a splendid place' and lists the bright colours on show: the carpet, chairs and tables are 'crimson', the ceiling is 'pure white' and 'bordered by gold', and the chandelier is described as 'a shower of glass-drops hanging in silver chains'. The use of these bright colours, and in particular gold and silver, helps to create the **image** of an incredibly luxurious home with expensive furnishings. By describing the Lintons' drawing room in this way, Brontë shows the reader not only the lavish lifestyle that Edgar is used to, but also, through Heathcliff's awed response, that he is not used to such things.

b Use the notes you created about the characters of Edgar and Isabella to write a similar paragraph about the contrast between Heathcliff and the Lintons. Don't worry if you are not familiar with the novel; use the evidence that you have been given.

> **Key terms**
>
> **Drawing room:** A room with comfortable furniture, used for entertaining guests
>
> **Image / Imagery:** A word or phrase that prompts the reader to imagine the way that something looks, sounds, smells, feels or tastes

Reading for deeper meaning

A02	Understand the meanings of literary texts and their contexts, and explore texts beyond surface meanings to show deeper awareness of ideas and attitudes.

The starting point of reading anything is to understand its surface meaning. You are probably already very good at understanding the surface meaning of many texts, but this might be complicated by your set texts likely coming from many different historical periods, places and cultures. This means that they might refer to objects or ideas with which you are not familiar; therefore, you need to have some understanding of the context in which they were written.

It might also mean that some of the language used is unfamiliar to you. Consider this famous line spoken by Juliet in Shakespeare's *Romeo and Juliet*:

> O Romeo, Romeo, wherefore art thou Romeo?
>
> William Shakespeare, from *Romeo and Juliet*

The word 'wherefore' here seems instinctively as though it might simply be an old-fashioned way of saying 'where', and so it is commonly misunderstood. Its real meaning is 'why'. Juliet is asking Romeo why he is Romeo – or, more specifically, why he has to be a Montague, a member of the family that is feuding with Juliet's own family, the Capulets.

You are also probably already very good at understanding deeper meanings, too. Think about these common phrases:

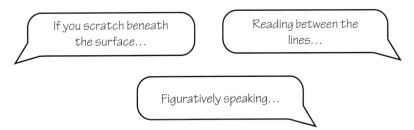

If you scratch beneath the surface…

Reading between the lines…

Figuratively speaking…

Because 'good' literature is often crafted to convey many layers of meaning in concise and sometimes very subtle ways, you must be alert and careful as a reader. The more you advance as a reader, the more you will detect these layers and become aware of such features as **subtexts**. You will become more able to engage actively with a text and develop skills such as **inference**. You will also learn to consider contexts such as the race, gender and age of the author and how these too impact on the meaning of a text.

> **Key terms**
>
> **Subtext:** A less obvious or unspoken meaning in a text
>
> **Infer:** Reading between the lines of a text to find clues to understand more than is said directly

Appreciating how writers use language, structure and form

A03	Recognise and appreciate ways in which writers use language, structure and form to create and shape meanings and effects.

A literary text is a crafted piece of work. This means that the writer has paid careful attention to **language choices**, **structure** and the form of the literary text because they all have to work together to convey meaning in the text.

> **Key terms**
>
> **Language choices:** The specific words that a writer chooses to use to convey particular ideas
>
> **Structure:** The sequence of ideas in a text and how it is put together

LANGUAGE

Words are the primary building blocks that writers use to tell a story or present ideas. Therefore, it is important to consider the language choices that an author makes, to think about why they decided to use the words that they did and try to explain the effects that these choices create.

The kind of features you might identify, and that you will have the opportunity to discuss in the later units of this book, include the use of adjectives, imagery, **metaphors** and **similes**, **hyperbole**, contrasting language and **personification**.

Key terms

Metaphor: A description of one thing as another thing that is mostly unrelated to make a comparison that highlights the similarity between the two things

Simile: A comparison of one thing to another, using the word 'as' or 'like' – 'They are *like* pale hair' is an example of a simile; the comparison gives emphasis to a description or makes it more vivid, but similes are generally thought of as less powerful than metaphors

Hyperbole: Exaggerated claims or statements, not meant to be taken literally

Personification: The description of an object or animal as if they have human characteristics

---

Exercise 2

Read this short description of Santiago, the **protagonist** of Ernest Hemingway's *The Old Man and the Sea*.

> The old man was thin and gaunt with deep wrinkles in the back of his neck. The brown blotches of the benevolent skin cancer the sun brings from its reflection on the tropic sea were on his cheeks. The blotches ran well down the sides of his face and his hands had the deep-creased scars from handling heavy fish on the cords. But none of these scars were fresh. They were as old as erosions in a fishless desert.
>
> Everything about him was old except his eyes and they were the same color as the sea and were cheerful and undefeated.
>
> Ernest Hemingway, from *The Old Man and the Sea*

a What is your general impression of Santiago? Explain your ideas with references to the passage.

b What literary devices can you identify in Hemingway's description? How do these devices help Hemingway create the impression of Santiago you described in part **a**? Write a sentence for each device. An example has been provided for you.

The use of the adjective 'gaunt' emphasises that Santiago is unhealthy and has suffered – perhaps he is unable to feed himself sufficiently.

Key term

Protagonist: A main character in a literary text

STRUCTURE

The way a literary text is structured is important too. Look at these images of a house under construction.

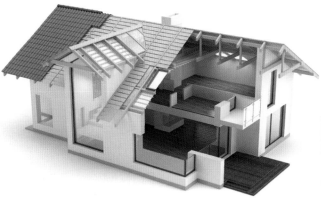

Before a house is constructed there is a plan or design drawn up by a skilled and trained person – an architect. When it is constructed there are many elements to its structure:

» Large elements of the structure include features like the roof, internal and external walls and floor.
» Medium-sized elements of the structure include the windows, stairways, doors and a heating system.
» Small elements of the structure include features like the individual bricks, the cement and the floorboards.

To understand how a text in literature is structured, try thinking of it as a big, beautiful architect-designed house that you are going to explore. You are going to try to understand how the architect has designed the text and how they have made each element work in structural harmony with other elements of the house.

Like the structure of a house, the structure of a text can be thought of as having large, medium-sized and small elements. You will learn about these elements and how to write about them in the units that follow.

Exercise 3

The following are all structural devices of a text.

full stops	chronological order	scenes	beginning	symbolism
resolution	paragraphs	monologue	dramatic irony	repetition

Write down three headings, as shown below:

Large	Medium-sized	Small

Put each structural device under the appropriate heading. You may not have come across the words in red before, so you might want to ask another person in the class or your teacher what they mean, or look them up in the glossary at the back of this book.

You will notice that some structural devices could go under a few headings, for example 'repetition', depending on whether it is repetition of single words, repetition of ideas or ongoing repetition of large parts of the text (for example, a **refrain** in a poem). Share your work with the rest of the class and explain the decisions you have made.

> **Key term**
>
> **Refrain:** A short part of a poem (or song) that is repeated between stanzas, like a chorus

FORM

Form is linked to structure. Look back to the pictures of a house under 'Structure'. The completed house is the final form towards which all the structural elements contributed.

The three main forms you will study in this course are poetry, prose and drama. However, within each of these forms, there are many subforms, each with their own rules and **conventions**.

> **Key term**
>
> **Conventions:** Typical features found within a literary genre

Exercise 4

Here are some poetic forms that you might have come across in your earlier years at school. See if you can remember what they are and what was particular about their form. Use a table like the one below to record your thoughts. The first one is done for you.

Poetic form	Description
Shape (also called 'concrete')	*A poem where the words take the shape of the object they are describing; for example, a poem about a tomato would appear as a circular shape on the page and may even take red colouring for its lettering.*
Haiku	
Limerick	
Acrostic	
Ballad	

There are many other very popular poetic forms, some of which you may come across in your set poem collection.

Here are three of the most common poetic forms that you might find in traditional English poetry:

» Sonnet (Petrarchan)
» Sonnet (Shakespearean)
» Ballad.

Here we will take a closer look at a Shakespearean sonnet, to allow you to familiarise yourself with some of the features you should be thinking about when considering a poem's form.

This is Shakespeare's 'Sonnet 130':

Sonnet 130

My mistress' eyes are nothing like the sun;
Coral is far more red than her lips' red;
If snow be white, why then her breasts are dun;
If hairs be wires, black wires grow on her head.
I have seen roses damasked, red and white,
But no such roses see I in her cheeks;
And in some perfumes is there more delight
Than in the breath that from my mistress reeks.
I love to hear her speak, yet well I know
That music hath a far more pleasing sound;
I grant I never saw a goddess go;
My mistress, when she walks, treads on the ground.
   And yet, by heaven, I think my love as rare
   As any she belied with false compare.

Key terms

Syllables: The sound elements in a word; for example, the word car|rot has two syllables in it and the word pot|a|to has three syllables in it

Metrical feet: Groups or units of two or three stressed or unstressed syllables; they are repeated in lines of poetry to form the poem's rhythm

Iambs: Metrical feet made up of two syllables: an unstressed one followed by a stressed one

Iambic pentameter: A line of poetry that contains five iambs

Metre: The rhythmic structure of a line of poetry

Rhyme scheme: The pattern of rhymes at the end of each line in poetry

Volta: An Italian word that means 'turn'; it is a 'turn' in thought or ideas

Sonnets are the traditional form for love poetry and Shakespeare's sonnet here is no exception: it is a love poem. If you read the poem carefully (it's best to read it out loud) you will notice that it is very carefully crafted.

» Count the number of **syllables** on each line (you should find that there are ten).
» Each line is divided into five **metrical feet** of two syllables each.
» These feet are called **iambs** and they are made up of two syllables: an unstressed syllable followed by a stressed syllable.
» Lines of five iambs are called **iambic pentameter**.

Look at the first line again and read it out loud.

    My **mis** | tress' **eyes** | are **no** | thing **like** | the **sun**

The syllables in bold are the accented ones and the vertical lines divide up the five feet.

The **metre** isn't the only pattern. There is more to notice.

» Sonnets are always 14 lines long.
» Shakespeare's sonnets take the following **rhyme scheme**: abab cdcd efef gg.
» Just before the last two lines of a Shakespearean sonnet, there is a **volta**.

If you read the first 12 lines, you will see that Shakespeare is telling us that his loved one is an ordinary mortal woman. He does not idealise her looks. He even says she has bad breath! However, there is a little twist in the last two lines where he tells us that his loved one is as wonderful as any woman who has been misrepresented by idealised comparisons: in simple terms, he loves her for who she is.

Developing a personal response

A04	Communicate a sensitive and informed personal response to literary texts.

Exercise 5

> I'm definitely right! Pelé was the best footballer of all time.

> No, you're wrong – it was Diego Maradona.

The two people here are expressing a personal response (or personal opinion) based on what they have seen of the skill of the two footballers.
a How successful do you think they will be in persuading each other? Why will or won't they be?
b What kind of things do you think they will talk about to support their opinions?
c Explain to the class or another person sitting next to you what you think.

It is always important, when putting across a personal response to a literary text, that you make your arguments convincing. Your evidence, in the form of the language and structure of the text, needs to be careful and accurate and effectively explained. As you work through the units and the tasks in this book, your skills of critical evaluation will develop, and you will learn not only to make judgements about the effectiveness of the literature you are reading, but also to make informed personal responses based on the evidence you have found.

Exercise 6

Look at the words in this box. They are just some of the language and structural devices used by authors that you have to take into consideration when reading for meaning and communicating an informed personal response. Think about how they have been used in literary works you have already read in school or at home.

narrator	tone	viewpoint	language (choices)
rhyme (scheme)	symbolism	style	voice
juxtaposition	structure	form	rhythm

If you don't know what all these devices are or can't think of how they can be used to aid meaning in texts, don't worry: as you continue on your literature course, you will become far more skilled at understanding how writers use these devices. For now, if you wish, you can look up these words in the glossary at the back of the book and find out what they mean.

Overall, the most important exercise you can do to support your understanding of literature and develop confidence in analysing it is to read widely and often – this will help you to develop an understanding of the many and varied ways in which writers craft their work. The more experience you have of different types of literature, the more clearly you will be able to see what they are trying to do, and whether you think they have succeeded. You will find a wide variety of examples of literature from all over the world in this book, and regular suggestions for ways to take your learning further. Why not use them as a starting point for your own reading?

Unit summary

In this unit, you have:
- Thought about the importance of active and independent learning.
- Practised some of the skills covered by the Assessment Objectives.
- Begun thinking about some of the aspects of literature – language, structure and form – that you will need to consider throughout your course.

You will have many opportunities to develop the skills you have begun to use in this unit throughout your course, but be sure to speak to your teacher or classmates about anything you don't understand.

3

What is literature?

In this unit, you will:
- Think about different definitions of what is meant by the term 'literature'.
- Contemplate the purposes of literature.
- Consider what is meant by 'literary value'.
- Begin thinking about the three main literary forms and their characteristics.

The information in this section is based on the Cambridge IGCSE Literature in English syllabuses (0475/0992) for examination from 2020, the Cambridge O Level Literature in English syllabus (2010) for examination from 2023 and the Cambridge IGCSE World Literature syllabus (0408) for examination from 2022. You should always refer to the appropriate syllabus document for the year of your examination to confirm the details and for more information. The syllabus document is available on the Cambridge International website at www.cambridgeinternational.org.

What is literature? This is not as straightforward a question as it might appear. Historically, the word 'literature' was used to describe all writing. In recent centuries, however, it has taken on a more selective and less clear meaning. In this unit, we will think about some of the ways we can define what should or should not be classed as 'literature', before beginning a consideration of the types of literature that you will study as part of your course.

The purposes of literature

One way of thinking about what is meant by 'literature' is to think about its purpose or purposes. In Unit 1, we briefly considered the question 'Why study literature?'. The reasons given, based on the aims of the Cambridge IGCSE Literature in English (0475/0992), Cambridge O Level Literature in English (2010) and Cambridge IGCSE World Literature (0408) syllabuses, included the notion that an appreciation of literature can aid our personal growth. The exercise below is designed to help you think about how literature can help you develop a greater understanding of human concerns.

Exercise 1

A fictional character called Atticus Finch, from the novel *To Kill a Mockingbird* by Harper Lee, spoke the following words to his young daughter, Scout. He was trying to teach her a life lesson after she had experienced difficulties with her school teacher, some of her school friends and neighbours.

> 'You never really understand a person until you consider things from his point of view... until you climb in his skin and walk around in it.'
>
> Harper Lee, from *To Kill a Mockingbird*

Many people would agree with Atticus. Do you? Think about the following questions.
a What life lessons do you think Atticus was trying to teach Scout?
b In what ways do you think reading literature helps a person to learn these life lessons?

Of course, this isn't the only reason to read. Literature may serve other purposes for readers.

Exercise 2

Here are some quotations from famous people about their perceptions of the purpose of literature. In pairs or small groups, discuss the quotations, thinking about the following questions.
a What do you think these people meant by their words?
b Based on your own reading experiences, do you agree with what they say?

> Nowadays I know the true reason I read is to feel less alone, to make a connection with a consciousness other than my own.

▲ Zadie Smith

> Books allowed me to see a world beyond the front porch of my grandmother's shotgun house [and] the power to see possibilities beyond what was allowed at the time.

▲ Oprah Winfrey

> Books and all forms of writing are terror to those who wish to suppress truth.

▲ Wole Soyinka

> Books are the mirrors of the soul.

▲ Virginia Woolf

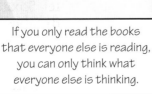

> If you only read the books that everyone else is reading, you can only think what everyone else is thinking.

▲ Haruki Murakami

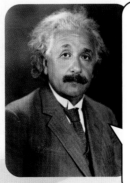

> Somebody who only reads newspapers and at best books of contemporary authors looks to me like an extremely near-sighted person who scorns eyeglasses. He is completely dependent on the prejudices and fashions of his times, since he never gets to see or hear anything else.

▲ Albert Einstein

Share your views with the class.

Literary value

Another criterion that is sometimes used to define what we mean by literature is the notion of literary value or worth. A novel, play or poem should only be considered 'literature' if it is of a high enough standard. However, rather than clarifying the issue, this approach only leads to further questions; principally 'How do we measure literary worth?'.

Exercise 3

How do we judge whether a prose, poetic or dramatic text has literary value or is worth studying? With a partner, rank the following criteria and then explain to the class why you have ranked them in this order.

» How well the text has stood the test of time
» Whether it merits more than one reading
» Whether it has a certain originality.

The list above is by no means exhaustive. How a text impacts on us as readers could be another criterion, but that could be what we call a 'value judgement', as we all like to read different types of literature.

Literary forms

A final way of thinking about what constitutes literature is simply to think about the kinds of literature we study as part of this academic field. Literature is divided into forms. The forms of literature that you will be learning about on your course are:

» Poetry
» Prose (short stories and novels)
» Drama.

Exercise 4

You are studying a broader range of literature than we tend to read at home and for our own purposes. Most private reading of literature is of prose. Fewer people tend to read poetry than prose and very few people indeed read drama texts. With a partner, discuss the reasons for the following:

» Most people who read literature read prose texts.
» Relatively few people read drama texts. (Think about what dramatists actually write their texts for, and the reason for the low numbers here might be more obvious than you think.)
» Reading all three **genres** in school might be considered important.

Share your ideas with the class.

Key term

Genre: A category of literature

POETRY

What is poetry?

Poetry is a form of literature in which ideas, meanings or emotions are expressed through language and rhythm. As you saw in Unit 2, poetry can take many different forms – sonnets, ballads, haiku, acrostics, plus many more – and each has its own set of rules or conventions regarding the number of lines, the number of syllables, the rhyme scheme used, and so on. In addition, several of the poems in this book are composed in something called **free verse**. Note that this does not mean that you don't need to consider their structural qualities, only that they don't follow regular patterns of metre or rhyme. Poems in free verse may still use metre, rhythm and rhyme to convey feelings or ideas, but perhaps not in a traditionally identifiable way.

Some of the features you will need to consider when studying poems include:

» **The language that the poet uses:** Typically speaking, the language used in poetry will be more figurative than in other literary forms. This means that it does not simply present a literal meaning, but rather uses literary devices such as metaphors and similes to create associations between different items and, by doing so, creates a strong impression for the reader of the person, place or object being described. Think, for example, of perhaps the most famous simile in English poetry, William Wordsworth's 'I wandered lonely as a cloud'. Why does Wordsworth compare himself to a cloud? Perhaps he is saying he is wandering aimlessly, in the same way that a cloud is blown by the wind without any set direction or destination. Perhaps he is saying that he is daydreaming and not paying attention to the real world around him, that he has his 'head in the clouds', so to speak. Can you think of any other possible interpretations?

Poets will often also appeal to our **senses** through the use of imagery, language that describes sensations that we experience through our five senses. For example, a poet might create a visual image of something by using words that describe its colour, or they might recreate sounds through the use of **onomatopoeic** language.

» **The way the poem looks and sounds:** As we have seen, poetry comes in many different shapes and sizes. The more poems you study, the better you will get at identifying the features that are characteristic of different forms. However, it is not enough simply to identify a poem's form. You also need to be able to explain why the poet has used that form and how it contributes to the impression that they wish to convey. Be sure to think about the way a poem looks on the page: are the lines and **stanzas** consistent in their lengths? Count the syllables in each line: are there the same number (of syllables) or do they follow a regular pattern? Why might that be the case? Or why not? It might be that a poem composed in a regular form exhibits a certain level of confidence or clarity of thought on the poet's part, while a poem that breaks from its form, or is composed in free verse, deals with subject matter that cannot be so easily represented, or emotions that cannot be so easily contained.

It is also a good idea to get into the habit of reading poems aloud, so that you get a clearer sense of the poem's rhythm and rhyme scheme, as well as the sounds of the specific words the poet has used, for example whether they are **alliterative** or **assonant**. Again, this will help you get a sense of the

Key terms

Free verse: A form of poetry that takes no particular shape, rhythm, metre or rhyme

Senses: Sight, smell, hearing, touch and taste

Onomatopoeia: Language that sounds like the idea it describes; 'crackle' is an example of onomatopoeia (make sure you can spell the term correctly)

Stanza: A group of lines in a poem, similar to a paragraph in a prose text; common stanza lengths are two, three, four, six or eight lines – in popular music, we often call stanzas 'verses'

Alliteration: The repetition of consonant sounds at the beginning of words or stressed syllables in adjacent words

Assonance: The repetition of vowel sounds in adjacent words

Key term

Turning point: A point in a literary text at which an idea or an attitude is changed or reversed

emotional or mental state of the poet, or a persona the poet has adopted, in relation to the subject matter. Do they seem in control of their thoughts and feelings? It might be that their words say one thing, but the structure or rhythm of the poem betrays their true feelings. Or perhaps a change of heart reveals itself in a structural **turning point** or formal shift in the poem.

» **The themes and ideas that the poem explores:** You will find, when you read your set poems and the poems in this book, that they are packed with dense layers of meaning and that there are new ideas and interpretations to explore with each subsequent reading of a poem. Even when a poem appears fairly straightforward in its meaning, you need to consider what the poet's motivation may have been for writing it; perhaps it explores a deeper issue relating to human nature or the natural world, or perhaps it relates to the historical or political context in which it was written, or to the author's own unique perspective on the world, whatever that may be.

This is not an exhaustive list and there are many other aspects of poetry that you will encounter and consider throughout your course.

Objectives

The reading experiences and tasks in Units 4 to 10 of this book have been carefully selected and put together to build up your skills and prepare you for writing about both your set poems and unseen poems.

In the Poetry section of this book you will:
» read a range of poems from different periods and cultures
» identify quotations that demonstrate a poem's meaning and learn how to use them when writing about poetry
» explore layers of meaning within poems
» analyse how poets use language, structure and form to create meaning
» use appropriate terminology when writing about poetry
» develop a sensitive and informed personal response to poetry.

Where will students be assessed on skills in writing about poetry?

Students following Cambridge O Level Literature in English (2010) or Cambridge IGCSE Literature in English (0475/0992) are examined on their set poetry texts in Paper 1 – Poetry and Prose. Depending on the route they are following for the Literature in English qualification, they may also be required to:
» respond to an unseen poem or extract from a poem in Paper 4 – Unseen

OR
» submit an assignment based on poetry in Component 5 – Coursework.

Your teacher will be able to tell you which route you are following for your O Level or IGCSE syllabus and where you will be required to respond to poetry texts.

Students following the Cambridge IGCSE World Literature syllabus (0408) are required to respond to an unseen poem in Paper 2 – Unseen Poetry and may be required to write about their poetry set texts in Paper 3 – Set Text. Your teacher will be able to tell you whether you will be required to write about poetry in Paper 3 – Set Text.

PROSE

What is prose?

The word 'prose' refers to language that is written or spoken in a natural way, in contrast to the rhythms of poetry. Most of what you read will be expressed in prose: websites, newspapers, magazines and non-fiction books (including this one). In your Cambridge IGCSE Literature in English (0475/0992), Cambridge O Level Literature in English (2010) or Cambridge IGCSE World Literature (0408) course, your prose reading will be in the form of short stories, extracts from longer prose works and novels that tell the stories of imaginary characters and worlds (although some will be based on or inspired by the authors' real-life experiences).

Some of the features you will need to consider when studying prose fiction include:

» **The perspective from which the story is told:** The perspective from which a work of prose fiction is narrated can drastically affect the way that the events of the story are presented to the reader. There are two principal types of **narrator** that you are likely to encounter in your course: **first person** and **third person**. A first-person narrative is told from the perspective of a character in the story; this will likely be the protagonist of the story, but it doesn't have to be. This type of narrative is easily identifiable by the use of the word 'I' by the narrator to refer to himself or herself. In such stories or novels, the reader only has access to the experiences and thoughts of the narrator; we see events through their eyes, so to speak. This might have the effect of creating greater sympathy in the reader for the character, but it can also serve to expose their flaws. In some cases, the reader may have reasons to question whether the narrator is being entirely truthful; in others, the reader may know something that the narrator does not seem to. If the narrator is a child, for example, the reader may have a clearer understanding of the events that they are describing than they do themselves.
A third-person narrative is told from a perspective outside the world of the story. In this type of narrative, the narrator refers to all the characters by their names, or by appropriate pronouns – he, she, they, and so on – and rarely refers to himself or herself. A third-person narrator is sometimes referred to as an **omniscient narrator** as they are not limited in their descriptions of the world they are presenting, or the actions, words or thoughts of their characters. Nevertheless, for the sake of telling a story, they will normally focus on just a few characters.

Key terms

Narrator: The person who tells the story in a text; what happens is told in their words

First-person narrative: A narrative in which the events of the novel are told through a character actually in the novel – we see events and other characters through their eyes; first-person narrators communicate what they themselves think, experience and witness, as well as what they have been told or heard

Third-person narrative: A narrative that is not told from the perspective of a character in the story

Third-person omniscient narrator: 'Omniscient' means 'knows everything'; this kind of narrator knows everything about the characters – what they think and what they do and why; the narrator is the third person, meaning that they tell the story, but they are not in the story

» **The characters, their attitudes and actions:** The primary way in which authors of prose fiction explore ideas or themes is through the presentation of different characters and their various personalities and attitudes. When thinking about the ways in which characters are presented, you should think about what the author or narrator tells us about their personality and their appearance, as well as what they say, the way they interact with other characters and, depending on the type of narrator, any reported thoughts. Often, characters will be representative of broader ideas or attitudes, and their actions or the fates that they suffer will be indicative of the author's thoughts about a particular theme or topic.

You should also be alert to how a principal character is likely to change as a result of the events of a novel. You might be familiar with Harper Lee's novel *To Kill a Mockingbird*, which is referenced earlier in this unit. If so, think about the character Scout. At the beginning of the novel, Scout is a young child, who judges people based on appearances. She fears a character called Boo Radley because he leads an isolated existence in his house on the same street. By the end of the novel, Scout is older and comes to learn that Boo is a kind man, who has led a hard life.

» **The structure of a novel or short story:** As we saw in Unit 2, we can talk about the structure of a work of literature at various different levels, from individual sentences right up to an entire novel. Generally speaking, you should think about the way the writer has put the different parts of their story together to maximise the effects it has on the reader. At the narrative level, you should think about how the author sets up the world of the story, how they introduce the characters and their situations, as well as any **conflicts** they are involved in or obstacles that they face. You should consider the role of individual chapters or paragraphs in progressing the story towards a **climax** or **resolution**, and think about how the state of affairs has changed by the end of the story.

Again, this is not an exhaustive list and there are many other aspects of prose fiction that you will encounter and consider throughout your course.

Key terms

Conflict: A situation in which there is an obstacle between a character and that character's goal; the conflict may be external or internal

Climax: The most exciting point in a text or performance when dramatic tension has increased to its highest point

Resolution: The final part of a story, in which everything is explained or resolved; sometimes called the 'denouement'

Exercise 5

Look at these two quotations about poetry and prose from famous writers and think about the questions that follow.

Prose: words in their best order; poetry: the best words in the best order.

Always be a poet, even in prose.

▲ Samuel Taylor Coleridge

▲ Charles Baudelaire

a What do you think is meant by each of these quotations?
b What do think they say about the hierarchy of the different literary forms? Do you agree with their judgements?

Objectives

The reading experiences and tasks in Units 11 to 17 of this book have been carefully selected and put together to build up your skills and prepare you for writing about both your set prose texts and unseen prose extracts.

In the Prose section of this book you will:
» read a range of extracts from literary prose works of different periods and cultures
» identify important quotations in prose extracts and learn how to use quotations when writing about prose
» explore layers of meaning within extracts from prose texts
» analyse how authors of prose texts use language, structure and form to create meaning
» use appropriate terminology when writing about prose texts
» develop a sensitive and informed personal response to prose texts.

Where will students be assessed on skills in writing about prose texts?

Students following Cambridge O Level Literature in English (2010) or Cambridge IGCSE Literature in English (0475/0992) are examined on their set prose text in Paper 1 – Poetry and Prose. Depending on the route they are following for the Literature in English qualification, they may also be required to:

» respond to an unseen prose extract in Paper 4 – Unseen

OR

» submit an assignment based on a prose text in Component 5 – Coursework.

Your teacher will be able to tell you which route you are following for your O Level or IGCSE syllabus and where you will be required to respond to a prose text.

Students following the Cambridge IGCSE World Literature syllabus (0408) are required to respond to a prose text in Component 1 – Coursework and may be required to write about their prose set text in Paper 3 – Set Text. Your teacher will be able to tell you whether you will be required to write about your prose set text in Paper 3 – Set Text.

DRAMA

What is drama?

While most poetry and prose texts are written for a reader, it is important to remember that drama texts or plays are intended for performance on a stage. This has an impact on the way we read a dramatic text. As well as considering such features as language, structure and form when exploring meaning, we also need to think about how the play would appear to an audience. Ideally, you should try to watch performances of your set drama texts, so that you can get an impression of the effect that the different dramatic techniques create on an audience in a theatre when combined.

Some of the features you will need to consider when studying dramatic texts include:

» **The way the play is staged:** You need to be alert to what the dramatist tells us about **setting**, lighting, sound and props. Remember that, in contrast to the author of a piece of prose fiction, a dramatist cannot provide detailed descriptions of the setting or location of the action of their play: everything they want the audience to be aware of has to be seen or heard on stage. Different dramatists will provide varying levels of detail in their scripts about these various aspects of **staging**. Where a lot of detail has been provided, you should think about the significance of the dramatist's instructions in relation to the themes and ideas they want to explore. If the script does not include much in the way of staging instructions, you should try to watch a performance of the play, or a video of a performance, or look at still photographs of a performance of it, and evaluate the director's interpretation of the text and compare it with your own.

Key terms

Setting: The time, place and culture in which a text takes place

Staging: The process of designing the performance space in which a play takes place, taking into account the set, the lighting and the costumes

Soliloquy: A type of speech in which a character in a play reveals their thoughts and feelings by speaking alone on the stage

» **How the dramatist uses stage directions:** As above, a dramatist is usually unable to tell their audience exactly what is going on inside a character's head (although occasionally a character might give a **soliloquy**). Therefore, a writer will often include stage directions in their plays to instruct the actors how they ought to deliver a particular line, how they should move on the stage and how they should interact with other characters. Again, the level of detail provided varies by dramatist, but where stage directions are included you should think about why the writer has included them and consider the way an audience will interpret an actor's behaviour on stage. As always, watching a performance of the play will help you to understand the way that stage directions are interpreted and the effects that they create.

Again, this is not an exhaustive list and there are many other aspects of dramatic texts that you will encounter and consider throughout your course.

Objectives

The reading experiences and tasks set in Units 18 to 24 of this book have been carefully selected and put together to build up your skills and prepare you for writing about your dramatic texts.

In the Drama section of this book you will:
» read a range of extracts from drama texts of different periods and cultures
» identify important quotations in drama extracts and learn how to use quotations when writing about drama
» explore layers of meaning within extracts from drama texts
» analyse how dramatists use language, structure and form to create meaning
» use appropriate terminology when writing about drama texts
» develop a sensitive and informed personal response to drama texts.

Where will students be assessed on skills in writing about drama texts?

Students following Cambridge O Level Literature in English (2010) or Cambridge IGCSE Literature in English (0475/0992), depending on the route they are following for the Literature in English qualification, will either:
» respond to their two set drama texts in in Paper 2 – Drama

OR
» respond to one set drama text in Paper 3 – Drama (open text).

Depending on the route they are following, they may also be required to respond to a drama text for Component 5 – Coursework.

Your teacher will be able to tell you which route you are following for your O Level or IGCSE syllabus and where you will be required to respond to drama texts.

Students following the Cambridge IGCSE World Literature syllabus (0408) are required to respond to a drama text in Component 1 – Coursework and may be required to write about one of their drama set texts in Paper 3 – Set Text. Your teacher will be able to tell you whether you will be required to write about a drama text in Paper 3 – Set Text.

Unit summary

In this unit, you have:
- Thought about different definitions of what is meant by the term 'literature'.
- Contemplated the purposes of literature.
- Considered what is meant by 'literary value'.
- Begun thinking about the three main literary forms and their characteristics.

Now that you have completed the introductory units of this book, you should have a general overview of your course, what you will be studying and the skills you will need to develop. Be sure to refer back to these units as you need to throughout the course.

POETRY

4 'Phenomenal Woman': Focus on reading for meaning

In this unit, you will:
- Identify quotations that demonstrate a poet's meaning and learn how to use them when writing essays.
- Explore the ways in which a poem creates meanings, beyond its surface meaning.
- Examine how writers use language and structure to create and shape meanings.
- Develop a personal understanding of a poet's intentions.

As we will see throughout the Poetry section, poets use many tools and techniques to convey meaning in their work. Even if you understand all of the words in a poem, it might be that there are deeper meanings hinted at through the **language choices** a poet has made and the effects that these have on you as a reader. When considering the meaning of a poem, you should always think about how the poet's choice of language or **structure** impacts on your understanding of it, and how features like the sound and **rhythm** of the poem can be used to create a certain impression.

Maya Angelou (1928 to 2014) was an American poet and memoirist. The poem 'Phenomenal Woman' comes from a volume of poetry called *And Still I Rise* (1978). Angelou was a civil rights activist and her poems are often about black female empowerment.

> **Key terms**
>
> **Language choices:** The specific words that a writer chooses to use to convey particular ideas
>
> **Structure:** The sequence of ideas in a text and how it is put together
>
> **Rhythm:** Patterns in long and short sounds, words and lines in poetry

> **Glossary**
> **Phenomenal:** Extraordinary or exceptional

4.1 'Phenomenal Woman' by Maya Angelou

Pretty women wonder where my
    secret lies.
I'm not cute or built to suit a fashion
    model's size
But when I start to tell them,
They think I'm telling lies.
I say,   5
It's in the reach of my arms
The span of my hips,
The stride of my step,
The curl of my lips.
I'm a woman   10
Phenomenally.
Phenomenal woman,
That's me.

I walk into a room
Just as cool as you please,   15
And to a man,
The fellows stand or
Fall down on their knees.
Then they swarm around me,
A hive of honey bees.   20
I say,
It's the fire in my eyes,
And the flash of my teeth,
The swing in my waist,
And the joy in my feet.   25
I'm a woman
Phenomenally.
Phenomenal woman,
That's me.

Men themselves have wondered 30
What they see in me.
They try so much
But they can't touch
My inner mystery.
When I try to show them   35
They say they still can't see.
I say,
It's in the arch of my back,
The sun of my smile,
The ride of my breasts,   40

The grace of my style.
I'm a woman
Phenomenally.
Phenomenal woman,
That's me.   45

Now you understand
Just why my head's not bowed.
I don't shout or jump about
Or have to talk real loud.
When you see me passing   50
It ought to make you proud.
I say,
It's in the click of my heels,
The bend of my hair,
the palm of my hand,   55
The need for my care.
'Cause I'm a woman
Phenomenally.
Phenomenal woman,
That's me.   60

4.2 First impressions

Exercise 1

a Read the poem together as a class.
b On a scale of 1 to 4, how well do you understand this poem after a first reading?
   4 – I understand it perfectly.
   3 – I mostly understand it.
   2 – I understand some of it.
   1 – I don't understand any of it.
c Write down any words or phrases you didn't understand.
d Share your responses to **b** and **c** with your teacher and classmates and discuss anything you didn't understand. Reread the poem. How well do you understand it now?

Exercise 2

> **Key term**
>
> **Stereotype:** An idea or belief people have about an object or group that is based upon how they look on the outside; it may be completely untrue or only partly true

In 'Phenomenal Woman', Angelou describes how she doesn't conform to the **stereotype** of a beautiful woman, but celebrates her uniquely attractive womanly qualities.

a In small groups, discuss the following questions:
   i What are some different stereotypes? For example:
      – Stereotypes about women and men
      – Stereotypes about younger people and older people
      What stereotypes do people have about you that you disagree with?
   ii What are the dangers of stereotyping people?
   iii Can you think of any people (they can be private or public figures) whom you would consider 'phenomenal' because they show us that we are wrong to judge by stereotypes?
   Pick a spokesperson (your teacher may help with this) to share your ideas with the class.
b Reread 'Phenomenal Woman' as a class, thinking about the work you have just done on stereotypes.
c On your own, look at lines 1 to 2 again and write down one word and one short phrase from these lines that show a stereotypical view of a perfect woman.

Exercise 3

a The poem is quite long. It is broken down into four **stanzas**. Think about the way paragraphs are used in an essay. With a partner:
   – think about the reasons that we use paragraphs in our essays
   – discuss how paragraphs can help a reader to understand an essay
   – discuss any ways in which stanzas in poetry are different from paragraphs in essays.

> **TIP**
>
> When discussing ways in which stanzas in poetry are different from paragraphs in essays, a good starting point might be to think about any patterns you can see in the poem.

MAKING CONNECTIONS

To learn more about
how the structure of a
poem affects its deeper
meaning, look at Unit
5 on 'Island Man' by
Grace Nichols.

b 'Phenomenal Woman' is divided into four main stanzas, with the following
refrain separating them:

> I'm a woman
> Phenomenally.
> Phenomenal woman,
> That's me.

- In pairs, reread each stanza, one at a time. In no more than 12 words, sum
  up what each stanza is about. Write this down.
- Share your ideas with a larger group or the whole class.

Key terms

Stanza: A group of lines in a poem, similar to a paragraph in a prose text; common stanza
lengths are two, three, four, six or eight lines – in popular music, we often call stanzas 'verses'

Refrain: A short part of a poem (or song) that is repeated between stanzas, like a chorus

---

4.3 Finding evidence

Exercise 4

a i In each stanza, the speaker takes four lines to describe ways in which she
is attractive to men.
In pairs, look at one of the four descriptions below. Write down what the
speaker is telling us about herself that makes her so attractive. What do
you think is the most important word on each line in conveying why she
feels so positive about herself? What does it convey to you and how does it
link to the word 'phenomenal' in the title?

Stanza 1	Stanza 2
It's in the reach of my arms The span of my hips, The stride of my step, The curl of my lips.	It's the fire in my eyes, And the flash of my teeth, The swing in my waist, And the joy in my feet.
Stanza 3	**Stanza 4**
It's in the arch of my back, The sun of my smile, The ride of my breasts, The grace of my style.	It's in the click of my heels, The bend of my hair, the palm of my hand, The need for my care.

ii One of you should read your four lines of the poem out to the class. The
other should read out your answers to the question 'What makes the
speaker so attractive?'. Ask your class members if they agree with you and
whether they have any further ideas that you could add to your worksheet.

MAKING CONNECTIONS

Language that appeals to our **senses** is often referred to as an **image** or **imagery**. For a
more in-depth exploration of the way that poets use images in their work, see Unit 6 on Ted
Hughes's 'Thistles'.

b In the last stanza, the speaker addresses us, as readers, personally. Why do you think she does this? Reread the first six lines of this stanza and think about what she is saying to us here. Copy out the following statements and write T (for true), F (for false) or NS (not sure) next to each one:
 – The speaker thinks that other women like her bow their heads because they feel inferior.
 – The speaker thinks that she has no need to make a big effort to draw attention to herself.
 – The speaker thinks that all women apart from her like to shout.
 – The speaker thinks that we are proud of her confidence and her achievements.
 – The speaker may feel that she is addressing people who think she has no right to be this confident.
Share your responses with the rest of the class. Remember to try to give clear explanations for your responses.

c In pairs, discuss reasons why you think this poem is called 'Phenomenal Woman'. The following reasons could form the basis of your discussion. Which reason do you think is the best and why?
 – She is exceptionally attractive in her own unique way.
 – She is brave and doesn't care what others say or think.
 – She is a larger-than-life figure.
 – Any other reason.
Share your responses with the class.

d In pairs, prepare a performance of 'Phenomenal Woman'. You decide how you want to perform the poem. One way to perform the poem might be to take a stanza each. Another way might be for one person to read the whole poem, while the other mimes the parts of the other characters in the poem. Did you notice that when you read the poem out loud the rhythm allows you to feel the **narrator**'s confident stride as she walks in the street? Practise your performance, thinking about how Angelou wants the speaker to sound, and how you can best demonstrate her power, poise and confidence.
Share your performance with the rest of the class.

Key terms

Senses: Sight, smell, hearing, touch and taste

Image / Imagery: A word or phrase that prompts the reader to imagine the way that something looks, sounds, smells, feels or tastes

Narrator: The person who tells the story in a text; what happens is told in their words

4.4 Writing practice

Exercise 5

Look at this essay question.

> **Explore the ways in which Maya Angelou makes the speaker sound very attractive in this poem.**

TIP

Look for key words in essay questions. The key word here is 'attractive'. This should be the focus for your response. It is helpful to highlight or underline key words as you spot them.

Use a table like this to make points that you could use in your essay. Find an appropriate quotation to support each point and comment on how your chosen quotation helps Angelou to make the speaker sound very attractive. Make sure you use **quotation marks**. One example has been provided for you.

Point	Supporting quotation	Comment
She makes herself sound very confident	'the stride of my step'	She moves quickly and with broad steps, as if showing the world she has no fear.

Key term

Quotation marks: Punctuation that we use to show that the words we are writing down have been copied from the text (quotations); sometimes referred to as 'inverted commas' or 'speech marks'

TIP

The best quotations are often very short and only include the words we need to support our ideas.

Exercise 6

Read this student's opening paragraph of their response to the question in Exercise 5. Then look at the feedback given by the teacher.

a Discuss the teacher's feedback with your partner or group. How would you improve the student answer according to the teacher's advice?

b Share your ideas with the class.

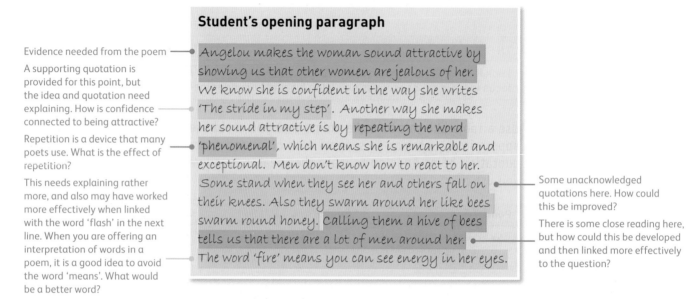

Student's opening paragraph

Evidence needed from the poem

A supporting quotation is provided for this point, but the idea and quotation need explaining. How is confidence connected to being attractive?

Repetition is a device that many poets use. What is the effect of repetition?

This needs explaining rather more, and also may have worked more effectively when linked with the word 'flash' in the next line. When you are offering an interpretation of words in a poem, it is a good idea to avoid the word 'means'. What would be a better word?

Angelou makes the woman sound attractive by showing us that other women are jealous of her. We know she is confident in the way she writes 'The stride in my step'. Another way she makes her sound attractive is by repeating the word 'phenomenal', which means she is remarkable and exceptional. Men don't know how to react to her. Some stand when they see her and others fall on their knees. Also they swarm around her like bees swarm round honey. Calling them a hive of bees tells us that there are a lot of men around her. The word 'fire' means you can see energy in her eyes.

Some unacknowledged quotations here. How could this be improved?

There is some close reading here, but how could this be developed and then linked more effectively to the question?

4.5 Set-text focus

Exercise 7

Consider the way that a person is presented in one or more of your set poems.

a Carry out the same task as in Exercise 3 in this unit to help you sum up the main ideas and how they develop or change between stanzas or through the poem.

b Consider what the poet wants us to think about the person in your chosen poem and what methods the poet uses to portray the person. Are there any patterns in and between stanzas that help the poet to present the person in this way?

c Create a table like you did in Exercise 5 in which you do the following:
   – In the left-hand column, list points that you want to make about how the person is presented.
   – Give short supporting quotations in the middle column.
   – In the right-hand column, give explanations / comment on the language / devices.

d Use your table to form the basis of an essay response.

Take your learning further

In another poem, called 'Still I Rise', Maya Angelou details a woman's steadfast resistance to attempts to belittle and subdue her, with references to African-American history, in particular slavery.

If you can, read the poem online.

1   The tennis player Serena Williams made a very powerful YouTube video adaptation of 'Still I Rise' in 2015. Watch the video on YouTube. How do Williams's performance of the poem and the accompanying visual images support its impact? Does the fact that a very successful modern-day American woman delivers the poem add anything to its meaning at all? Look at the lines of the poem that Williams misses out. Why might she have chosen to do this?
2   Think about how the messages and ideas in 'Still I Rise' impact on your understanding of the speaker in 'Phenomenal Woman' and her position.

Unit summary

In this unit, you have learned how to:
● Identify quotations that demonstrate a poet's meaning and how to use them when writing essays.
● Explore the ways in which a poem creates meanings, beyond its surface meaning.
● Examine how writers use language and structure to create and shape meanings.
● Develop a personal understanding of a poet's intentions.

Think about how you have demonstrated each of these skills in the exercises in this unit. Be sure to return to this unit once you have spent some time developing other skills, and apply your learning to this poem.

'Island Man': Focus on structure

In this unit, you will:
- Identify the use of structural devices in a poem and use them to support your argument or opinion.
- Think about how the structure of a poem contributes to its meaning.
- Explore the ways a poet uses structural devices to create and shape meanings and effect.
- Explain the effect that the structure of a poem has on you as you read it.

In Unit 4, you looked at stanzas and refrains in 'Phenomenal Woman'. Now we will look at other ways in which a poet can structure a poem, and how choices regarding structure can affect meaning and create effects in a poem.

Grace Nichols was born in 1950 in Guyana, a country in South America that has strong cultural and political ties with the Caribbean. She emigrated to Britain in 1977. Her poem 'Island Man' is about a man from the Caribbean who moved to London for economic reasons, but who struggles to adapt to the very different way of life.

> **Glossary**
>
> **North Circular:** The North Circular Road is a very busy ring road around central London

5.1 'Island Man' by Grace Nichols

(for a Caribbean island man in London who still wakes up to the sound of the sea)

Morning
and island man wakes up
to the sound of blue surf
in his head
the steady breaking and wombing   5

wild seabirds
and fisherman pushing out to sea
the sun surfacing defiantly
from the east
of his small emerald island   10
he always comes back   groggily groggily

Comes back to sands
of a grey metallic soar
        to surge of wheels
to dull North Circular roar   15

muffling muffling
his crumpled pillow waves
island man heaves himself

Another London day

5.2 First impressions

Exercise 1

The Caribbean comprises many countries, including Jamaica, the Bahamas and the Dominican Republic, to name but a few. They have a tropical climate and many sandy beaches. London is the capital city of the United Kingdom and one of the largest and busiest cities in Europe.

a Draw two mind maps. In the middle of one write 'Caribbean Island' and in the middle of the other write either 'London' or the name of another big city near to you.

b Add words that you associate with each place to the appropriate mind map. These could include:
- colours
- sounds
- sights
- activities
- lifestyle
- weather
- anything else.

One idea has been added to each mind map.

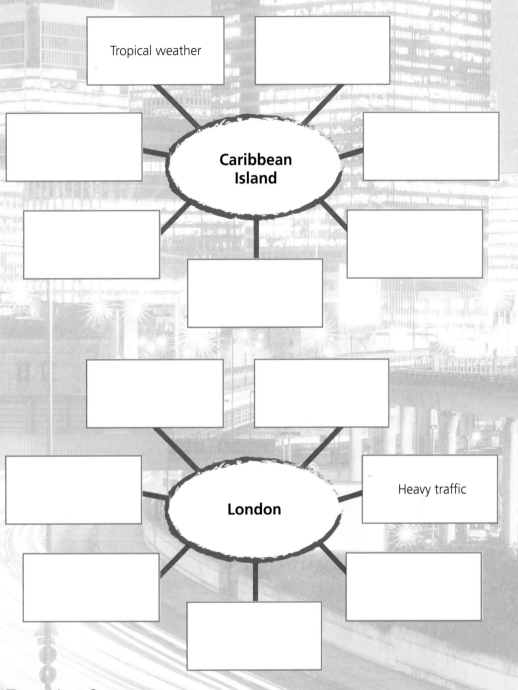

Tropical weather

Caribbean Island

London

Heavy traffic

Exercise 2

a With a partner, brainstorm:
- what you think is meant by the word 'structure' in relation to a poem or other literary text
- what features of a poem you would expect to consider if you were writing about a poem's structure.

Share your ideas with the rest of the class.

b Look at the table below. By yourself, or with a partner, match the structural device to its correct meaning.

Structural device	Meaning
1 form	**a** run-on lines
2 stanza	**b** writing something again
3 rhyme scheme	**c** pause in the middle of a line
4 refrain	**d** verse
5 rhythm	**e** pattern in the rhythm
6 metre	**f** physical shape of the poem
7 enjambment	**g** punctuation at the end of the line
8 end-stopped line	**h** patterns in the rhyme usually at the end of the line
9 caesura	**i** lines repeated, usually between stanzas
10 repetition	**j** placing two or more ideas side by side so the reader will compare them
11 juxtaposition	**k** moment in the poem where an idea or attitude is reversed
12 turning point	**l** beat and pace

c Look at the structural devices in either word cloud 1 or 2 opposite. Which devices do you think could be used to create the possible effects listed below each word cloud? You may decide that several devices could be used to create the same effect.

caesura
free verse
refrain
opening
enjambment **ending**
regular rhyme scheme
clear poetic form

▲ Word cloud 1

regular stanzas
cyclical or circular shape
chronological narrative
offset line **juxtaposition**
change in line length
irregular stanzas

▲ Word cloud 2

Possible effect
Indicates changes or movement of ideas in the poem
Emphasises a main idea
Answers a question posed in the poem or leaves the reader with something to think about
Suggests a flowing of ideas or emotion
Creates a sense of orderliness
Reflects a moment of **epiphany** in the poem
Sets up a scene or poses a question
May make the poem seem childish like a nursery rhyme

Possible effect
Draws attention to contrasting pairs of ideas
Suggests that the poet is exploring new ideas
Gives the poem a sense of telling a story or of time passing
Creates a sense of orderliness
Creates a sense of uncertainty
Suggests an idea linked to separation
Suggests that nothing changes

TIP

The effects given in the lists above are what we call 'general' or 'generic' effects'. When you write about the structural devices in a poem, you should try to explain as clearly as possible how they create effects that are specific to that poem.

Discuss with the rest of the class the matches you have made. Try to explain your reasons for the matches you made.

d Read the poem. While you are reading, think about the way Nichols has structured her poem, and the devices that you have discussed already in this exercise. Think about:
– how the poem is divided up, and into how many sections
– what devices Nichols uses to show the different divisions
– whether the layout of the words affects the way you read the poem
– whether you can find any other techniques, such as repetition or juxtaposition.

Make sure that, if you notice a device that Nichols uses, you also note down an explanation of the effect that it has on the way you read the poem.

Key term

Epiphany: A moment when a character in the text has a sudden insight or realisation that changes their view or understanding for the rest of the text

5.3 Finding evidence

Exercise 3

a Look at the first ten lines of the poem.

By yourself, or with a partner, think about and write down answers to the following:

i Where does Island Man wake up in his dreams?

ii Where does he wake up in reality?

iii Why do you think that Nichols calls him 'Island Man' instead of giving him a name?

iv What is the effect of opening the poem with the word 'Morning' on its own line?

v What sounds and sights has Island Man been dreaming about?

vi The word 'wombing' on line 5 is an unusual word. Comment on its possible meaning and use here.

vii Read the line 'the steady breaking and wombing' out loud and listen to the rhythm it creates. Pay particular attention to the **consonance** of the words 'breaking' and 'wombing'. What is the rhythm imitating here? How does it achieve this effect?

viii On line 8 the sun is **personified** when we are told that it surfaces 'defiantly'. What does this suggest to you about the sun?

ix What is the effect of referring to Island Man's island as his 'emerald island'?

x What would be lost if the whole poem were written out as one paragraph? Think about what is gained by having separate stanzas that look different on the page.

b In the second half of the poem, Nichols **juxtaposes** the reality of London with the dream of the Caribbean island.

i In small groups or pairs, discuss the following questions:

– Why are the words 'groggily groggily' repeated and offset from the rest of the line?

– What might the two lines 'Comes back to sands / of a grey metallic soar' mean? As a clue, focus on the two words 'sands' and 'soar' and see if you can work out what Nichols is trying to achieve here.

– Are there any other ways in which Nichols creates the effect that Island Man does not want to face his day at work?

ii Look at the whole poem again. Write down two words from each half of the poem that describe:

– a colour seen in London and a colour seen in the Caribbean

– a sound heard in London and a sound heard in the Caribbean.

iii Now look back to the mind maps you created in Exercise 1b. Compare your own ideas about London and a Caribbean island with Island Man's ideas. Do you and Island Man share the same ideas?

iv Look back to the work you have done on structure throughout Exercises 2 and 3. Share with a partner what you have learned about different structural devices and their effects in poetry. You should discuss structural devices generally and refer specifically to 'Island Man'.

Key terms

Consonance: The repetition of similar consonant sounds

Personification: The description of an object or animal as if they have human characteristics

Juxtapose: Putting two images or ideas that are not similar close together to create a contrasting effect

5.4 Writing practice

Exercise 4

Four students were set this essay question on the poem 'Island Man':

Explore how Nichols uses the structure of 'Island Man' to convey the differences between life in the Caribbean and life in London.

They had ten minutes to write one paragraph.

Here is what Student A wrote, along with some teacher comments:

> **Student A**
>
> The poem tells us all about a man who has been living on a Caribbean island and he has now moved to London. He doesn't like living in London because it's grey and noisy. The poem uses repetition with 'groggily groggily' and 'muffling muffling'. 'Island Man' has a cyclical shape. If a text has a cyclical shape it means that it begins and ends in the same place. A cyclical structure shows that nothing changes for Island Man.

You are showing a general understanding of what Island Man feels about London, which is good, but you need to link this comment to the question, which is about 'structure'. It would be a good idea to highlight the key words in the question to help you to focus clearly in your opening sentence.

Good. You have correctly identified a structural feature in the poem. You now need to write about the effect of the repetition here in telling us about how Island Man feels about London or the Caribbean.

This is getting better. You have correctly identified a feature and started to discuss its effect. You don't need to tell me what a cyclical shape is (I already know!). Can you include some more detail to tell us where Island Man is at the beginning and the end of the poem and expand on what you mean by 'nothing changes'?

a Rewrite Student A's paragraph with the improvements suggested by the teacher.

Now read what Student B wrote.

> **Student B**
>
> I really liked the poem 'Island Man'. I think the poet did a good job with language and structure and this really helped me to understand how much Island Man loved his lovely sunny island and hates the noise of the cars on the North Circular Road. I really liked the words 'breaking and wombing' because they made me feel like I was bobbing up and down on a wave. There is an offset line showing that Island Man feels he is being separated from the dream he is enjoying.

b i Imagine you are Student B's teacher. Write some helpful comments to Student B like Student A's teacher did. Remember to tell Student B what was good about their response as well as how it can be improved.
ii Now rewrite Student B's paragraph with your own suggested improvements.
iii Compare your work with a partner and see if you can help each other to improve this paragraph further.

Here is what Student C wrote, along with some teacher comments.

Student C

This is a strong opening that immediately addresses the question. Well done.

The structural features of 'Island Man' help a reader to understand how Island Man longs for his old island in the Caribbean and has difficulty in adapting to life in the city. The opening line is very short, containing just the one word 'Morning' which makes it stand out and means that Island Man has been rudely awoken from his pleasant dreams of his island. The cheerful greeting 'Morning' is answered at the end of the poem with Island Man's own unhappy thought of 'Another London day'. The use of **enjambment** makes the lines flow smoothly, just like the ocean in his dreams and the **onomatopoeic** word 'wombing' imitates the gentle sounds he can hear in his head.

This is an interpretation that would fit, but can you explain more effectively how this interpretation links to the evidence you have given ('Morning' being given its own line). Also, as you are offering an interpretation, could you find a better word than 'means'. Is there anything else you can say about the impact of the opening line?

Good idea. Can you expand on your comment here at all?

Noticing a contrast between the way the poem opens and closes can create the basis for a good structural point. Can you expand on what you mean here? How is contrast achieved?

Another good idea. Again, can you expand? What does the word 'wombing' also make you think of here and can you link your points in the last two sentences back to the question?

c Rewrite Student C's paragraph with the improvements suggested by the teacher.

Now read what Student D wrote.

Student D

It's clear that Island Man finds his life in London to be dismal and hectic and that he misses the life he used to lead in the Caribbean. The way that Nichols's poem is structured helps us to understand this. There is no clear form to the poem and it is written in **free verse** with very little rhyme. There is some internal rhyming ('breaking', 'wombing' and 'pulling'): the use of the present continuous here helps us to understand that the ocean's movements and the fishermen's toils are also continuous in Island Man's dreams. The offset words 'groggily groggily' show us how Island Man struggles to become part of his daily reality.

d i Imagine you are Student D's teacher. Write some helpful comments to Student D like Student C's teacher did. Remember to tell Student D what was good about their response as well as how it can be improved.
   ii Now rewrite Student D's paragraph with your own suggested improvements.
   iii Compare your work with a partner and see if you can help each other to improve this paragraph further.

Key terms

Enjambment: A sentence that runs on beyond the end of a line in poetry

Onomatopoeia: Language that sounds like the idea it describes; 'crackle' is an example of onomatopoeia (make sure you can spell the term correctly)

Free verse: A form of poetry that takes no particular shape, rhythm, metre or rhyme

---

5.5 Set-text focus

Exercise 5

Choose another poem from your set texts in which you feel that the structure of the poem plays an important role in conveying the poet's messages and ideas (your teacher may help you with this).

a Remind yourself of the different structural devices identified in Exercise 2.

b While you are reading the poem, jot down any structural devices you see, like you did in part **d** of Exercise 2, and think about the purpose they serve.

c Look at how the poem begins and ends. Has the poet changed their attitude or view by the end? If so, can you find the **turning point**?

d Look at the questions set in Exercise 3 of this unit. Can you set between five and ten similar questions to help a fellow class member understand the poem? Try to make at least half of your questions open questions, where there could be more than one answer.

e Swap your questions with someone else in the class. Answer them, then swap back and mark each other's answers.

Key terms

Turning point: A point in a literary text at which an idea or an attitude is changed or reversed

Rhyme scheme: The pattern of rhymes at the end of each line in poetry

Metre: The rhythmic structure of a line of poetry

Theme: A key idea or subject that is repeated throughout a text

Take your learning further

In this unit, you have been studying a poem written in free verse, a very common poetic form, particularly in poetry from the last century. However, there are many other very popular poetic forms, some of which you may come across in your set poem collection.

Here are three of the most common poetic forms that you might find in traditional English poetry:
- Sonnet (Petrarchan)
- Sonnet (Shakespearean)
- Ballad.

1 Carry out some research on these different forms. You might want to consider the following:
  – The form these poems take: length, **rhyme schemes**, **metre**, rhythm, stanza length
  – Any new technical terms associated with how these poems are structured
  – Any other particular features of each form
  – Similarities and differences between the forms
  – **Themes** and ideas commonly explored in these poems.

2 Design a worksheet to test someone in your class on the research you have done. Don't put the answers on your worksheet.
  a Swap your worksheet with another student and see how many of the questions you can answer without referring to your research.
  b Mark each other's worksheet. Did you get your answers all right?

Unit summary

In this unit, you have learned how to:
- Identify the use of structural devices in a poem and use them to support your argument or opinion.
- Think about how the structure of a poem contributes to its meaning.
- Explore the ways a poet uses structural devices to create and shape meanings and effect.
- Explain the effect that the structure of a poem has on you as you read it.

Think about how you have demonstrated each of these skills in the exercises in this unit. Be sure to think about the structures of the other poems included in this book and also to think about 'Island Man' in relation to some of the aspects of poetry discussed in other units.

6 'Thistles': Focus on language

In this unit, you will:
- Select words and phrases in a poem that support a certain reading.
- Identify ways that writers explore ideas beyond the surface meaning of a text.
- Examine how a writer's use of language – including metaphor, similes, personification and onomatopoeia – creates effects.
- Explain what a writer's use of imagery makes you think and feel, and how it does so.

Ted Hughes (1930 to 1998) was an English poet. A lot of his poetry is inspired by nature. Quite often in Hughes's nature poetry, we see images and ideas that make us compare the natural world with the human world.

Ted Hughes's birthplace is the Calder Valley in Yorkshire. Vikings were a very strong force in Yorkshire in the ninth and tenth centuries CE. Many battles were fought there and some Vikings settled in Great Britain.

Glossary

Guttural: A harsh or grating speech sound produced in the throat

Hoe: A tool used to cultivate land by digging up and destroying weeds

Viking: Pirates from Scandinavia (northern Europe) – they raided the coasts of other European countries in the 8th to 10th centuries and are often associated with physical strength and aggression

6.1 'Thistles' by Ted Hughes

Against the rubber tongues of cows and the hoeing hands of men
Thistles spike the summer air
And crackle open under a blue-black pressure.

Every one a revengeful burst
Of resurrection, a grasped fistful   5
Of splintered weapons and Icelandic frost thrust up

From the underground stain of a decayed Viking.
They are like pale hair and the gutturals of dialects.
Every one manages a plume of blood.

Then they grow grey like men.   10
Mown down, it is a feud. Their sons appear
Stiff with weapons, fighting back over the same ground.

6.2 First impressions

Exercise 1

a Read the poem together as a class.

b With a partner, talk for one minute about what you know about thistles. You could discuss:
  - where they tend to be found
  - what you think about them
  - what other people think about them.

c The poem compares thistles to Vikings. Look at the pictures below.

Why might it be appropriate to choose Vikings to compare to thistles? Take five minutes to write down as many similarities between them as you can think of. You might like to present your ideas in a mind map like the one below.

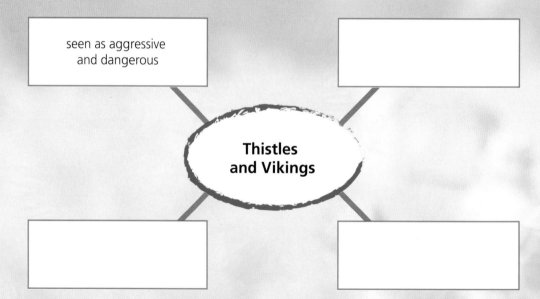

seen as aggressive and dangerous

Thistles and Vikings

6.3 Finding evidence

Exercise 2

We are told in line 1 that men are 'hoeing' the thistles.

a i In pairs, find words or short phrases in the first two stanzas that suggest the thistles are angry and dangerous. Write down what these words or phrases mean and comment on their effects. The first one has been done for you.

Word / short phrase	Meanings and effects
'spike'	Pierce with a sharp point. Makes us think the thistles are dangerous.

ii For each of the words or phrases you identified, think of alternative language that Hughes could have used. Why do you think he uses the words he does? For example, why does he use the word 'spike' rather than 'pierce' or 'impale'?

iii Hughes uses **metaphor**, personification and onomatopoeia in the first two stanzas. If you are not sure what these terms mean, have a look at the Glossary at the back of this book.

In pairs, identify one example each of metaphor, personification and onomatopoeia from the first two stanzas of 'Thistles'. To help you get started, one metaphor has been found for you.

Metaphor	'rubber tongues'
Metaphor	
Personification	
Onomatopoeia	

> **Key term**
>
> **Metaphor:** A description of one thing as another thing that is mostly unrelated to make a comparison that highlights the similarity between the two things: 'rubber tongues' in the poem 'Thistles' is an example of a metaphor – the cows' tongues are not really rubber, but we get a sense that they are soft and sensitive compared to the prickles of the thistles

b Now go back and reread stanza 1.

The **syntax** of stanza 1 creates an abrupt effect as the line opens with a **preposition** and the main subject comes much later.

i Rewrite stanza 1 as if it were a sentence in a prose text with the **subject** at the start.

ii Why do you think Hughes decided to start his poem with 'Against'?

iii What is the effect of telling us that the cows have 'rubber tongues' and that the men are hoeing with their 'hands'?

c Some people say that Hughes's use of language in the first two stanzas suggests he is using the description of men hoeing thistles as a way of describing the aggression of a real human war.

i On your own, look at stanzas 1 and 2 again and decide how much you agree with this idea.

ii Now copy out the table below. On your own, think about what Hughes might be saying about war in the first two stanzas and which of these statements most closely match his thoughts about war. Write numbers 1 to 4 by each statement, where number 1 most closely matches what he is saying and number 4 least accurately describes what he is saying.

Ted Hughes is saying this about war in stanzas 1 and 2	Number 1–4
War is a fight over land	
War is aggressive and violent	
War is unfair	
War can be justified	

iii Compare your table with the person you are sitting next to. Take it in turns to explain your thoughts and ideas to each other. Remember to refer to stanzas 1 and 2 as closely as you can to put across your ideas.

> **TIP**
>
> When you are explaining your ideas about a text, always remember to refer as closely as you can to it. Use specific words and phrases from it as examples.

> **Key terms**
>
> **Syntax:** The order of words in a sentence
>
> **Preposition:** A word, often short, that uses direction, location or time to link together words in the sentence; examples include 'on', 'in', 'before' and 'after'
>
> **Subject (of a sentence):** The person or thing doing the action described in a sentence; it can be a noun (for example, 'Thistles' in line 2 of the poem) or a pronoun (for example, 'it', 'they')

Exercise 3

a Now reread stanzas 3 and 4 carefully. In stanzas 3 and 4, Hughes seems to be telling us that long-dead Vikings buried under the ground are the source of the thistle's warlike features.

i Write a list of any words or phrases where you think Hughes is drawing direct comparisons between thistles and Vikings.

ii Check your list with the left-hand column opposite. Did you find all the images?

iii Pair the images with the ideas they create.

	Image		Idea
1	'the underground stain of a decayed Viking'	**a**	The Vikings brought a new language to the countries they invaded – a language of the throat, quite raspy and rough. The 'crack' that the thistle emits when it's crushed copies this sound.
2	'like pale hair'	**b**	New thistles are upright and equipped to fight all over again.
3	'the gutturals of dialects'	**c**	The new thistles will retaliate for their dead ancestors.
4	'a plume of blood'	**d**	As thistles age they lose their colour.
5	'grow grey like men'	**e**	Thistles grew from the remains of long-dead Viking warriors buried beneath the ground.
6	'Their sons'	**f**	Thistles have light-coloured spikes that are similar to the fair hair associated with people from north European (Scandinavian) countries.
7	'stiff with weapons'	**g**	Thistles have reddish-purple flowers, which are like the feathers that are worn as a sign of honour on a warrior's helmet. This could also suggest blood cascading (pluming) from the head of a wounded warrior.
8	'fighting back'	**h**	The seeds from the old thistles create new thistles.

b A student said: 'The language of stanzas 3 and 4 is very thought-provoking and creates a feeling of sadness.'
  i Do you agree with the student's words about stanzas 3 and 4? Can you say on a scale of 1 to 10 how sad it makes you feel (where 10 is saddest)? Explain your response to the class.
  ii Are there any other feelings that the language in stanzas 3 and 4 creates? Explain to the class your response by referring closely to the poem and the language of the poem.

TIP

Whenever you are explaining your ideas, it is important to keep your focus on the language used in the poem.

6.4 Writing practice

Exercise 4

a Look at this essay question.

Explore how Hughes makes the thistles sound like fierce warriors in this poem.

   i On your own, copy the question down and read it carefully. It is important to show that you know and understand the whole poem, but it is also important that you focus on the question set. Highlight the key words in the question and make sure that you know what you will be writing about.

   ii Now that you have worked out what the key words in the question are, copy out and, in pairs, complete the following table to plan your essay.

  iii You should both write down your language choices in the left-hand column and give the meaning of each choice in the right-hand column. If you can, try to comment on the effect of each choice too. Help each other to find the best language choices and to find the best way to express their meanings (and effects).

> **TIP**
>
> Keep your language choices short. Only include the words you want to talk about.

Language that makes the thistles sound like 'fierce warriors'	Meanings (and effects)
'spike (the summer air)'	This means that the prickles from the broken thistles are filling the air. (The effect is to make them sound dangerous like flying weapons.)

This table is a useful planning tool because it helps you to see the content of your essay at a glance.

> **TIP**
>
> If you are asked for the 'meaning' of a word or phrase, you should put it in your own words or paraphrase it. You have to be careful to make sure your meaning makes sense in the context of the whole poem.
>
> If you are asked for the 'effect' of a word or phrase, you should write about how it makes the reader feel or how it influences the way we interpret the poem.

iv Now that you have completed the table, try to write five paragraphs on your own (one for each row of the table) to answer the essay question. Remember to use quotation marks around each quotation. You could start your essay with the following sentence: 'Hughes makes effective use of language in order to make the thistles sound like fierce warriors…'

b Look at this essay question.

How does Hughes's language create strong feelings about war in 'Thistles'?

i On your own, copy the question down and read it carefully. As in part **a**, it is important to show that you know and understand the whole poem, but it is also important that you focus on the question set. Highlight the key words in the question and make sure that you know what you will be writing about.

ii Now that you have worked out what the key words in the question are, copy out and complete the following table to help you plan your essay. Your earlier work in '6.3 Finding evidence' will help you. Spend about 15 minutes on this table.

Strong feeling	Language	Comment on how the language choice creates the strong feeling

This table helps you to see your essay content at a glance and is a useful planning tool.

Exercise 5

The following paragraphs are taken from the middle of student answers to the essay question:

How does Hughes's language create strong feelings about war in 'Thistles'?

a In pairs, read all three partial responses and agree which you think is best and which you think needs most improvement.

b Number them 1, 2 and 3 (where 1 is the best and 3 is the weakest).

c Write down **one** point that is good about each response and **one** point that could be improved.

d Share your thoughts about the responses with a bigger group or the whole class.

Key terms

Simile: A comparison of one thing to another, using the word 'as' or 'like' – 'They are *like* pale hair' is an example of a simile; the comparison gives emphasis to a description or makes it more vivid, but similes are generally thought of as less powerful than metaphors

Pathos: A feeling of sadness or pity created by a writer through their use of language or other devices

Student response A

This poem uses metaphors like 'splintered weapons'. This is a metaphor because it is comparing the prickles of a thistle to a weapon without using the word 'as' or 'like'. This causes strong feelings about war because metaphors are better than **similes**. I liked the way Ted Hughes compared them to Vikings in the poem. He did this because there are dead Vikings buried where he used to live in Yorkshire.

Student response B

The poem makes me feel sad about war because people die in violent ways. The 'plume of blood' makes me think of blood coming out of a warrior's head and 'mown down' makes me think of a lot of people just all killed at once. It's like they were all just killed in the way we chop down grass. There are other images that make me feel sad like 'rubber tongues' because I think of the thistles prickling the soft tongues of the cows.

Student response C

At the end of the poem, the main feeling is sadness in contrast to the anger felt previously at the apparent malice of the thistles for their continued attacks on human men trying to work the land. Now we see them as generation after generation of freedom fighters, engaged in a constant cycle of fighting for, and losing, the ground they occupy. **Pathos** is created in such images as 'grow grey like men' and 'Their sons'. This personification enables us to see how the fight is a life-long battle and seems to be their only reason for existence, passed on down the generations. That they can be 'mown down' suggests that they are easily eradicated and their fight is pointless.

6.5 Set-text focus

Exercise 6

Choose a poem from your set-text list that makes effective use of language.

a Draw a mind map with a central word saying what the poem is about (for example, Nature, Love, Happiness). On your mind map link short quotations to your central word, where you think the poet has made effective language choices that help you to understand what the poem is about.

b Put these language choices into a table and comment on their meanings and effects.

c With your partner, discuss any strong feelings that the language choices in the poem create. (Look back to your work on 'Thistles' in '6.3 Finding evidence' to help you with this.)

d With your partner, discuss whether the language choices help you to see any change in the poet's thoughts, or if the poet keeps to the same idea throughout. (Again, look back to your work on 'Thistles' in '6.3 Finding evidence' to help you with this.)

e Write a plan for one of the two essay questions below:

What feelings does [poet's name] make the reader feel in [title of poem]? How does the poet's use of language create those feelings?

OR

How does [poet's name] use language to create strong feelings about [word in your mind map] in [title of poem]?

Take your learning further

1 Write up one of your essay plans as a full essay. You should think of using at least a paragraph for each row of language and comments. If your plan took 15 minutes to write, you should spend about half an hour on your essay.
2 Some poets romanticise nature or write about it in a sentimental way. Hughes's nature poems are the opposite: he is inspired by the rawness of nature and often writes in very **explicit** detail about his subject. Read some of Hughes's other nature poems and decide how his use of language affects how we interpret nature in each poem. Does the language sometimes suggest that he is writing about something else in the human world and using nature to help us think about the human world?

Key term

Explicitly: In a way that is clear and precise, requiring little interpretation

Unit summary

In this unit, you have learned how to:
- Select words and phrases in a poem that support a certain reading.
- Identify ways that writers explore ideas beyond the surface meaning of a text.
- Examine how a writer's use of language – including metaphor, similes, personification and onomatopoeia – creates effects.
- Explain what a writer's use of imagery makes you think and feel, and how it does so.

Think about how you have demonstrated each of these skills in the exercises in this unit. How do the other poets studied in this section use language to create meanings and effects?

7 'Search for My Tongue': Focus on themes and ideas

In this unit, you will:
- Make direct and indirect references to a poem to illustrate your ideas about the themes and ideas explored within it.
- Develop a deeper awareness of the ideas discussed in a poem by looking beyond its surface meaning.
- Explore the ways a poet uses language and structure to present ideas and explore themes.
- Communicate personal opinions about certain themes, based on your reading of the poem.

In Units 5 and 6, you have looked at how structure and language in poetry help a poet to convey meaning. In this unit you will be further developing these skills, so that you can write effectively about the themes and ideas explored by poets in your set texts. A theme is an idea that runs through a work of literature. A work of literature can have main themes and minor themes depending on how important you think they are to the text.

Sujata Bhatt was born in 1956 in Ahmedabad, the largest city in the Indian state of Gujarat, where her mother tongue was Gujarati. Later, her family lived for some years in the United States, where she learned English. She now lives in Germany.

In 'Search for My Tongue', Bhatt studies the impact on a person who has emigrated as a child to a country where a completely different language is spoken.

Glossary
Mother tongue: The first language we learn from birth

7.1 'Search for My Tongue' by Sujata Bhatt

You ask me what I mean
by saying I have lost my tongue.
I ask you, what would you do
if you had two tongues in your mouth,
and lost the first one, the mother tongue,   5
and could not really know the other,
the foreign tongue.
You could not use them both together
even if you thought that way.
And if you lived in a place you had to   10
speak a foreign tongue,
your mother tongue would rot,
rot and die in your mouth
until you had to spit it out.
I thought I spit it out   15
but overnight while I dream,

munay hutoo kay aakhee jeebh aakhee bhasha
may thoonky nakhi chay
parantoo rattray svupnama mari bhasha pachi aavay chay
foolnee jaim mari bhasha nmari jeebh   20
modhama kheelay chay
fullnee jaim mari bhasha mari jeebh
modhama pakay chay

it grows back, a stump of a shoot
grows longer, grows moist, grows strong veins,   25
it ties the other tongue in knots,
the bud opens, the bud opens in my mouth,
it pushes the other tongue aside.
Everytime I think I've forgotten,
I think I've lost the mother tongue,   30
it blossoms out of my mouth.

7.2 First impressions

Exercise 1

Read the poem. The middle stanza is a transliteration of Gujarati, Sujata Bhatt's mother tongue. Unless you speak Gujarati yourself, you probably won't understand it. Don't worry about that for now.

a In pairs or small groups, discuss the following ideas:

   i What do we mean by a person's 'culture'?

   ii Is a person's 'sense of identity' the same as their culture?

   iii How important to your culture and your sense of identity is the language you speak?

   Share your ideas with the class. Remember to try to give reasons for what you say. You might want to give examples from your own life and experience.

b **i** By yourself or with a partner, think about the phrase 'mother tongue'. What does the word 'mother' make you feel about the first language we learn?

   ii By yourself or with a partner, brainstorm any situations in which you might not be able to speak in your mother tongue. Write them down.

   iii Write down a few words that describe how you might feel if you were in a situation where you couldn't speak in your mother tongue.

   Share your responses with the class.

c Reread the poem slowly with the thoughts and ideas you discussed in **a** and **b** in mind.

   i How does the title 'Search for My Tongue' help you to understand what the poem is about and how the poet feels? Is there a reason why the poem isn't called 'Search for My Mother Tongue'?

   ii Do you think you might be able to work out what the middle stanza is saying? Tell your teacher if you think you know.

7.3 Finding evidence

Exercise 2

a Loss of identity is a main theme in 'Search for My Tongue'. Make a mind map with 'Themes' in the middle. Put 'Loss of identity' on the mind map. See if you can identify three more themes and put them on too.

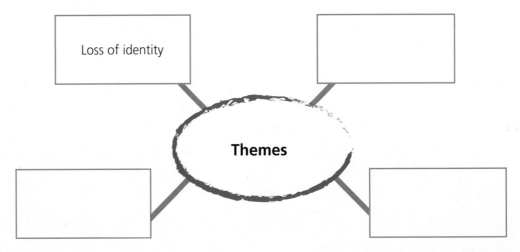

b i At the beginning of the poem, the speaker seems to be talking to an unknown person whom she calls 'you'. Write down what you think was the conversation between the speaker and the person she is addressing just before the poem starts. This only needs to be a few lines long.

ii On your own, or with a partner, paraphrase what the speaker is saying in lines 3 to 7. Try to use your own words as much as possible.

iii Think about lines 8 and 9. Here the speaker is saying that you can't use two languages at once, and she adds 'even if you thought that way'. Discuss with your partner what 'even if you thought that way' might mean. If you are learning a foreign language in school, it might help to consider which language you think in when you try to speak or write in that foreign language.

iv Reread lines 10 to 14. The poet uses a metaphor to suggest that her mother tongue is a plant that will 'rot' and die because it is not given an opportunity to be used (and flourish and grow). Look at the images of plants below. Which ones would you link with the 'foreign tongue'? Which ones would you link with the 'mother tongue'? Explain your reasons to the class.

v At the end of the first stanza, the poet uses the verb 'spit' in the phrase 'spit it out' to tell us how she thought she had forgotten her mother tongue. Spitting is often seen as offensive behaviour or as a way of getting rid of something unwanted in the mouth. With a partner or by yourself, think about and write down:
   – why you think the poet uses the word 'spit' here
   – the effects of repeating words like 'spit' and 'rot'; think about:
      – how the words sound when you speak them
      – the way they make you feel when you think about them.

Exercise 3

Look at the Gujarati lettering below. Underneath each line of original Gujarati is an English transliteration, which helps an English speaker to know how to pronounce the Gujarati letters.

મને હુતું કે આબ્‌બી જીભ આબ્‌બી ભાષા

(munay hutoo kay aakhee jeebh aakhee bhasha)

મેં થૂંકી નાબી છે

(may thoonky nakhi chay)

પરંતુ રાત્‌રે સ્‌વપ્‌નાંમાં મારી ભાષા પાછી આવે છે

(parantoo rattray svupnama mari bhasha pachi aavay chay)

ફૂલની જેમ મારી ભાષા મારી જીભ

(foolnee jaim mari bhasha nmari jeebh)

મોઢામાં બીલે છે

(modhama kheelay chay)

ફૂલની જેમ મારી ભાષા મારી જીભ

(fullnee jaim mari bhasha mari jeebh)

મોઢામાં પાકે છે

(modhama pakay chay)

a With a partner, or by yourself, consider why the poet has written the middle section in Gujarati, using English letters underneath to show you how to pronounce it. It might help you to think about what might have been lost to the poem if the Gujarati section weren't there. Tell the class your thoughts.

b The final stanza, in English, is a translation of the Gujarati section. Think about the structure of the poem. Why does the Gujarati section feature in the middle of the poem? Why does it come before its English translation?

Exercise 4

Reread the last stanza. Here the metaphor of plants and flowers is extended.

a Think about the images used here and decide which of the following comments you feel best describe the effects of these images. Copy out the table. Use the numbers 1 to 5 (where 1 is most true and 5 is least true). Explain your responses to the class.

Comment	Number 1–5
Describing her tongue as a plant is using an image from nature, which makes us feel that it is natural for your mother tongue to stay with you forever.	
Using an image of her tongue as a plant makes us think of the cyclical nature of life: how, like plants grow and then die, her own sense of identity in this foreign country grows strong but then is lost.	
The image of her tongue as a flower that 'blossoms' makes us think of something beautiful to look at.	
The image of her tongue as something that grows and won't stop growing until the other tongue is killed by it tells us how powerful her connection is to the culture of her birth country.	
The image is a rather frightening one that suggests the lack of control we have over our thoughts and dreams while we sleep.	

b Do you have any other thoughts that are different from the ideas in the table? Share them with the class.

c Write down one word that you think describes the **tone** of the speaker's voice in the last stanza. Share your word with the class. Try to use examples from the poem to explain your choice of word.

> **Key term**
>
> **Tone (of voice):** A character's personality conveyed by language choices for speech and thoughts; it can change over the course of a text

> **TIP**
>
> To help you work out the tone of voice in the last stanza, consider the effects of such structural devices as listing and repetition, as well as the language choices and images. Look back to Units 5 and 6 where structural devices and use of language are covered.

> **MAKING CONNECTIONS**
>
> Grace Nichols also explores themes of cultural identity and separation in 'Island Man' (Unit 5). Compare and contrast the methods the two poets use to convey their similar themes.

7.4 Writing practice

Exercise 5

a Some students, who found the poem 'Search for My Tongue' quite difficult, made the following comments. Try to write some advice that would help each student understand and appreciate the poem better.

Student A:

> I didn't understand the middle verse at all and so I didn't see why it needed to be there, especially when I realised that the last verse is just saying the same in English.

Student B:

> Why is the poet saying that she has two tongues in her mouth? I think that gives the reader a rather ugly image, as if the poet feels like she is some kind of alien creature.

Student C:

> My English teacher is always telling me to write concisely and not repeat myself, so why does the poet keep repeating words like 'grow' and 'open' in the last stanza?

b Look at the following essay title:

Explore the ways in which Bhatt uses powerful words and images in 'Search for My Tongue'.

i Here are the first two paragraphs of a student's response to this essay title. Read them and think about the questions in the annotations.

Student response

In the poem 'Search for My Tongue' the poet repeats words like 'mother' and 'foreign' to make clear the contrast in the way she feels about the two languages she speaks or used to speak. The word 'mother' tells us how her first language made her feel nurtured and expresses her love for her former culture. The word 'foreign' ironically suggests her detachment from the language of the country she lives in now, and her sense that she will never truly belong to this culture. The poet also repeats the strong word 'lost' to stress what she believes has happened to her mother tongue. This is a blunt, simple everyday word, but it powerfully suggests the finality of her detachment from her former language and culture.

In lines 12–16, the poet uses the metaphor of a dead plant to describe her tongue. The image makes the reader think that a battle has taken place between the 'foreign tongue' and the 'mother tongue' and that the foreign tongue has won. This could make the reader perceive the foreign tongue as some kind of weed or parasite that has surrounded and preyed on her mother tongue. Again, she uses repetition, this time of the strong words 'rot' and 'spit'. Both words are rather **colloquial** and blunt and suggest that she is obliged to treat her mother tongue as something undesirable in her mouth that she has to get rid of quickly.

Ironically: why has the student used this word here? What is ironic about the point being made?

Suggests: Why is 'suggests' often a better word to use than a word like 'means' in an essay like this?

Powerfully: Why has the student used this word?

Could make: See the comment on 'suggests' above. Why are modal verbs like 'could' often better in an essay like this?

ii Underline the key words in the essay title. Think about what should go into the third and fourth paragraphs of this essay. Make a planning table like the one below.

Powerful words and images	Comments

iii Write the third and fourth paragraphs to the essay. Spend 20 to 30 minutes on this.

iv Swap your work with a partner. Read each other's work. Did you cover the same ideas? What did you like about your partner's work? What might your partner have done to make their work even better?

> **Key term**
>
> **Colloquialism:** An informal, chatty or slang word or phrase, which we tend to use more in speech than in writing

7.5 Set-text focus

Exercise 6

Choose another poem from your set poem collection in which the themes and ideas are thought-provoking.

a Make a mind map of the themes like you did in Exercise 2a in this unit.

b Make a planning table like you did in Exercise 5bii in which you choose powerful language and images that you think help the poet to convey their ideas. Remember to complete a comment column on the right-hand side.

c Consider any other powerful devices the poet uses to convey their ideas. How is the poem structured? Are there any patterns?

d Using the work you did in Exercise 5b to help you, write an essay response to the question:

Explore the ways in which [poet's name] uses powerful words and images in [title of poem].

Take your learning further

A number of poets have explored their feelings about how their language affects their sense of belonging and how they are perceived in a country.

Tom Leonard is a Scottish poet whose poem 'The Six O'clock News' questions whether BBC newsreaders should all speak in one 'official' dialect or whether they should be allowed to speak in the dialect they grew up with.

Rita Joe came from Cape Breton Island in Nova Scotia. She was of Mi'kmaq background, meaning that her family were descendants of the indigenous people of this part of Canada. She spoke the local language. When she was orphaned, aged ten, she was sent to the Shubenacadie Residential School, where she was not allowed to speak her own language and had to learn another culture. Her poem 'I Lost My Talk' is about this experience.

Either:
- Read 'The Six O'clock News' (out loud if you can) or listen to a reading of the poem on YouTube.

Or:
- Read 'I Lost My Talk' (out loud if you can) or listen to a reading of the poem on YouTube.

In what ways do you think Leonard's or Joe's messages about their language / dialect are similar to Bhatt's? In what ways are they different? Explain your ideas.

What do you learn about the importance of language to a person's sense of identify and self-worth after reading these poems?

Key term

Dialect: A form of language that has some differences in vocabulary and grammar and that is spoken by people in a specific social group or from a specific place

---

Unit summary

In this unit, you have learned how to:
- Make direct and **indirect references** to a poem to illustrate your ideas about the themes and ideas explored within it.
- Develop a deeper awareness of the ideas discussed in a poem by looking beyond its surface meaning.
- Explore the ways a poet uses language and structure to present ideas and explore themes.
- Communicate personal opinions about certain themes, based on your reading of the poem.

Think about how you have demonstrated each of these skills in the exercises in this unit. You will need to be alert to the themes and ideas that writers are exploring in all of the texts you study on this course. You may also want to think about Bhatt's poem in more depth in relation to some of the other aspects of poetry focused on in this section.

Key term

Indirect reference: Using some of the same words as the writer but in a different form; quotation marks are not required for an indirect reference

8

'Elegy For My Father's Father': Focus on character and perspective

In this unit, you will:
- Show detailed knowledge of a poem, supported by reference to the text.
- Understand a poem and its contexts and explore beyond surface meanings to show deeper awareness of the speaker's ideas and attitudes.
- Recognise and appreciate ways in which a poet uses language, structure and form to create character and perspective.
- Examine different interpretations of a poem and consider which you think is most insightful.

Key terms

Perspective: Like a lens through which readers view characters and events in a text; the perspective of a text is created by the speaker: we interpret the characters and events based on what the speaker shows and tells us

Protagonist: A main character in a literary text

In Units 5 and 6, you looked at how structure and language help to convey meaning in poetry. In Unit 7, you practised the skills you developed by writing about themes and ideas in a poem. Now you will be looking at how a poet uses language and structure to create a character or voice, as well as the **perspective** from which the themes and ideas of the poem are addressed. There will be opportunities to build on the skills you are still developing to write about characters in your set poems.

James K. Baxter (1926 to 1972) was a New Zealand poet. His grandfather, John Baxter, the **protagonist** of this poem, was born in Scotland and emigrated to New Zealand in his early twenties. John Baxter died in 1939 in Dunedin, New Zealand, when his grandson would have been about 13 years old. The grandson is the speaker in this poem.

Glossary

Elegy: A sad poem, usually used to lament the death of a loved one

Cairn: A Scottish word, meaning a mound of stones built by people as a burial mound or memorial

Pipes: Bagpipes, a musical instrument associated with Scotland; they are often played ceremonially at funerals

Aaronsrod: A plant that naturally grows much taller than other plants: Aaron was a biblical figure and the brother of Moses, who led the Israelites out of Egypt and into the Promised Land; like Moses's rod, Aaron's rod had miraculous powers, demonstrated during the Plagues of Egypt – on one occasion, instructed by God, Aaron threw down his rod in front of the Egyptian Pharaoh and it turned into a serpent that ate all the other serpents conjured by Pharaoh's sorcerers; the rod is also a natural symbol of authority, as the tool used by a shepherd to correct and guide his flock, as well as being a plant that naturally grows much taller than other plants

Sods: Turf, pieces of grass attached to the soil

Burning-glass: A large lens used to catch the sun's rays to create fire in olden days

8.1 'Elegy For My Father's Father' by James K. Baxter

He knew in the hour he died
That his heart had never spoken
In eighty years of days.
O for the tall tower broken
Memorial is denied: 5
And the unchanging cairn
The pipes could set ablaze
An aaronsrod and blossom.
They stood by the graveside
From his bitter veins born   10
And mourned him in their fashion.
A chain of sods in a day
He could slice and build
High as the head of a man
And a flowering cherry tree   15
On his walking shoulder held
Under the lion sun.
When he was old and blind
He sat in a curved chair
All day by the kitchen fire.   20
Many hours he had seen
The stars in their drunken dancing
Through the burning-glass of his mind
And sober knew the green
Boughs of heaven folding   25
The winter world in their hand.
The pride of his heart was dumb.
He knew in the hour he died
That his heart had never spoken
In song or bridal bed.   30
And the naked thought fell back
To a house by the waterside
And the leaves the wind had shaken
Then for a child's sake:
To the waves all night awake   35
With the dark mouths of the dead.
The tongues of water spoke
And his heart was unafraid.

8.2 First impressions

Exercise 1

> **Key term**
>
> **Assuming a persona:** Taking on the identity of another person

In poetry, there is always a speaker. However, there can be different types of speaker:

» The poet speaking in their own voice

» The poet **assuming a persona** to speak

» The poet as a detached voice speaking about someone or something else.

a You have studied four poems so far in this section of the book: 'Phenomenal Woman', 'Island Man', 'Thistles' and 'Search For My Tongue'. You may also have studied additional poems in the 'Take your learning further' exercises of each unit. Working with a partner:

   i Look back to the poems you have read so far and decide which type of speaker each poet has chosen for their poem.

   ii Discuss the effects of having this type of speaker for each of these poems. Share with the rest of the class what you have discussed. Remember to base what you say on evidence from each poem.

b Look at the title of the poem by James K. Baxter. By yourself, or with a partner:

   i Work out what you think the poem is going to be about, just from its title.

   ii Think about what calling his grandfather 'my father's father' suggests about the poet's relationship with his grandfather.

c Read the poem 'Elegy For My Father's Father' slowly and carefully. Think about the following questions:

   i How helpful was the title to you in understanding what the poem is about?

   ii What type of speaker does the poem use?

   iii What parts of the poem were straightforward to follow? Which words or lines could you not understand?

Share your thoughts with the class or your teacher.

Exercise 2

The poem is presented in one single stanza. However, there are five sections to the poem; the beginning of the first line of each is given in the table below. Each section shows a movement in the poet's thoughts.

Copy the table and, in the right-hand column, summarise what you think Baxter is describing in each of the five sections. The first section is done for you.

Section	Begins with...	Summary of what Baxter is describing
1	'He knew in the hour'	The last hour of his grandfather's life in which he has awareness that he has never shared his emotions with his family
2	'O for the tall tower'	
3	'A chain of sods'	
4	'When he was old and blind'	
5	'He knew in the hour'	

8.3 Finding evidence

Exercise 3

In this unit we are considering how a poet creates a character. In this case, there are two main characters to consider: the speaker (the grandson) and the protagonist (the grandfather).

We are also considering perspective. In this case, the perspective we receive is the grandson's. As you work through the exercises below, you may find yourself wondering whether the way the grandson presents his grandfather shows a change in perspective at different points in the poem. Also, you will notice that the grandson often writes as if he knows what his grandfather thought.

a Reread section 1 (lines 1 to 3) of the poem. Consider the phrase 'eighty years of days'. With a partner:
  i Think about what is odd about this phrase. What would be a more normal way of writing it?
  ii Discuss the effect of this phrase. Think about what would have been lost if another more usual phrase had been used.
b Reread section 2 (lines 4 to 11). The language of this section is **elevated**, or what we would call written in an **epic style**. Write down your responses to the following questions:
  i The metaphor of a 'tall tower' that is now 'broken' describes the grandfather who was once a big strong man and is now weak and dying. Does the writing **style** here affect your thoughts on Baxter's perspective on his grandfather?

Key terms

Elevated language: Language that is formal and dignified; there is no use of slang or informal words – because of its heightened formality, elevated language can feel unfamiliar and difficult to relate to; James K. Baxter had a love for Classical and Romantic poetry, which often uses flourishes like those we see in 'Elegy For My Father's Father'

Epic style: A style of writing associated with long narrative poems set in ancient times about extraordinary characters who perform heroic deeds; it includes elevated language, with many metaphors and similes as well as rhetorical flourishes and old-fashioned word order

Style: The way in which an author writes, determined by the sort of language they tend to use, the way they structure sentences and by any other writing patterns that commonly appear in their text

ii The reference to a 'cairn' and 'pipes' reminds us that the grandfather spent his youth in Scotland. The 'cairn' appears to be the only memorial to his death and, instead of having bagpipes to play him out in a formally commemorative way, there is just the 'aaronsrod' and the naturally growing 'blossoms'. Write down some adjectives to describe how the landscape is presented.

▲ A cairn in Scotland   ▲ A man playing the bagpipes   ▲ An Aaron's rod plant

iii The people who attend the memorial are described as 'They'. We are told that they were 'From his bitter veins born', so they must be his children and grandchildren. Discuss with your partner:
   1 the effect of the use of the word 'They'
   2 the effect of the use of the phrase 'his bitter veins'
   3 what 'mourned him in their fashion' might mean.

Exercise 4

Reread section 3 (lines 12 to 17) of the poem and then read the following responses to these lines by some students.

Student X:

> These lines made me feel respect for the grandfather as he worked very hard all day creating a 'chain of sods'. The word 'chain' makes me think he placed these pieces of turf carefully and in intricate designs, like jewellery. We are told that he carried a 'cherry tree' on his shoulder, so he must have been very strong. The heat beating down on him is described as 'lion sun', suggesting it was very powerful and oppressive to work in.

Student Y:

> At first I thought the grandfather was not a likeable man because he didn't show any feelings and his family didn't give him a good send-off when he died. But these lines remind me that he lived at a time over a hundred years ago when men had to provide for their families and spent their days engaged in hard physical labour, while the women were expected to be nurturing and involved with looking after children. Families relied on the **patriarch** to appear tough and strong, so that must have made it hard for men to show their feelings.

Student Z:

> This section of the poem is sandwiched between the section describing his very low-key funeral and the section describing his frailty and helplessness as an old man. Structurally this draws attention to the contrast between the grandfather in his youth and in his later years. Active verbs such as 'slice' and 'build' contrast with the stillness and inactivity at his funeral and with the silent introspection of the old man sitting in the kitchen.

MAKING CONNECTIONS

Did you notice that, like Baxter, Nichols seems to know the thoughts and feelings (even the dreams!) of the character she is describing in 'Island Man' (Unit 5)? How does Nichols make the reader feel about Island Man through this approach? Do you think she knows him personally? If you think she doesn't know him personally, why has she chosen to write about him as if she does?

All of these students offer interesting thoughts and ideas about this section of the poem. With a partner, think about how well each student:

» shows detailed knowledge of the content of the poem and supports ideas by reference to the text
» explores the poem's **contexts** and beyond surface meanings to understand attitudes and ideas
» recognises the ways Baxter uses language and structure to convey meaning and create effects
» offers an informed personal response.

Key terms

Patriarchal: A society ruled or controlled by men; the patriarch is the male head of the family

Context: The circumstances around a text; for example, the writer's life or the historical background

---

Exercise 5

a Reread the first three lines of section 4 (lines 18 to 20). Write down two ways in which the grandfather's life has changed now that he is old.

Reread the next seven lines of section 4 (lines 21 to 27). The speaker enters his grandfather's mind to tell us what he believes his grandfather is thinking and feeling as he sits silently in the kitchen. This gives the reader another perspective from which to view the old man's character.

The images in this part of the poem can be interpreted in more than one way – they are **ambiguous**. As a critical reader, you will need to decide on your own personal interpretation of the poem, basing it on evidence you find in the text.

b The table below contains the opinions of a few critics about some of Baxter's imagery. In a small group, discuss the critics' interpretations and decide which ones work best for you. Do you have any other ideas about how these images might be interpreted? Explain your reasons using evidence from the text.

Image	Critic 1	Critic 2	Critic 3
The stars in their drunken dancing	I take this to be a metaphor for fate and time passing. The stars engage in 'drunken dancing' because his memories are now confused and don't follow a **chronological order** anymore.	The old man worked long hours outdoors. He is remembering the beautiful stars in the sky and the way they twinkled.	
the burning-glass of his mind	This tells us that, although the grandfather spoke very little, his mind is still very intense as he tries to process these confusing memories.	The memories are seared into his mind, as if a burning-glass is being used to focus them.	
knew the green Boughs of heaven folding The winter world in their hand.	The 'winter world' is a metaphor for the grandfather's old age and he sees 'heaven' as a new springtime coming to carry him away.	These images from nature remind us that this was the world the grandfather had known and loved. Even though he is now blind, he knows that the seasons are changing and he remembers the country scenes he would see as a younger man. In New Zealand you can see the Aurora Australis on some long winter nights: the 'green / Boughs of heaven' are a reference to this occurrence.	I agree with Critic 1, but I see 'The winter world' as a metaphor for the grandfather's cold heart. His death would allow his locked-up spirit to run free, as if it were springtime.
The pride of his heart was dumb.	Sadly, he had no way of expressing the things that meant most to him.	He never bragged about his achievements but was quietly satisfied by what he had done in his life.	I was interested in the word 'pride'. Pride is one of the seven deadly sins and too much pride [hubris] comes before a fall. Maybe the grandfather was so blinded by pride that he didn't know how much he neglected his family. The 'fall' is the way they treated his memory after his death.

c   Has this new perspective from which the grandfather is presented changed
your view of his character at all? Why? Why not?
Choose a group spokesperson (your teacher might help you with this) and
share your ideas with the class.

Key terms

Ambiguous: Not having one obvious meaning, or open to interpretation

Chronological order: Events related in the sequence that they happened

---

Exercise 6

Reread section 5 (lines 28 to 38).

a   The poem has a circular shape. It brings us back to the point where it started
by repeating the first two lines. Discuss with a partner why you think the
poet has structured his poem like this and what effect he might be trying
to achieve.

In section 5 (lines 28 to 38) the speaker is still inside the mind of the
grandfather and recreating for the readers what he believes his grandfather was
thinking and experiencing immediately before he died.

b   Match these lines from the last ten lines of the poem with the emotions the
grandfather is experiencing. You can choose more than one if you wish, but be
ready to explain your choice(s).

i   his heart had never spoken
In song or bridal bed.
And the naked thought...

ii   [Thought] fell... thought fell back
To a house by the waterside
And the leaves the wind had shaken
Then for a child's sake:
To the waves all night awake
With the dark mouths of the dead.

iii   The tongues of water spoke
And his heart was unafraid.

triumphant
soothed
peaceful
resigned
guilty
regretful
nostalgic
confused

c   Are there any other adjectives that you
think are appropriate to describe the
grandfather's feelings in this section of the
poem? Share them with the class.

d   As you saw before, the poem is written in one stanza of 38 lines. It has no
clear rhyme scheme and is written in free verse. With your partner, discuss
why you think Baxter has chosen this form for his poem.

8.4 Writing practice

Exercise 7

Look at this essay question:

Explore the ways in which Baxter makes the character of his grandfather so interesting in 'Elegy For My Father's Father'.

a As you have done in previous units, highlight the key words in the question.
b As you have done in previous units, make a planning table for this essay. Spend 10 to 15 minutes on your planning table.
c Share your planning table with a partner. Help each other to fill in any gaps. Suggest any improvements that could be made to your partner's planning table.
d Write the opening two paragraphs of this essay then swap your work with your partner again to compare what you have written. Try to help each other to find ways to improve the work already done. Discuss the plan for the rest of the essay.
e Spend 30 to 35 minutes writing up your full response to this essay question.

8.5 Set-text focus

Exercise 8

Select one of your set-text poems in which your perspective on a character or event changes during the course of the poem (your teacher may help you with this).

a Like you did in Exercise 1b, use the title of the poem to give you clues about what the poem is about and the poet or persona's perspective on the event or character.
b If the poem is written as one stanza or is quite challenging to interpret, try to break it down into sections, as we did in Exercise 2 (your teacher may help you with this). Try to get an overview of what each section is about.
c From whose **viewpoint** is the poem written – the poet's own viewpoint or from that of an assumed persona?
   – If you think it is the poet's own voice, is the perspective a present-day perspective, or is it a perspective from the past? How does the perspective change in the course of the poem?
   – If you think that the speaker is an assumed persona, what evidence can you find for this?
d What methods and devices does the poet use to convey character and perspective? Consider language and structure.
e Look at the work you did in Exercise 5b. Are there any different ways of interpreting the perspective in which this event or character is presented? Explore these different interpretations and decide which ones you like best.

Key term
Viewpoint: The thoughts and feelings that a character has towards a situation

Take your learning further

The poem 'Follower' by Seamus Heaney is about Heaney's relationship with his father, both in early childhood and later life. Like Baxter's grandfather, Heaney's father was very hardworking and skilled at farm work. He was also a man who showed very little emotion. There are many readings of 'Follower' on YouTube, often with good accompanying visual images. Find a reading to listen to or find a copy of the text online to read.

- Examine the perspectives from which Heaney presents the characters of both his father and himself in 'Follower'.
- Compare and contrast the ways in which the grandfather in 'Elegy For My Father's Father' and the father in 'Follower' are presented.

Unit summary

In this unit, you have learned how to:

- Show detailed knowledge of a poem, supported by reference to the text.
- Understand a poem and its contexts and explore beyond surface meanings to show deeper awareness of the speaker's ideas and attitudes.
- Recognise and appreciate ways in which a poet uses language, structure and form to create character and perspective.
- Examine different interpretations of a poem and consider which you think is most insightful.

How well do you think you have demonstrated each of these skills? What were you good at? Are there any that you struggled with?

'London's Summer Morning': Focus on setting and mood

In this unit, you will:
- Use quotations and indirect references to support your ideas about the mood of a poem.
- Think about the ways a poet uses settings to convey moods and ideas, beyond the surface meaning.
- Explore how a poet uses language and structure to create a sense of time and place and communicate mood.
- Communicate the moods that a poem suggests to you and explain your opinions.

Key terms

Setting: The time, place and culture in which a text takes place

Mood: In literature, the mood is the atmosphere or feeling created in the writing by the author through such features as setting, description or the attitudes of characters

In Unit 5, you read 'Island Man' by Grace Nichols. In the poem, Island Man wakes up in his London home in the 20th century. The noises of the cars outside on the main road and the busy atmosphere make him feel stressed and unhappy. In 'London's Summer Morning', another speaker wakes up in London on a busy, noisy morning, a difference being that this time the **setting** is the 18th century. Another significant difference, as we will see in this unit, is the **mood** in the two poems.

To explore the contexts of your set poems effectively, you need to be able to discuss setting; and to explore beyond a surface meaning you need to develop a good awareness of mood. Your work in this unit will help you to develop these skills.

Mary Robinson (1757 to 1800) was an English poet. She was also well known as an actor, dramatist and novelist as well as being a celebrity figure of the day. In 'London's Summer Morning' (1795), she writes a description of early-morning street life in a way that is very vivid and evocative, especially for anyone reading her poem over two centuries later.

Glossary

List: Listen to / hear

Sultry: Hot and humid

Chimney-boy: In the 18th century young boys were trained to climb chimneys to clear them of soot

Milk-pail: A large tin or wooden vessel used to carry milk

Impervious: Can't be penetrated or seen through

Hackney-coaches: Four-wheeled carriages pulled by horses; they could take up to six passengers

Trunk-makers: People who make large hinged boxes; the boxes would usually carry clothes

Coopers: People who made wooden barrels and other similar containers

Ruddy: Red-faced

'Prentice: Shortened form of 'apprentice': a young person learning a trade

Band-box: A round-shaped hat box

Awning: A canopy used to protect merchandise

Damsel: A young unmarried woman

Limy snare: A trap for insects made from a sticky substance

Venturous: Daring, prepared to take risks

Discordant: Jarring, out of tune

Pilfered: Stolen

Base domestic spoiler: A thief who has stolen from the household they work in

9.1 'London's Summer Morning' by Mary Robinson

Who has not waked to list the busy sounds
Of summer's morning, in the sultry smoke
Of noisy London? On the pavement hot
The sooty chimney-boy, with dingy face
And tattered covering, shrilly bawls his trade,   5
Rousing the sleepy housemaid. At the door
The milk-pail rattles, and the tinkling bell
Proclaims the dustman's office; while the street
Is lost in clouds impervious. Now begins
The din of hackney-coaches, waggons, carts;   10
While tinmen's shops, and noisy trunk-makers,
Knife-grinders, coopers, squeaking cork-cutters,
Fruit-barrows, and the hunger-giving cries
Of vegetable-vendors, fill the air.   15
Now every shop displays its varied trade,
And the fresh-sprinkled pavement cools the feet
Of early walkers. At the private door
The ruddy housemaid twirls the busy mop,
Annoying the smart 'prentice, or neat girl,   20
Tripping with band-box lightly. Now the sun
Darts burning splendour on the glittering pane,
Save where the canvas awning throws a shade
On the gay merchandise. Now, spruce and trim,
In shops (where beauty smiles with industry)   25
Sits the smart damsel; while the passenger
Peeps through the window, watching every charm.
Now pastry dainties catch the eye minute
Of humming insects, while the limy snare
Waits to enthral them. Now the lamp-lighter   30
Mounts the tall ladder, nimbly venturous,
To trim the half-filled lamps, while at his feet
The pot-boy yells discordant! All along
The sultry pavement, the old-clothes-man cries
In tone monotonous, while sidelong views   35
The area for his traffic: now the bag
Is slyly opened, and the half-worn suit
(Sometimes the pilfered treasure of the base
Domestic spoiler), for one half its worth,
Sinks in the green abyss. The porter now   40
Bears his huge load along the burning way;
And the poor poet wakes from busy dreams,
To paint the summer morning.

9.2 First impressions

Exercise 1

In this unit we will be considering settings and how they contribute to the mood in a poem. When writing about the setting of a text, you would usually consider two things:

» place
» time.

a By referring to the title only, write down the setting for 'London's Summer Morning' by referring to the place and time.

Writing about mood is sometimes considered a bit more difficult. You could start to understand how to write about mood by considering the moods of people.

▲ Angry

▲ Unhappy

▲ Excited

b Copy and complete the table, adding four more words to describe a positive mood and four more words to describe a negative mood.

Positive mood	Negative mood
relaxed	stressed

In poetry, the mood is the atmosphere or feeling created in the writing by the author through such features as:

» setting
» language choices
» attitudes of characters.

In addition, poetry often uses very subtle methods to create mood. Language and structural devices are carefully selected. You may already have noticed that poets often use far fewer words than prose writers use to create mood. Look back to the poems you have read in Units 4 to 8. They are 'Phenomenal Woman', 'Island Man', 'Thistles', 'Search For My Tongue' and 'Elegy For My Father's Father'.

c Look at these extracts from the poems you have already read. Using references to setting, language, attitudes and any other methods you can see, match each extract to an appropriate mood word from the word cloud. You may choose more than one mood word if you like, or use the same mood word twice.

i From 'Phenomenal Woman':

I say,
It's the fire in my eyes,
And the flash of my teeth,
The swing in my waist,
And the joy in my feet.

ii From 'Island Man':

to surge of wheels
to dull North Circular roar

muffling muffling
his crumpled pillow waves
island man heaves himself

Another London day

iii From 'Thistles':

Against the rubber tongues of
cows and the hoeing hands
of men
Thistles spike the summer air
And crackle open under a
blue-black pressure.

iv From 'Search for My Tongue':

it grows back, a stump of a shoot
grows longer, grows moist, grows strong veins,
it ties the other tongue in knots,
the bud opens, the bud opens in my mouth,
it pushes the other tongue aside.

overwhelmed
celebratory
rejoicing confident empowered
anxious
sombre resigned
triumphant
despondent
confused vengeful

v From 'Elegy For My Father's Father':

> O for the tall tower broken
> Memorial is denied:
> And the unchanging cairn
> The pipes could set ablaze
> An aaronsrod and blossom.

Make sure you find evidence for the mood words you choose and share your reasons for your choices with the class.

d With setting and mood in mind, read 'London's Summer Morning' slowly and carefully. Make a note of the sights, sounds and actions that contribute to the mood.

9.3 Finding evidence

Exercise 2

You will often find that the setting changes in the course of a poem. In 'London's Summer Morning' the time and place change by just small amounts.

a In pairs complete the following tasks:
  i Find the short key word repeated throughout the poem that indicates a small shift in time.
  ii Discuss the exact length of time you think the poem covers.
  iii Find two places where you think the setting has changed from the actual street to somewhere inside.
  Share your findings with the class.

b Using the short key word you have found in part **a**, create a **storyboard** with eight frames to mark the small time and location shifts you have found in the poem. You can use stick men to draw the characters if you wish, but try to make their occupation clear, for example by giving the chimney-boys a brush for the chimneys.

> **Key term**
>
> **Storyboard:**
> Resembling a cartoon strip in a magazine, it has a number of boxes (frames) in which a story is told through pictures; the skill in putting together a storyboard lies in picking the most important moments to represent – film-makers often use storyboards

---

TIP

A storyboard tells a story in pictures (called 'frames'). Your storyboard of 'London's Summer Morning' will need to have large frames to capture as much of the activity in the poem as possible. Remember to read the poem carefully to make sure you get the setting correct, for example we don't actually see the chimney-boys on the chimneys – we see them on the hot street shouting for business.

Your storyboard should have helped you to gain an overview of all the activities in the poem and the sequence in which they happen.

MAKING CONNECTIONS

A poem in which the mood changes between the beginning and the end is 'Search for My Tongue' (Unit 7). Bhatt initially seems confused and unhappy but by the end feels triumphant and reassured. Are there mood changes in any of the other poems you have read?

c Copy and complete the table, adding four more words or very short phrases (no more than four words each) that you can find in the poem to go under each heading.

Sounds	Sights	Activities
'bawls'	'sultry smoke'	'twirls the busy mop'

You could probably add far more words and short phrases to each column. What do these words tell you about the mood in the street? Did you notice that not only are there small shifts in time and place, but there are also shifts in mood? It is common for mood to change during the course of a text.

d Choose words from the box below that you think best match the mood of each frame in your story board. You may find that you want to use more than one word for each.

Mood words			
loud	active	suffering	cheerful
enticing	refreshing	irritating	excited
warm	peaceful	inquisitive	busy
chaotic	awed	confused	dismayed
sympathetic	thoughtful	painful	annoying

Share your chosen evidence with the class. Be ready to explain why you have chosen your words. While you were doing this work, did you think of any further words to describe the mood at any point in the poem? Share any further words with the class.

Now think about the form and structure of the poem and how they help convey mood.

e With a partner, discuss the effects of:
  i   the form of the poem as one stanza
  ii the use of enjambment
  iii the placing of the short key word that you found in part **a** within the lines of the poem.

f Get into small groups. Each group should take one or two (consecutive) frames from one of their storyboards and rehearse a performance of the activities described in those frame(s). When you are ready, perform your frame(s) to the class, starting with frame 1. One member of the group should read out the relevant section in the poem while the others play the roles of the characters. When acting your role, try to help your audience feel the mood of the poem too.

9.4 Writing practice

Exercise 3

A student had the following question set for homework:

> **How does Mary Robinson convincingly convey the active street life in 18th-century London?**

The student said:

> I've highlighted 'active street life' as my key words, but I don't know how to do this question. I've just been studying how to write about setting and mood, but it doesn't say anything here about setting and mood. I don't know what to do.

a The student's friends gave her the following pieces of advice. Rank them from 1 to 5, where 1 is the best piece of advice and 5 is the worst. Discuss with a partner your reasons for how you have ranked the advice and share these reasons with the class.

Student A:
> Don't worry. You know the poem really well so just start at the beginning and work your way through it, a line at a time. Make sure you include everything you know about the poem.

Student B:
> Open your essay with 'Mary Robinson convincingly conveys the active street life in 18th-century London by giving us a clear sense of setting and mood'.

Student C:
> You are being asked about setting and mood, but just not in those actual words. The word 'street' is the setting and 'active' is a description of the mood. Think of it like that and you will be fine.

Student D:
> Write about the language used to describe the street and the structural devices the poet uses to show shifts in time and place. I really like the listing of all the vehicles and the jobs, as it gives an impression of hustle and bustle, which means the same as 'active'.

Student E:
> Draw a planning table and put your quotations and comments in it. Remember to link your comments to the question.

b Are there any questions you have about approaching this essay question? Write them down. Swap your questions with another student and see if you can answer them. Share your questions and answers with the class.

c Based on the discussions you have had, and the work you have done in this unit, spend 45 minutes writing your own response to this essay question.

9.5 Set-text focus

Exercise 4

Choose one of your set poems where you think there is a strong sense of setting and mood (your teacher may help you with this).

a Identify the setting in time and place. Are there any changes of setting? How does the poet signal these changes?

b How do the settings and the descriptions of the settings contribute to the mood?

c Look closely at how language choices, form and the use of structure contribute to the mood and how the reader reacts to the setting.

d Think back to Unit 4 where you studied 'Phenomenal Woman'. In this poem the rhythm contributed significantly to our image of a powerful woman striding confidently in the street. How does the rhythm in your set poem help the poet to achieve their effects?

e Be ready to use appropriate quotations and to refer closely to your poem.

f Plan a response to the following question in relation to your poem:

How does [poet's name] convey strong feelings about a place and time in [title of poem]?

Take your learning further

1 Other English poets have written about the city of London. Two well-known poems are 'London' (1794) by William Blake and 'Composed upon Westminster Bridge, September 3, 1802' by William Wordsworth. Read both or one of these two poems. Compare and contrast one or both with 'London's Summer Morning' by considering the:
   - descriptions of the settings
   - mood created in the poems
   - language choices and structural devices.

2 Read the poem 'City Johannesburg' by the South African poet Mongane Wally Serote. The poem is set during the Apartheid era and is about the relationship between the speaker, a black South African man, and the city he travels daily to work in, Johannesburg. Compare and contrast 'City Johannesburg' with 'London's Summer Morning' by considering the:
   - descriptions of the settings
   - mood created in both poems
   - relationship the poets have with the cities they are writing about.

Unit summary

In this unit, you have learned how to:
- Use quotations and indirect references to support your ideas about the mood of a poem.
- Think about the ways a poet uses settings to convey moods and ideas, beyond the surface meaning.
- Explore how a poet uses language and structure to create a sense of time and place and communicate mood.
- Communicate the moods that a poem suggests to you and explain your opinions.

Think about how you have demonstrated each of these skills in the exercises in this unit. You might like to build on the work you did in Exercise 1 by thinking in more depth about how the other poets studied in this book use settings to create moods.

'Dark August': Focus on developing a personal response

In this unit, you will:
- Use quotations and indirect references to support your personal response to a poem.
- Explore a poem beyond its surface meaning and think about different interpretations of it.
- Explain how a poet uses literary devices to create a particular response.
- Communicate a sensitive and informed personal response to a poem.

Now that you have studied a number of poems and acquired the necessary skills to write about different aspects of a poem, you are going to put your skills together to develop a sensitive and informed personal response. A personal response could be as simple as 'I like this poem' or 'I don't like this poem', but clearly this would not meet the requirement of being 'sensitive' or 'informed'. A sensitive and informed personal response to a text comes from reading the text closely, thinking critically about meanings and interpretations and reading or listening to the views of others. The process of engaging with a poem that has a number of layers and points of interest to think about and respond to can be very fulfilling for a reader.

Derek Walcott (1930 to 2017) was a poet and dramatist from the Caribbean Island of St Lucia. In 'Dark August' he writes about a time of sadness, but the mood changes as he becomes reconciled with the situation.

10.1 'Dark August' by Derek Walcott

So much rain, so much life like the swollen sky
of this black August. My sister, the sun,
broods in her yellow room and won't come out.

Everything goes to hell; the mountains fume
like a kettle, rivers overrun; still,   5
she will not rise and turn off the rain.

She is in her room, fondling old things,
my poems, turning her album. Even if thunder falls
like a crash of plates from the sky,

she does not come out.   10
Don't you know I love you but am hopeless
at fixing the rain? But I am learning slowly

to love the dark days, the steaming hills,
the air with gossiping mosquitoes,
and to sip the medicine of bitterness,   15

so that when you emerge, my sister,
parting the beads of the rain,
with your forehead of flowers and eyes of forgiveness,

all will not be as it was, but it will be true
(you see they will not let me love   20
as I want), because, my sister, then

I would have learnt to love black days like bright ones,
The black rain, the white hills, when once
I loved only my happiness and you.

10.2 First impressions

Exercise 1

Read the poem 'Dark August'. Below are some students' initial responses to it.

Read the students' responses. Is your initial response to the poem similar to any of the student responses? Do you have a different first response? Share your thoughts with the class.

Student A:

> When I first read this poem, I thought it was about the poet's sister who is sulking in her room and remembering better days from the past. The bad weather is a metaphor for his very sad feelings while she is in a bad mood with him. At the end of the poem, she forgives him, but he explains that he's done a lot of thinking and their relationship has now changed.

Student B:

> I thought that the poem was about losing someone, maybe the end of a love affair. While he was with his lover, the poet felt like he had sunshine and happiness in his life, but now the person has gone, it is like the sun has gone into mourning along with him because all there is is bad weather. The sun is a metaphor for how he feels. At the end of the poem, he is starting to come to terms with his loss, but he explains that the experience has changed him, and he will never feel sunshine dominating his life the way he did in the past.

Student C:

> I think this poem is reflecting on our modern way of life. There are images from nature and images of manmade things like kettles and plates. The sun is grieving because nature is no longer dominant in our lives and never will be again. At the end of the poem the sun forgives the man but there is an understanding that humankind will never go back to a more natural lifestyle.

As you can see, these students have responded to the poem in different ways. Their responses do show interpretative skill, overview and some sensitivity to the language of the poem, but these are just first responses, so they are not very well-informed responses yet. The students need to read the poem again, thinking about the language and structural devices that the poet has used, and find evidence for their responses. They may find that their initial thoughts and interpretations are refined as they attempt a deeper reading of the poem – or they may even change their minds completely.

10.3 Finding evidence

Exercise 2

a As noted in the previous unit, it is often a good idea to start by considering how the title of the poem helps you understand the poem's content. Depending on where you live in the world, August can be a summer month or a winter month. In St Lucia, August is summer time, but it is also in the middle of hurricane season, so there can be torrential rain and powerful winds.

Discuss with a partner what the title might tell you about the poem's content.

b You should be able to identify the form of this poem as free verse. If not, have a look back to Unit 5. Discuss with a partner how the form of this poem might help you to make your first impressions of what it is about.

c The poem is also written in **tercets**, meaning that, even though it is in free verse, there is some clear pattern throughout. There is also a turning point in the poem (see Unit 5). With your partner, see if you can find the turning point and notice whereabouts in the poem it comes structurally.

Key term

Tercet: A three-line stanza; it is sometimes known as a 'triplet' – other stanza lengths are couplets (two lines), quatrains (four lines), quintains (five lines), sestets (6 lines), septets (7 lines) and octets (8 lines)

d Look back to the work you did on mood in Unit 9. Copy the table below and use it to identify what the mood is as the poem develops towards the turning point. Write down your evidence and comment on how this helps you to understand the mood. Only go as far as the turning point in the poem.

Stanza	Mood	Evidence	Comment

Share your work with the class.

Exercise 3

a Make notes about what you think the poet is saying in stanzas 5 to 8 (lines 13 to 24). Use the words from the poem's turning point to help you to decide what the speaker's attitude is in these last four stanzas.

b Write down answers to the following questions:
  i Stanzas 2 and 5 both use images from nature that suggest inclement and stormy weather. Compare how the poet presents the weather in each stanza. How does the poet's choice of imagery reflect the difference in his attitude in the two stanzas?
  ii Thinking back to your work in the previous exercises, who or what do you think the 'sister' is now? Has your view on who or what the 'sister' is changed?
  iii What are the effects of the 'sister' being described as 'parting the beads of the rain' and wearing a 'forehead of flowers'?
  iv What does the description 'eyes of forgiveness' suggest about what the sister has been thinking and feeling while shut in her room?
  v Who do you think the 'they' might be in stanza 7 and why do you think this?
  vi The poet uses a number of contrasts in the last stanza. Identify the contrasts and explain the effects of them.
  Share your responses with the class

10.4 Writing practice

Exercise 4

Look back to the initial responses Students A and B made in Exercise 1. Then read the revised responses that the students made.

Student A feels her initial response to the poem was pretty accurate and she does not wish to interpret the poem any differently. However, she has read the poem again, and found more evidence to support her view:

> I originally thought that the poem was about a disagreement between the poet and his sister and I still can see a lot of evidence that this is what it is about. However, I have thought a bit more deeply about the poem and found more evidence to back up my interpretation. Here is an outline of the points I would make to support my interpretation.

Student A's notes

1 The poet clearly thinks the world of his sister as he calls her 'the sun', which is an image of light and life giving.
2 However, she is very temperamental and there is a lot of evidence that he really suffers during her fits of anger.
3 The gloom and angry emotions in the house are very evident. While his sister is sulking and refusing to leave her room, the writer also feels turbulent emotions, as we see through his imagery in stanza 2.
4 He thinks that it doesn't matter what he says or does; he can't make her feel better or want to leave her room, and some of the imagery suggests his desperation about this.
5 Then he comes to realise that even though he loves his sister, he can't change her tendency to have episodes like this. This is a moment of epiphany for him.
6 This epiphany comes in the very middle of the poem, so that the reader receives a balanced view of the suffering he experienced before and his feelings of acceptance afterwards.
7 When his sister has got over her anger, and comes out of her room to make her peace, he realises that there has to be compromise in the way he deals with her fluctuating moods.
8 He resolves that in future he won't allow her changeability to affect his emotions so much – he will just accept that this is the way his sister is.

Student B has changed his mind about his initial response to the poem. He now says:

> I originally thought this poem was about the loss of a loved person, but I now think it's about the loss of the poet's creativity. This is an outline of the points I would make to support my interpretation.

Student B's notes

1 The sun was the inspiration for the poet's creativity, and he calls her his 'sister' because of the very close relationship they have had. It is as if they have always shared the same house and have always been there for each other.

2 The sun inspired him to write warm, happy poetry. Now that he is no longer inspired to write such poetry, he feels anger and despair. This is reflected through the **pathetic fallacy** of stanza 2.

3 The room the sun has shut herself in suggests his inability to access the inspiration to write.

4 The sun, because of the close relationship she has with the poet, shares his grief, powerlessness and sense of loss, which is why she is described as 'fondling old things, / my poems'.

5 However, through experiencing pain and anger, the poet discovers another inspiration for his poetry writing: he can also write about these emotions and not just happiness.

6 The idea that he finds inspiration through negative emotions is powerfully conveyed throughout the poem when he uses his most poetic imagery to describe such things as 'the swollen sky', 'the steaming hills', mountains that 'fume' and thunder that 'falls / like a crash of plates'.

7 He says that he will 'sip the medicine of bitterness'. This metaphor suggests that the bitterness he has experienced will be the source of his healing. The word 'sip' suggests the small mouthfuls he has to take to learn how to write differently.

8 Ironically, because he has found inspiration for his poetry again, the sun is appeased and comes out of her room ready for the role she has always played as the poet's constant companion. She looks beautiful and is conciliatory.

9 He explains that, although he will always love the warm inspiration she gave him, he has found other equally beautiful sources for creative release.

10 The use of enjambment throughout the poem suggests how his emotions are overflowing and running on quickly.

a In small groups, or in pairs, discuss the revised responses of Students A and B.
  i Do you find any points of agreement with either or both of them?
  ii Which personal response do you find to be more 'sensitive' and 'informed'? Why do you think this?
  iii Can you offer another interpretation of the poem, which takes into account the whole poem, including the turning point?
b The writing of Students A and B is in note form at present. More needs to be done to develop a critical response that analyses the language and structural devices used.
  Either:
  – Choose one of the plans and write it up fully as an extended analysis (allow yourself 30 minutes for this).
  Or:
  – Make your own plan for your own interpretation of the poem (you might want to use a planning table like those in previous units or a point-by-point plan like the ones above) and then write it up fully as an extended analysis (allow yourself 45 minutes for this).

10.5 Set-text focus

Exercise 5

Think about all the features of poetry that you have learned to analyse in this Poetry section. You have developed a number of skills allowing you to write about language and structural devices as well as improving your ability to respond critically to a poem. Your essay-writing skills have improved too: you now know that you should choose the best points that you are confident of writing about as well as focusing closely on the question set. You have also learned about the importance of planning your essay response and how to construct a plan.

Now look at your set-text poems.

Either:
a **i** Find a poem among your set poems where the weather plays a significant role. Compare how the weather is used in that poem with how it is used in 'Dark August'.
  ii Write a response to the essay question below:

Explore how [poet's name] makes powerful use of the weather in [title of poem].

Or:
b **i** Find a poem among your set poems that conveys strong emotion. Compare how the emotion is conveyed in that poem with how it is conveyed in 'Dark August'.
  ii Write a response to the essay question below:

Explore the ways in which [poet's name] convincingly portrays strong emotions in [title of poem].

Take your learning further

1   Derek Walcott was an admirer of another Caribbean poet, the Jamaican reggae singer / songwriter Bob Marley (1945 to 1981). In 1991, on a BBC Radio 4 programme called 'Desert Island Discs', Walcott described the 'haunting' nature, 'poignancy' and 'accuracy' of 'No Woman, No Cry', a song in which Marley depicts the life he used to live in the poor capital of Jamaica, Kingston, as a struggling poet and singer. The poem is a call to a woman in his life to be positive and not to grieve the bad times.
    Find the lyrics to 'No Woman, No Cry' and read them alongside an audio recording of the song. Consider why Walcott may have considered this poem / song so powerful. Does it have the same impact on you? Why? Or why not?

2   Choose a poem you have already read and worked on in this section of the book. Now that you have a more confident grasp of the skills you need to analyse a poem, can you see how your personal response to the poem could be improved? Make notes on how you could have written more effectively and demonstrated a more informed response to the poem.

Unit summary

In this unit, you have learned how to:
● Use quotations and indirect references to support your personal response to a poem.
● Explore a poem beyond its surface meaning and think about different interpretations of it.
● Explain how a poet uses literary devices to create a particular response.
● Communicate a sensitive and informed personal response to a poem.

Think about how you have demonstrated each of these skills in the exercises in this unit. Now that we have reached the end of the Poetry section, be sure to look back to the poems you have studied and think about how the different skills you have developed can be combined to create a sensitive and informed personal response to each.

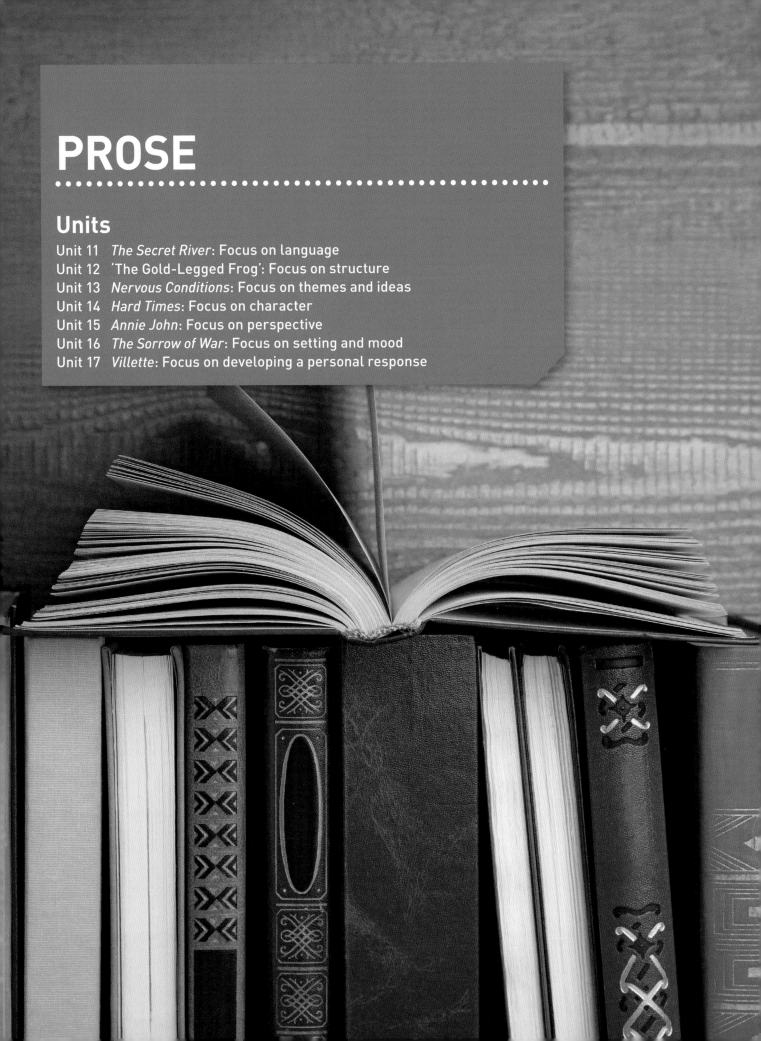

PROSE

....

Units

The Secret River: Focus on language and meaning

In this unit, you will:
- Use quotations and indirect references to demonstrate the ways that a writer uses language and communicates meanings.
- Think about how an author's use of language reveals deeper meanings.
- Identify features of language – such as metaphor, personification and hyperbole – and explain how they are used to create effects.
- Describe the ways a writer's use of imagery appeals to your senses and justify your reaction with textual evidence.

Glossary

Hugger-mugger: Arranged in a close-together, confused way

Mouldering: Decaying slowly

Tannery: A place or building where animal hides and skins are tanned to make leather

Shambles: A place where animals are slaughtered for meat

Malting: A building in which malt – an ingredient in beer – is made or kept

Miasma: A polluting smell

Turnips and beets: Vegetables

Stagnant: Water that is not flowing so it is often dirty and smelly

Steeple: A pointed roof found on a church

Vertiginous: Causing dizziness

Pew: A bench with a back for people to sit on in church

Void: A completely empty space

Britches: Trousers

As we will see in the coming units, authors of prose fiction have a range of tools they can use to communicate meaning, one of the most important of which is language. As a critical reader, you need to be able to look beyond the surface level of a text to see not just what facts you are being told **explicitly**, but also what the author's careful **language choices** help you to understand **implicitly**. Devices that an author might use, and which we will explore in this unit, include **metaphor**, **simile**, **personification**, **hyperbole**, **sibilance** and **imagery**.

The Secret River is a prize-winning novel by Kate Grenville, an Australian author. The story was inspired by the life of Grenville's great-great-great-grandfather who was sent from England to Australia in 1806 as punishment for a crime. The same happens to the **protagonist** of *The Secret River*, William Thornhill.

This extract is from the start of the novel and shows William growing up in London, England. By studying it closely and thinking about the language that Grenville uses, we can learn a lot about the character's feelings and the world in which he lives.

Key terms

Explicitly: In a way that is clear and precise, requiring little interpretation

Language choices: The specific words that a writer chooses to use to convey particular ideas

Implicitly: In a way that is not direct or obvious

Metaphor: A description of one thing as another thing that is mostly unrelated to make a comparison that highlights the similarity between the two things

Simile: A comparison of one thing to another, using the word 'as' or 'like' – 'They are *like* pale hair' is an example of a simile; the comparison gives emphasis to a description or makes it more vivid, but similes are generally thought of as less powerful than metaphors

Personification: The description of an object or animal as if they have human characteristics

Hyperbole: Exaggerated claims or statements, not meant to be taken literally

Sibilance: The repetition of sibilant consonants such as 's', 'z' or 'sh'

Image / Imagery: A word or phrase that prompts the reader to imagine the way that something looks, sounds, smells, feels or tastes

Protagonist: A main character in a literary text

11.1 From *The Secret River* by Kate Grenville

In the rooms where William Thornhill grew up, in the last decades of the eighteenth century, no one could move an elbow without hitting the wall or the table or a sister or a brother. Light struggled in through small panes of cracked glass and the soot from the smoking fireplace veiled the walls. 5

Where they lived, down close to the river, the alleyways were no more than a stride across, and dimmed even on the brightest day by the buildings packed in hugger-mugger. On every side it was nothing but brick walls and chimneys, cobblestones and mouldering planks where old whitewash marked the grain. There were the terraces of low-browed 10 houses hunched down on themselves, growing out of the very dirt they sat on, and after them the tanneries, the shambles, the glue factories, the maltings, filling the air with their miasmas.

Down beyond the tanneries, turnips and beets struggled in damp sour fields, and between the fields, enclosed behind their hedges and walls, 15 were the boggy places too wet to plant in, with rushes and reeds where stagnant water glinted.

The Thornhills all stole turnips from time to time, running the risk of the dogs getting them, or the farmer hurling stones. Big brother Matty bore a scar on his forehead where a stone had made a turnip less tasty. 20

The highest things were the steeples. There was nowhere to go in all these mean and twisted streets, even out in the marshy low ground, where some steeple or other did not watch. As soon as one of them was hidden by the elbow of a lane there was another staring down from behind the chimneys. 25

And under the steeple, the House of God. William Thornhill's life had begun, as far as his own memory of it was concerned, with the grandest house that God had: Christ Church beside the river. The building was so big it made his eyes water. On the gateposts there were snarling stone lions that his mother lifted him up to look at, but they made him cry 30 out in fear. The vertiginous lawn seemed to engulf him as he stood in its emptiness. The bushes stood guard in a line, and tiny insects of humans laboured up the vast steps of the entrance far away. He was dizzy, lost, hot with panic.

Inside the church he had never seen such a vault of ceiling and 35 such light. God had so much space it could frighten a boy from Tanner's Lane. Up at the front were complicated carvings: screens, benches, a great construction that towered over the people sitting in the pews. It was a void into which his being expanded without finding a boundary, all in the merciless light that blasted down from the huge windows and left 40 everything cold, with no kindly shadows anywhere. It was a place with no charity in its grey stones for a boy with the seat out of his britches.

He could not understand any of it, knew only that God was as foreign as a fish.

11.2 First impressions

Exercise 1

How can writers create layers of meaning?

a Compare the two images. As a class, think of as many words as you can to describe the feelings you associate with each image.

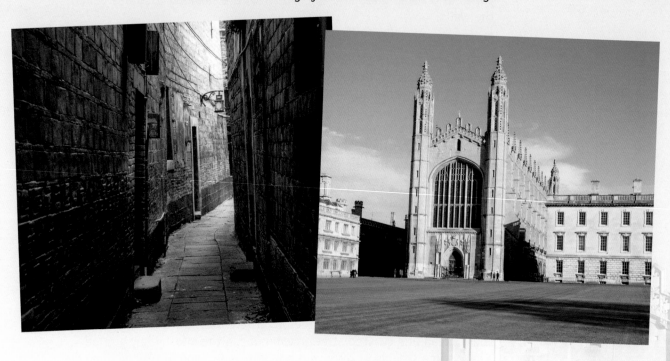

b Which image would you expect to make you feel:
   – hope
   – fear?

c Now read the extract. As you read, make a note of the adjectives Grenville uses to describe the different settings. How do they compare with the words you listed above? Is there anything surprising about the language that Grenville uses?

11.3 Finding evidence

Exercise 2

MAKING CONNECTIONS

For more information about language devices such as personification, metaphor and imagery, look at 'Thistles' by Ted Hughes in Unit 6.

Read the first three paragraphs of the extract again. Copy and complete the following table, identifying the language devices used (consider hyperbole, imagery, metaphor, personification and sibilance). Then add one or two sentences about each quotation, explaining how Grenville's use of language helps to convey meaning. One answer has been written for you.

Quotation	Language device	Effect
a 'no one could move an elbow without hitting the wall or the table or a sister or a brother'		
b 'Light struggled in through small panes of cracked glass'	personification	This quotation tells us that William's home is very dark and suggests that his family cannot afford big windows or to keep them repaired. Grenville's use of personification in her description of the struggling light adds to the feeling that life is very difficult for William's family.
c 'the soot from the smoking fireplace veiled the walls'		
d 'mouldering planks where old whitewash marked the grain'		
e 'low-browed houses hunched down on themselves, growing out of the very dirt'		
f 'turnips and beets struggled in damp sour fields'		

Exercise 3

Look at the descriptions of the churches in the second half of the extract, and in particular the description of Christ Church.

a What are William's general feelings towards these buildings? Identify phrases from the text to support your ideas.

b Working with a partner, write each phrase onto a separate sticky note.

c Arrange the notes into an order that shows the effectiveness of each phrase in creating this impression.

d Write a short paragraph explaining how one of the phrases creates a particular effect.

e How is Christ Church different from William's home? For each of the quotations in Exercise 2, find another that describes Christ Church. Discuss with your partner how the quotations in each pair contrast with each other.

Key term

Setting: The time, place and culture in which a text takes place

MAKING CONNECTIONS

Much of the passage from the beginning of *The Secret River* is devoted to describing two contrasting places: William Thornhill's family home and the church that he attends. For a more in-depth exploration of the ways in which writers use **settings** to create effects, see Unit 16 on Bảo Ninh's *The Sorrow of War*.

Exercise 4

Think about Grenville's presentation of the character of William Thornhill in this passage.

a What **themes** and ideas do you think Grenville is exploring through the character of William Thornhill, based on this short extract? What is his relationship with or attitude to each of these themes?

Look at the final line of the extract. Grenville uses a simile to describe William's confusion about God: '[He] knew only that God was as foreign as a fish'.

b What do you think is meant by this simile? Explain your answer with reference to the rest of the passage.

> **Key term**
>
> **Theme:** A key idea or subject that is repeated throughout a text

11.4 Writing practice

Exercise 5

Now that you have looked at the extract in detail, look at this essay question:

How does Grenville use words and images to powerful effect in this part of the novel?

a Highlight the key words in the question.

b Write a brief plan of how you would answer the question; use a mind map or a bullet point list – not sentences. Pay close attention to the key words you have highlighted and make sure you address them (look at the Tip box for more help). Check that you have included relevant quotations and ideas from the work you have already done.

> **TIP**
>
> This type of question is quite general and gives you scope to explore aspects of the extract that you are interested in and that you feel are most important. However, there are still some key words in the question. 'Words' and 'images' indicate that your response should be focused on Grenville's use of language, and on explaining how she uses certain devices to convey meanings or create certain effects. The phrase 'powerful effect' implies that you should communicate a personal response, describing what Grenville's use of language makes you feel and explaining how her writing creates this impact.

Exercise 6

Read a student's first draft of their response to the question. Then look at the feedback given by their teacher.

a Discuss the teacher's feedback with your partner or group. How would you improve the student's answer according to the teacher's advice?

b Share your ideas with the class.

Student's first draft

Can you give further examples of the senses that Grenville uses? What is the overall effect created by her use of the senses in the extract?

You have not given any quotations to show how the church is frightening. Can you find some?

You need to use a quotation here to show how enormous William feels the church is. Don't forget to discuss the personification of the steeples!

Grenville shows that William's family is poor by using powerful adjectives such as 'cracked' and by describing the 'mouldering planks'. This is one example of Grenville using the senses. The people living there do not seem to have much money because there is lots of dirt.

The churches sound really frightening especially Christ Church because it is really big. William is really scared of the lions. It does not sound like it is a very nice place.

Why is this adjective powerful and how does it show they are poor?

What does the word 'mouldering' mean? What does 'mouldering planks' suggest about the way these Londoners are living? What is suggested by the old age of the 'whitewash'?

What method does Grenville use to describe the houses: 'low-browed houses hunched down on themselves'? What effect is created by the image?

Key term

Senses: Sight, smell, hearing, touch and taste

Exercise 7

The student rewrote the response after feedback.

a What changes do you notice between the student's first draft and the second?

b Read the annotations to see the improvements. Are these the same changes you noticed?

Student's second draft

The response is organised into paragraphs now; the ideas about the quotations are more developed.

Key term

Indirect reference: Using some of the same words as the writer but in a different form; quotation marks are not required for an indirect reference

This is an **indirect reference** to 'struggled' in line 14.

In the first few paragraphs, Grenville's use of language and imagery suggests that William's family is very poor and that their home is not very pleasant. For example, she describes the house's window as 'cracked'. This suggests that the family is unable to afford repairs to their home and make do with what they have. The sharp 'c' sounds of the monosyllabic adjective almost echo the sound of the glass when it was broken, thus reinforcing the house's dilapidated state.

Grenville intensifies this impression by describing the house's planks as 'mouldering' showing that the house is rotting away. Perhaps the people once had enough money to paint their houses but the 'old whitewash' has now faded so much it just marks the grain of these rotting planks; the family's situation has perhaps got worse over time.

Grenville uses the sense of sight to convey this impression, but she also uses other senses: the fields are 'damp' and 'sour'. The sense of touch here is coupled with the sense of taste to show that the land surrounding the houses is also poor; it is hardly good enough for the struggling turnips.

TIP

It is good practice to include some indirect references as well as quotations. The relevant quotation is 'turnips and beets struggled in damp sour fields'. The student chose to reference indirectly the quotation with the related word 'struggling'.

Overall there is a sense of crushing and inescapable poverty. Its symptoms, dirt and darkness are all around: inside the house where soot 'veiled the fireplace' and outside too where the houses seem to grow from the dirt. When Grenville personifies the 'low-browed houses hunched down on themselves', the depressed **mood** created by 'low' and 'hunched' conveys the terrible and persistent burden of the pressure that weighs down on these Londoners.

Grenville also personifies the church steeples: they watch, hide and stare. This personification creates a sense of fright: it is as if William cannot escape their influence. The young William has a literal belief in God living within the churches and Christ Church is 'the grandest house that God had'. The sheer contrast between the size of the church – '[it] was so big it made his eyes water' – and the claustrophobic, 'hugger-mugger' alleyways of his home frightens him and induces 'panic'. He is intimidated by the space, the light and the coldness of the place which has 'no charity in its grey stones for a boy with the seat out of his britches'.

William's fear of Christ Church in London foreshadows his ongoing struggle to find his place in the world. After years of struggle, William succeeds in building a splendid house in New South Wales. But this house is a 'speck' on land in 'another world' belonging to the Darug people. William continues to be anxious about his place in the world even after it becomes 'his'.

Another indirect reference, this time to 'watch', 'hidden' and 'staring' in lines 23 to 24.

*A sensitive and informed personal response. This **cross-referencing** shows a thorough understanding of the novel.*

*It is good to include some information about **context** but – as here – the references should be brief and used to support your ideas.*

Key terms

Mood: In literature, the mood is the atmosphere or feeling created in the writing by the author through such features as setting, description or the attitudes of characters

Foreshadow: Hinting at something to come in the future

Cross-referencing: Referring to another text or another part of the same text to draw attention to a similarity or difference

Context: The circumstances around a text; for example, the writer's life or the historical background

Exercise 8

Now you have practised thinking critically about another student's response to the question, do the same for your plan.

Discuss your plan with a partner and compare it to theirs. If you were writing a full response to the question, what would you remove or add to your plans? Try to find at least three good points and three points that you would improve.

11.5 Set-text focus

Exercise 9

Consider the language choices in your prose set text.

a Choose an extract from your prose text in which the writer uses powerful imagery or makes interesting word choices. Your teacher may be able to help you with this.

b Create a table like the one in Exercise 2 and find quotations in your chosen extract that use a variety of language devices. Make sure you note down the effect that each quotation has rather than just making a list.

c Consider how you think the author has used language to help convey meaning. In what significant ways has the author used language to explore certain themes or describe characters and settings?

d Look at the following essay question, based on the one used in '11.4 Writing practice', and think about it in relation to your set text and the extract you have chosen:

How does [writer's name] use words and images to powerful effect in this part of the novel?

Plan a response to this essay question using the evidence and ideas you found in parts **a** to **c**. Then write an essay responding to this question.

Take your learning further

The novel *The Secret River* imagines the conflict between English settlers of Australia, such as William Thornhill, and the aboriginal Australians. An extract on Kate Grenville's website shows the drama of William meeting an aboriginal person for the first time.

1 Read the extract: **https://kategrenville.com.au/books/the-secret-river**
2 If you can, act out the extract.
3 How does the language used in this extract add to your understanding of the character of William?

Unit summary

In this unit, you have learned how to:
● Use quotations and indirect references to demonstrate the ways that a writer uses language and communicates meanings.
● Think about how an author's use of language reveals deeper meanings.
● Identify features of language – such as metaphor, personification and hyperbole – and explain how they are used to create effects.
● Describe the ways a writer's use of imagery appeals to your senses and justify your reaction with textual evidence.

Think about how you have demonstrated each of these skills in the exercises in this unit. Be sure to return to this unit once you have spent some time developing other skills in the remainder of the Prose section and apply your learning to the extract from *The Secret River*.

12 'The Gold-Legged Frog': Focus on structure

In this unit, you will:
- Identify the uses of structural devices in a short story.
- Explore a text beyond its surface meaning to show a deep awareness of ideas and attitudes.
- Recognise and appreciate ways in which an author uses structural devices to create and shape meanings and effects.
- Describe your personal response to a text in terms of structural devices.

In this unit we will look at ways in which a writer can **structure** a prose text and how choices about structure can affect the text's meaning and have an impact on the reader. There are four main points to consider when we are looking at structure in a prose text. They involve the organisation of words and ideas at:
» sentence level
» paragraph level
» extract level
» whole-text level.

The way the author of your prose set text crafts their work or puts it together is an important consideration. A complete short story has been provided here to help you develop the skills you need to write about structure.

'The Gold-Legged Frog' was written by Thai short-story writer Khamsing Srinawk, born in 1930. The story focuses on an ordinary village man in Thailand, who has to struggle to feed his family, including five children. He faces oppression from many angles, including extremes of weather, poverty, petty officialdom and, ultimately, what the man himself calls 'luck' or fate.

Glossary

Pall: A dark cloud of dust; it can also be a cloth spread over a coffin

Portent: A sign or warning that something significant (usually disastrous) is going to happen

Want: Lacking something necessary, usually food and water

Paddy fields: Fields where rice is grown

Land snail: A snail that lives on land rather than in the sea

Razor clam buried waiting for the rains: Clams usually thrive in the sea, so a clam on land in hot weather would be in need of the rain

Faith-healers: People who use either the power of prayer or divine ritual to help heal a sick person

Herbalists: People who use natural medicines from plants to help heal a sick person

Baht: Currency of Thailand

Taciturn: Uncommunicative, saying nothing or very little

Guffaws: Loud rude laughter

12.1 'The Gold-Legged Frog' by Khamsing Srinawk

The sun blazed as if determined to crisp every living thing in the broad fields. Now and again the tall, straight, isolated sabang and payom trees let go some of their dirty yellow leaves. He sank exhausted against a tree trunk with his dark blue shirt wet with sweat. The expanse around him expressed total dryness. He stared at the tufts of dull grass and bits of straw spun in a column to the sky. The brown earth sucked up into the air cast a dark pall over everything. A whirlwind. He recalled the old people had told him this was the portent of drought, want, disaster and death, and he was afraid. He was now anxious to get home; he could see the tips of bamboo thickets surrounding the house far ahead looking like blades of grass. But he hesitated. A moment before reaching the shade of the tree he felt his ears buzz and his eyes blur and knew it meant giddiness and sunstroke. He looked at the soles of his feet blistered from the burning sandy ground and became indescribably angry – angry with the weather capable of such endless torture. In the morning the cold had pierced his bones, but now it was so hot he felt his head would break into bits and pieces. As he remembered the biting cold of the morning, he thought again of his little son. 5

10

15

That same morning he and two of his small children went out into the dry paddy fields near the house to look for frogs for the morning meal. The air was so chilly the two children on either side of him shivered as they stopped to look for frogs hiding in the cracks of the parched earth. Each time they saw two bright eyes in a deep crack, they would shout, "Pa, here's another one. Pa, this crack has two. Gold-legged ones! Hurry, Pa." 20

He dashed from place to place as the voices called him, prying up the dry clods with his hoe. He caught some of the frogs immediately, but a few jumped away as soon as he began digging. It was the children's job to chase and pounce on them. Many got away. Some jumped into different fissures obliging him to pry up a new cake of earth. If his luck was good, besides the frog, he would find a land snail or a razor clam buried waiting for the rains. He would take these as well. 25

30

The air was warming and already he had enough frogs to eat with the morning rice. The sound of drumming, the village chief's call for a meeting, sounded faintly from the village. Vague anger again spilled over as his thoughts returned to that moment. If only he had gone home then the poor child would be all right now. It was really the last crack. As soon as he poked it, the ground broke apart. A fully grown gold-legged frog as big as a thumb leaped past the bigger child. The younger raced after it for about twelve yards when it dodged into the deep hoofprint of a water buffalo. The child groped after it. And then he was shocked almost senseless by the trembling cry of his boy, "Pa, a snake, a snake bit my hand." 35

40

A cobra spread its hood, hissing. When finally able to act, the father with all his strength brought the handle of his hoe three times down on the back of the serpent leaving its tail twitching. He carried his child and the basket of frogs home without forgetting to tell the other to drag the snake along as well. 45

On the way back his son cried softly and moaned, beating his chest with his fists and complaining he could not breathe. At home, the father summoned all the faith-healers and herbalists whose names he could think of and the turmoil began.

"Chop up a frog, roast it, and put it on the wound," a neighbour called out. 50

When another shouted, "Give him the toasted liver of the snake to eat," he hurriedly slit open the snake to look for the liver while his wife sat by crying.

The later it got, the bigger the crowd. On hearing the news, all the neighbours attending the village chief's meeting joined the others. One of them told him he had to go to the District Office in town that day 55
because the village chief told them it was the day the government was going to hand out money to those with five or more children, and he was one who had just five. It was a new shock.

"Can't you see my boy's gasping out his life? How can I go?"

"What difference will it make? You've called in a lot of doctors, all of them 60
expert."

"Go, you fool. It's two hundred baht they're giving. You've never had that much in your life-time. Two hundred!"

"Leave this for a bit," another added. "If the boy dies, you'll be out, that's all." 65

"I won't go," he yelled. "My child can't breathe and you tell me to go. Why can't they give it out some other day? It's true I've never had two hundred baht since I was born, but I'm not going. I'm not going."

"Jail," another interjected. "If you don't go, you simply go to jail. Whoever disobeyed the authorities? If they decided to give, you have to 70
take; if not, jail."

The word "jail" repeated like that affected him, but still he resisted.

"Whatever it is, I said I'm not going. I don't want it. How can I leave him when he's dying?" He raised his voice. "I'm not going."

"You go. Don't go against the government. We're subjects." He turned to find 75
the village chief standing grimly at his side. His voice dried up immediately.

"If I don't go, will it really be jail?" he asked.

"For sure," the village chief replied sternly. "Maybe for life."

That was all there was to it. Dazed, he asked the faith-healers and neighbours to take care of his son and left the house. 80

He reached the District Office almost at eleven and he found a group of his neighbours who had also come for the money sitting in a group. They told him to address the old deputy district officer which he did.

"I am Mr. Nark Na-ngarm, sir; I have come for money, the many children money." 85

The deputy district officer raised his fat face to stare at him for a moment then spoke heavily. "Idiot, don't you have eyes to see people are working. Get out! Get out and wait outside."

"But sir, my child is dying." But he cut himself short when he thought perhaps if the official suspected that his child had died there would be trouble. The deputy officer looked down at his paper and went on scribbling. Nark dejectedly joined the group outside. "All one does is suffer, born a rice farmer and a subject," he thought. "Poor and helpless, one's mouth stained from eating roots when the rice has run out, at the end of one's tether, you turn to the authorities only to be put down." The official continued to write as if there were no groups of peasants waiting anxiously. A few minutes after twelve, he strode from the office but had the kindness to say a few words.

"It's noon already. Time for a break. Come back at one o'clock for it."

Nark and his neighbours sat there waiting till one o'clock. The taciturn deputy on returning called them all to sit on the floor near him. He began by asking each of them why they had so many children. The awkward replies of the peasant brought guffaws from the other officials who turned to listen to the embarrassing answers. At last it had to be his turn.

"Who is Mr. Nark Na-ngarm?"

"I am, sir," he responded with humility.

"And now why do we have such a lot of children?"

Several people tittered.

"Oh, when you're poor, sir...," he burst out, his exasperation uncontrollable.

"What the hell's it got to do with being poor?" the deputy officer questioned in a voice that showed disappointment with the answer.

"So poor and no money to buy a blanket. The kids just keep coming."

Instead of laughter, dead silence, finally broken by the dry voice of the blank-faced deputy, "Bah! This joker uses his wife for a blanket."

The wind gusted again. The sabang and payom trees threw off a lot of leaves. The spears of sunlight still dazzled him. The whirlwind still hummed in the middle of the empty rice field ahead. Nark left the shade of the tall tree and went through the flaming afternoon sunshine heading for his village.

"Hey, Nark..." The voice came from a group of villagers still some distance away. It was topped by another.

"You sure are lucky." The words raised his spirits. He smiled a little before repeating expectantly, "How was I lucky, how?"

"The two hundred baht. You got it, didn't you?"

"I got it. It's right here." He patted his pocket.

"What luck! You sure have good luck, Nark. One more day and you'd have been out by two hundred baht."

90

95

100

105

110

115

120

125

12.2 First impressions

Exercise 1

a The following are some of the structural devices that you will come across in prose texts.

comma foreshadowing change of narrator

simple sentences paragraph lengths juxtaposition

listing anaphora flashback word order

direct speech

opening of a text

Copy and complete the table, adding the structural devices above under the appropriate heading. The first one has been done for you.

Sentence level	Paragraph level	Extract level	Whole-text level
	Simple sentences		

> **Key term**
>
> **Simple sentence:** A sentence that has a subject and a verb but no connectives (for example 'and' or 'but')

It may be possible to put some of the structural devices under more than one heading. Be ready to explain your reasons for this.

b As you are probably aware, there are more structural devices than can be listed here. See if you can add one more structural device of your own under each heading.

Share your ideas with the class.

c Now read the short story 'The Gold-Legged Frog'. This is a complete text, not an extract. As you read, make notes on anything you notice of interest structurally, at sentence, paragraph and whole-text levels. Be prepared to talk about two structural devices and their effects with the rest of the class.

12.3 Finding evidence

Exercise 2

Did you notice that there was a **flashback** in the short story?

a Identify the line at which Nark Na-ngarm has a flashback to an event from earlier that day. Identify the line at which the reader is brought back to the present time.

b Reread up to the flashback and reread the end section (the point at which we are brought back to the present time). In pairs or small groups, discuss:
- how the author shows that the narrative has returned to the present time at the end
- how the description at the beginning prepares us for the end – you might notice such techniques as foreshadowing; repetition; descriptions of Nark's mood; descriptions of nature and their effects
- the impact on the reader of the use of flashback.

Key term

Flashback: When a writer describes an event from an earlier point in time than the main story; flashbacks may be used to present a character's memories

Exercise 3

When we write about structure at sentence or paragraph level, it is usual to combine comments on language with comments on structure.

Look at paragraphs 2 to 4. To create **pathos** around both Nark and his children, Srinawk uses a number of language choices and **structural techniques** at sentence and paragraph level.

Copy and complete the table below, giving examples of Srinawk's use of language and structural devices, as well as a comment on how each one helps to create pathos. One has been added for you.

Language or structural device	Example	Comment on how this helps to create pathos
Direct speech	'Pa, here's another one. Pa, this crack has two. Gold-legged ones! Hurry, Pa.'	We can hear the childlike excitement of his son and his extreme desire to help his father. Repetition of 'Pa' emphasises their close relationship.

Key terms

Pathos: A feeling of sadness or pity created by a writer through their use of language or other devices

Structural techniques: The ways in which an author structures their writing

Direct speech: A character's actual words, put inside speech marks

Exercise 4

Reread from line 46 to the end of the story. Here Srinawk explores the themes of poverty, death and social oppression. His main structural device is direct speech, to convey the attitudes of the village people, the officials and Nark himself.

a By looking at **what** they say and **how** they say it, discuss in pairs or small groups what we learn about the differences between these people in their attitudes towards:
  – poverty
  – death
  – social oppression.
Make notes on what you find for each of these themes. Share your ideas and evidence with the rest of the class.

The use of flashback can be a powerful tool, as we have seen in this short story. The way a story ends is important too, as it can leave a lasting impression on the reader.

b How effective do you find the ending of this short story (from line 122 to the end of the story)? Think about this by yourself or with a partner and write down your thoughts about the ending. Share these thoughts with the class. Points to consider might be:
  – Did the author provide some clues as to what might happen at the end (but not in a way that would spoil the ending)?
  – Was there a twist at the end?
  – Did the ending leave you with something to think about or a strong feeling?

> **TIP**
>
> When discussing direct speech, remember to consider **how** the characters speak as well as **what** they say. For example, in this story, some of the features you might discuss include:
> - **tone of voice** ('yelled', 'sternly')
> - use of a **rhetorical question** ('How can I leave him when he's dying?')
> - use of punctuation and repetition ('Get out! Get out...')

> **MAKING CONNECTIONS**
>
> As you can see from your work in Exercise 4, structural devices, as well as features such as language and **characterisation**, can be used to explore themes in your set prose text. More work on using structural devices, language and characterisation to explore themes can be found in Unit 13.

> **Key terms**
>
> **Tone (of voice):** A character's personality conveyed by language choices for speech and thoughts; it can change over the course of a text
>
> **Rhetorical question:** A question that does not require an answer
>
> **Characterisation:** The ways in which a writer presents a character to an audience

12.4 Writing practice

Exercise 5

Now that you have looked at the story in detail, look at this essay question based on an extract from 'The Gold-Legged Frog'. We are using lines 53 to 114.

How does Srinawk create a sense of poverty and intimidation at this moment in the short story?

a Copy the question and highlight the key words.
Notice that there are two key words in this question – 'poverty' and 'intimidation' – and that, although they are connected, they are not **synonymous**. It would be a good idea to deal with them separately in your response.

Key term

Synonymous: Has the same meaning as another word

---

b Complete two planning tables, one for each of these two themes, with evidence that you can use in your response relating to the different characters. For each piece of evidence, provide a comment about how it creates a sense of poverty or intimidation. Here are examples of planning tables with one line in each completed for you.

Poverty		
Character	**Evidence**	**Comment**
Nark Na-ngarm		
Villagers	'Go, you fool. It's two hundred baht they're giving. You've never had that much in your life-time. Two hundred!'	'[F]ool' – language suggests that the villager can't believe that someone as poor as Nark would put his dying child before the opportunity to have money; repetition of 'two hundred' and use of exclamation mark stresses the importance of such a sum of money to impoverished rice farmers.
Deputy district officer and officials		

Intimidation		
Character	Evidence	Comment
Nark Na-ngarm		
Villagers	"'Jail,' another interjected. "If you don't go, you simply go to jail. Whoever disobeyed the authorities? If they decided to give, you have to take; if not, jail.'"	Use of direct speech containing repetition of the word 'jail', repeated structures ('if...') and rhetorical question conveys a sense of urgency and panic, which in turn leads the reader to understand how these people are oppressed
Deputy district officer and officials		

Exercise 6

A student has finished completing the planning table, but still has a number of questions to ask the teacher. Here they are, with the teacher's answers.

Student:

I never know how to start my essays. How do I start this one?

Teacher:

Rather than sitting thinking about this for too long, you can use the wording of the question to get started, for example 'Srinawk creates a sense of poverty and intimidation at this moment through his use of language and structural devices'. Your opening to an English Literature essay doesn't have to be an exciting one, just one that shows you mean business!

Student:

I noticed that the deputy district officer is described quite a lot. He has a 'fat' face and he is 'taciturn' and 'blank-faced'. I am sure these details wouldn't be included by Srinawk if they weren't important, but what can I say about them?

Teacher:

Well-spotted details. I think you could say a few things linked to poverty and intimidation.

'Fat face' could suggest that the deputy is well-fed compared to Nark. Did you notice that just a few sentences later Nark reflects on his frequent experience of hunger ('one's mouth stained from eating roots when the rice has run out')? This close **juxtaposing** of ideas draws attention to how very poor Nark is compared to the deputy. This means you could make a language and a structural point out of these details

'Taciturn' and 'blank-faced' both suggest the deputy's boredom and indifference to his job. You could link this to 'intimidation' because a kinder official would be making more effort to help the poor villagers feel welcome and entitled to their money, instead of making them feel like they shouldn't even be there. There is a **semantic field** of language linked to indifference surrounding the deputy and his fellow officers.

Student:

I have found lots of quotations to support the idea that the villagers and Nark are intimidated by the officials. Shall I list all of them?

Teacher:

Listing a lot of quotations is probably not a good idea, especially if they are all illustrating the same point. I would be selective and choose just a small number (one or two). Use the ones that you have most to say about because it is your analysis of the quotations that matters most. Short quotations integrated within your sentences are nearly always better than long ones that are set out at the end of your sentences.

> **Key terms**
>
> **Juxtapose:** Putting two images or ideas that are not similar close together to create a contrasting effect
>
> **Semantic field:** A group of words connected by meaning

a Read through the teacher's advice and discuss with a partner how useful the advice is for your own essay-writing, both in response to this particular essay question and in general, thinking about your prose set text. Write down anything you don't understand about the advice and share it with your teacher and the class.

b Write an introductory paragraph in response to the essay question in Exercise 5. Copy the teacher's recommended first sentence, then add three or four sentences of your own explaining how you will answer the question.

12.5 Set-text focus

Exercise 7

Consider the use of direct speech in your prose set text.

a Choose an extract from your prose text where the writer uses a lot of **dialogue**.

b Consider how the dialogue here helps to:
  - reveal a character / the characters
  - move the **plot** along
  - develop themes.

  Make a table. Copy out any effective quotations from your chosen extract in the left-hand column. Comment on the right about how they help to reveal characters, move the plot along and / or develop a theme.

c Discuss with a partner the relevance and importance of these quotations to your set text. Consider the following points in your discussion:
  - The best quotations are usually short – could any of your quotations be shortened without losing the evidence you want to provide?
  - Were there other quotations in the extract that might have illustrated your points better than the ones you have chosen?

d Turn over the paper you were working on or close your book. Spend five to ten minutes with a partner testing each other on how well you can remember the quotations you have written down.

> **Dialogue:** A conversation between two or more people that is presented in a text; in prose texts, dialogue is often written as direct speech
>
> **Plot:** The main events in a play or other text that interrelate to make the story

Take your learning further

1   Put the short story 'The Gold-Legged Frog' into a **storyboard** of eight frames. Select the content of each frame by choosing eight of the most significant moments in the story.
2   Caption each frame with a quotation from the text that sums up that key moment.
3   In a group, choose whose storyboard you wish to use to act out the story.
4   Did acting out the story help you to sympathise more with any of the characters?

Key term

Storyboard: Resembling a cartoon strip in a magazine, it has a number of boxes (frames) in which a story is told through pictures; the skill in putting together a storyboard lies in picking the most important moments to represent – film-makers often use storyboards

Unit summary

In this unit, you have learned how to:
● Identify the uses of structural devices in a short story.
● Explore a text beyond its surface meaning to show a deep awareness of ideas and attitudes.
● Recognise and appreciate ways in which an author uses structural devices to create and shape meanings and effects.
● Describe your personal response to a text in terms of structural devices.

Think about how you have demonstrated each of these skills in the exercises in this unit. You will need to keep the structural concerns discussed in this unit in mind when studying the prose extracts in the following units.

Nervous Conditions: Focus on themes and ideas

In this unit we will be examining, in an extract from a prose text, how a writer explores themes and ideas. A theme in a prose text is a recurring idea that the writer explores. Major themes will probably be present throughout the text. Minor themes may be explored in just a small section of the text. Being able to examine the themes of your set text through use of character, structural devices and language choices enables you to demonstrate a deeper knowledge of your text and an understanding of the author's intentions.

Nervous Conditions was the debut and prize-winning novel of Zimbabwean novelist Tsitsi Dangarembga (born 1959), and is the first of a trilogy of semi-autobiographical novels written by her. It was published in 1988.

The novel is semi-autobiographical and is set in post-colonial Rhodesia (present-day Zimbabwe) in the 1960s. It tells the story of Tambu and her extended family and is narrated by Tambu herself. The extract is from early on in the novel. Tambu's brother, Nhamo, is away being educated at a missionary school run by their uncle, Babamukuru. Tambu is resentful because, although she was extremely successful in the year she spent at a local school (this is what she means by 'my Sub A performance' in the extract), her parents have decided that they can only afford to keep Nhamo at school. Tambu has to learn her role as a woman instead. Maiguru is Babamukuru's wife.

Glossary

Lucrative: Producing a lot of money

Aiwa!: An expression of frustration

Sub A: The first year of kindergarten or pre-school

The Mission: Mission schools were set up by white Christian missionaries and existed to educate and help in the westernisation of local children; Babumukuru was installed as headteacher at the Mission school by the white authorities

13.1 From *Nervous Conditions* by Tsitsi Dangarembga

Fortunately, my mother was determined that year. She began to boil eggs, which she carried to the bus terminus and sold to passengers passing through. (This meant that we could not eat them.) She also took vegetables – rape, onion and tomatoes – extending her garden so that there was more to sell. Business was fair, and good during public holidays, when visitors from as far as Salisbury, Fort Victoria, Mount Darwin and Wankie would be tempted to buy a little extra to take home with them. In this way she scraped together enough money to keep my brother in school. I understood that selling vegetables was not a lucrative business. I understood that there was not enough money for my fees. Yes, I did understand why I could not go back to school, but I loved going to school and I was good at it. Therefore, my circumstances affected me badly. 5

10

My father thought I should not mind. 'Is that anything to worry about? Ha-a-a, it's nothing,' he reassured me, with his usual ability to jump whichever way was easiest. 'Can you cook books and feed them to your husband? Stay at home with your mother. Learn to cook and clean. Grow vegetables.' 15

His intention was to soothe me with comforting, sensible words, but I could not see the sense. This was often the case when my father spoke, but there had not before been such concrete cause to question his theories. This time, though, I had evidence. Maiguru was educated, and did she serve Babamukuru books for dinner? I discovered to my unhappy relief that my father was not sensible. 20

I complained to my mother. 'Baba says I do not need to be educated,' I told her scornfully. 'He says I must learn to be a good wife. Look at Maiguru,' I continued, unaware how viciously. 'She is a better wife than you!' 25

My mother was too old to be disturbed by my childish nonsense. She tried to diffuse some of it by telling me many things, by explaining that my father was right because even Maiguru knew how to cook and clean and grow vegetables. 'This business of womanhood is a heavy burden,' she said. 'How could it not be? Aren't we the ones who bear children? When it is like that you can't just decide today I want to do this, tomorrow I want to do that, the next day I want to be educated! When 30

35

there are sacrifices to be made, you are the one who has to make them. And these things are not easy; you have to start learning them early, from a very early age. The earlier the better so that it is easy later on. Easy! As if it is ever easy. And these days it is worse, with the poverty of blackness on one side and the weight of womanhood on the other. Aiwa! What will help you, my child, is to learn to carry your burdens with strength.'   40

I thought about this for several days, during which I began to fear that I was not as intelligent as my Sub A performance had led me to believe, because, as with my father, I could not follow the sense of my mother's words. My mother said being black was a burden because it made you   45 poor, but Babamukuru was not poor. My mother said being a woman was a burden because you had to bear children and look after them and the husband. But I did not think this was true. Maiguru was well looked after by Babamukuru, in a big house on the Mission which I had not seen but of which I had heard rumours concerning its vastness and   50 elegance. Maiguru was driven around in a car, looked well-kempt and fresh, clean all the time. She was altogether a different kind of woman from my mother.

13.2 First impressions

Exercise 1

Read the extract from *Nervous Conditions*, keeping the idea of theme in your mind.

a This extract is just a small section of the novel. What do you learn from this extract of the themes that the novel will cover? Draw a mind map with the words 'themes and ideas' in the middle. How many themes can you see here that you expect to be developed in the novel?

Nervous Conditions – themes and ideas

b A **narrator** is a person who tells a story. The extract is a **first-person narrative**. Read the definition of 'first-person narrative' in the key terms box. In a pair or a small group, discuss how a first-person narrative can be effective. Do you think there are any disadvantages to a first-person narration? Share your thoughts with the class.

> **Key terms**
>
> **Narrator:** The person who tells the story in a text; what happens is told in their words
>
> **First-person narrative:** A narrative in which the events of the novel are told through a character actually in the novel – we see events and other characters through their eyes; first-person narrators communicate what they themselves think, experience and witness, as well as what they have been told or heard

13.3 Finding evidence

Exercise 2

a   Read the first paragraph of the extract again.
Copy out the following statements and write T (true), F (false) or NEE (not enough evidence) by each one. **Only** refer to the first paragraph for your answers.

   i   Tambu's mother thinks her son's education is important.

   ii Tambu thinks her mother is a good mother.

   iii Tambu believes that her brother's education is more important than hers.

   iv Selling vegetables was less lucrative during public holidays.

   v   Tambu has been arguing with her mother.

   Share your answers with the class. Remember to have your evidence ready.

b   In paragraphs 2, 4 and 5, we learn about Tambu's parents' attitudes to such topics as:

   i   being a woman   iii education

   ii being a man   iv being black.

   Write at least one sentence in relation to each of these points, stating what Tambu's parents believe.

c   Look again at what Tambu's mother says in paragraph 5.

   i   Do you think that Tambu's mother intends to be kind by giving her this advice?

   ii Are there any differences in the way Tambu's mother and father speak to Tambu about education and womanhood?

   iii Is it possible to have some sympathy with Tambu's parents' views?

   Discuss these questions with a partner then share your thoughts with the class. Remember to find evidence for what you say.

> **TIP**
>
> Remember that when considering a character's intentions, you should look not just at what the character says, but how they are presented as saying it. Look, for example, at language choices, repetition for effect, punctuation and **syntax**.

Key terms

Syntax: The order of words in a sentence

Oxymoron: Two opposing words put together for effect, for example 'bitter sweet'

Perspective: Like a lens through which readers view characters and events in a text; the perspective of a text is created by the speaker: we interpret the characters and events based on what the speaker shows and tells us

d   Now look at Tambu's reactions to her parents in paragraphs 3, 4 and 6. Discuss the following with a partner or in a small group:

   i   What does Tambu mean when she says her parents' advice and explanations don't make 'sense' (lines 19 to 20 and 42 to 45)? Think about this in context.

   ii What does the **oxymoron** 'unhappy relief' mean in the sentence: 'I discovered to my unhappy relief that my father was not sensible'?

   iii What does Tambu think of Babamukuru and his wife Maiguru and how does she use her uncle and his wife to support her arguments?

e   Think back to the work you did in Exercise 1 part **b**. Since reading this extract and working through the tasks in Exercise 2, have you had any further thoughts about how a first-person narrative can be an effective way of exploring themes and ideas? Discuss with a partner:

   i   the use of a female narrator in helping the author to explore such themes as social injustice and poverty

   ii the use of the naive **perspective** of a child to explore these themes.

13.4 Writing practice

Exercise 3

Look at this essay question:

In what ways does Dangarembga make you strongly sympathise with Tambu and her mother at this moment in the novel?

The key words in this question are 'strongly sympathise' and the focus is on the characters of Tambu and her mother.

A student has spent 15 minutes putting together a planning table for this essay. Their teacher has written comments on the planning table.

What I need to cover	How Dangarembga makes us *strongly sympathise* with **Tambu** and her **mother**	A good idea to put the question into your planning table with the key words and focus characters' names highlighted.
Focus on the question – how we are made to sympathise with the two people	We are made to sympathise with Tambu and her mother for similar reasons but also for different reasons: their lives as women, their lives because they are black and because they don't have much money	This is a strong opening because it suggests to me that you are going to focus closely on the essay title set. I like the idea that you will be dealing with the mother and daughter separately. It is true that they share reasons why we should sympathise with them, but there are also differences.
Reasons for sympathy	Tambu – very bright, brother's education a greater priority, low expectations of her parents, confused by her parents' advice (contrast B and M's lives) Mother – works hard for little money; spends it all on Nhamo's education; resigned to her life as a black woman ('poverty of blackness' and 'weight of womanhood' – balancing of phrases suggests they are equal burdens); frustrated tone to Tambu	A lot of things to focus on here. I think that this will be your biggest section. Don't forget to consider 'how' as well as 'what'. Comment on the devices, techniques and language the narrator uses to convey the things you have noted.
First-person narrative	Tambu's **viewpoint**, so we gain insight into her feelings about her own situation (bearing in mind she is a child and can't have an adult perspective)	Good. Make sure you link this to the question. Think about how the first-person narrative helps us to feel sympathy for Tambu. Find evidence for that. We have to **infer** what her mother might really feel through the way she speaks to Tambu and her actions.
Father's attitude	'Can you cook books and feed them to your husband?'	This looks unfinished, as it is just a quotation. Does the father's attitude to Tambu (he is rather flippant) add to the sympathy we feel?

Key terms

Viewpoint: The thoughts and feelings that a character has towards a situation

Infer: Reading between the lines of a text to find clues to understand more than is said directly

Have you thought about how you might conclude this (if you have time)? The question uses the phrase 'strongly sympathise'. Is there a case to be made for one character eliciting more sympathy than the other?

Write your own response to the essay title. You can use the planning table provided and spend about 30 minutes or you can make your own planning table and spend a total of about 45 minutes.

13.5 Set-text focus

Exercise 4

These exercises will help you to learn and think more deeply about your prose set text.

a   Find an extract in your set text where the narrator makes us feel sympathy for a character or characters. Apply the question set in Exercise 3 to your chosen passage, substituting in the relevant author's and characters' names.

OR

b   Find an extract in your set text where the theme of poverty is explored. Write a response to the following question:

In what ways does [author's name] convincingly portray the effects of poverty at this moment in the novel?

OR

c   Find an extract in your set text where education or school life is felt to be important to a character or characters. Write a response to the following question:

In what ways does [author's name] vividly convey to you the significance of this moment for [name of character]?

Whichever essay you choose to write, remember to create a planning table that includes a 'focus on the question' section. You should also consider:

» the impact of a first or **third-person narrative**
» any other language, techniques and devices used by the author.

> ### Key terms
>
> **Third-person narrative:** A narrative that is not told from the perspective of a character in the story
>
> **Third-person omniscient narrator:** 'Omniscient' means 'knows everything'; this kind of narrator knows everything about the characters – what they think and what they do and why; the narrator is the third person, meaning that they tell the story, but they are not in the story

> **MAKING CONNECTIONS**
>
> In some other units in the Prose section, the extracts take different types of third-person narrators. In Unit 16, the narrative in *The Sorrow of War* is third person, but it is a 'limited' third-person narrative. This means that the narrator knows the thoughts, feelings, judgements and experiences of one character (Kien). However, the narrator does not know, for example, what the truck driver is thinking as they drive into the jungle. In Unit 14, the narrator in *Hard Times* is a **third-person omniscient narrator**, which means that the narrator knows exactly what all the characters think and feel and what they are like as people: there is very little room for the reader to make their own judgements about characters and their actions.

Take your learning further

There are always 'two sides to every story'. *Nervous Conditions* examines an experience from a young girl's perspective. It is very easy to judge her father as a rather flippant and even unkind person in the way he dismisses her desire for what many of us nowadays consider a fundamental human right – education.

In the poem 'How To Be A Man', the contemporary Indian poet Simar Singh examines the pressures on 21st-century men, in particular the effects on the mental health of men as a consequence of gender roles and expectations.

There are performances of the poem by Singh himself on YouTube. Listen to the poem or look it up on the internet.

Look back to the ideas that were generated by your discussions about Tambu's father. Does Singh's poem help you to see that there might be another side to her father that Tambu can't know about? Or perhaps you think that Tambu's father is not deserving of our sympathy. Why not?

Unit summary

In this unit, you have learned how to:
● Use references to an extract from a novel to discuss themes and ideas discussed in the text.
● Explore the text beyond surface meanings to show deeper awareness of themes, ideas and attitudes.
● Recognise and appreciate ways in which authors use language, structure and form to create effects and explore themes.
● Communicate a sensitive response to themes and ideas, informed by references to the text.

Think about how you have demonstrated each of these skills in the exercises in this unit. You will need to be alert to the themes and ideas that writers are exploring in all of the texts you study on this course.

14

Hard Times: Focus on character

In this unit, you will:
- Show detailed knowledge of the content of an extract from a prose text, supported by reference to the extract.
- Think about the ways in which characters are presented, beyond their surface appearances.
- Recognise and appreciate ways in which a writer uses language, structure and form to reveal character.
- Communicate a sensitive and informed personal response to the ways in which characters are described.

In the previous unit, you saw how a writer explores themes and ideas through the actions and attitudes of their characters. When studying any prose text, you will need to think about the way the author describes their characters, what they show them doing and report them saying, as well as their relationships with other characters. You should also be prepared to think about how characters change throughout the text you are studying and what their development says about the attitudes they hold or the ideas they represent.

Hard Times is a novel by the well-known Victorian English author, Charles Dickens (1812 to 1870). Dickens is considered by many to be the greatest English novelist of his time, and many of his fictional characters are well known today. Dickens was also a social critic and he campaigned extensively for children's rights, education and other social reforms.

This extract is from near the start of the novel and shows a young girl called Sissy Jupe being interrogated by Mr Gradgrind, the man in charge of the school Sissy attends. Mr Gradgrind is portrayed as a cold and practical man with no interest in promoting imagination and ideas in the school he presides over. Sissy is the daughter of a circus performer.

Glossary

Curtseying: The act of bending one's knee and bowing one's head to acknowledge someone's superiority

Calling: Way of life, career

Breaks horses: Teaches horses to accept a saddle and bridle and the weight of a human riding on their back

The ring: The circular arena in a circus where acts are performed

Farrier: Someone who puts shoes on horses

Behoof: Benefit

Pitchers: Containers for holding liquid; this is used as a metaphor here – the children are

seen as empty receptacles for Mr Gradgrind's words of wisdom (Dickens is being ironic)

Irradiated: Lit up

Interval: Aisle separating the groups of boys and girl

Quadruped: Four-legged animal

Graminivorous: Animal that eats grass

Grinders: Teeth that gnash together to break down food

Eye-teeth: Very sharp, pointed teeth

Incisive: Sharp teeth at the front of the mouth

Shod: Wearing (horse) shoes

14.1 From *Hard Times* by Charles Dickens

'Girl number twenty,' said Mr. Gradgrind, squarely pointing with his square forefinger, 'I don't know that girl. Who is that girl?'

'Sissy Jupe, sir,' explained number twenty, blushing, standing up, and curtseying.

'Sissy is not a name,' said Mr. Gradgrind. 'Don't call yourself Sissy. Call yourself Cecilia.'   5

'It's father as calls me Sissy, sir,' returned the young girl in a trembling voice, and with another curtsey.

'Then he has no business to do it,' said Mr. Gradgrind. 'Tell him he mustn't. Cecilia Jupe. Let me see. What is your father?'   10

'He belongs to the circus, if you please, sir. He rides the horses.'

Mr. Gradgrind frowned, and waved off the objectionable calling with his hand.

'We don't want to know anything about that, here. You mustn't tell us about that, here. Your father breaks horses, don't he?'   15

'If you please, sir, when they can get any to break, they do break horses in the ring, sir.'

'You mustn't tell us about the ring, here. Very well, then. Describe your father as a horsebreaker. He doctors sick horses, I dare say?'

'Oh yes, sir.'   20

'Very well, then. He is a veterinary surgeon, a farrier, and horsebreaker. Give me your definition of a horse.'

(Sissy Jupe thrown into the greatest alarm by this demand.)

'Girl number twenty unable to define a horse!' said Mr. Gradgrind, for the general behoof of all the little pitchers. 'Girl number twenty possessed   25
of no facts, in reference to one of the commonest of animals! Some boy's definition of a horse. Bitzer, yours.'

The square finger, moving here and there, lighted suddenly on Bitzer, perhaps because he chanced to sit in the same ray of sunlight which, darting in at one of the bare windows of the intensely white-washed room,   30
irradiated Sissy. For, the boys and girls sat on the face of the inclined plane in two compact bodies, divided up the centre by a narrow interval; and Sissy, being at the corner of a row on the sunny side, came in for the beginning of a sunbeam, of which Bitzer, being at the corner of a row on the other side, a few rows in advance, caught the end. But, whereas the girl   35
was so dark-eyed and dark-haired, that she seemed to receive a deeper and

more lustrous colour from the sun, when it shone upon her, the boy was so light-eyed and light-haired that the self-same rays appeared to draw out of him what little colour he ever possessed. His cold eyes would hardly have been eyes, but for the short ends of lashes which, by bringing them into immediate contrast with something paler than themselves, expressed their form. His short-cropped hair might have been a mere continuation of the sandy freckles on his forehead and face. His skin was so unwholesomely deficient in the natural tinge, that he looked as though, if he were cut, he would bleed white.

40

45

'Bitzer,' said Thomas Gradgrind. 'Your definition of a horse.'

'Quadruped. Graminivorous. Forty teeth, namely twenty-four grinders, four eye-teeth, and twelve incisive. Sheds coat in the spring; in marshy countries, sheds hoofs, too. Hoofs hard, but requiring to be shod with iron. Age known by marks in mouth.' Thus (and much more) Bitzer.

50

'Now girl number twenty,' said Mr. Gradgrind. 'You know what a horse is.'

14.2 First impressions

Exercise 1

How do we learn about characters in a text? In most prose fiction texts there are three main ways that we learn about characters. We learn about them through:

» what they say and how they say it
» what they do
» what the narrator tells us about them.

a In the table below, the quotations are being used to reveal something about each character. Copy and complete the second two columns of the table, identifying which of the methods of characterisation above is being used in each case. The first one is done for you.

Quotation	Character	Method of characterisation
Jane threw her book down angrily on the table.	Jane	What they do
I always thought of Robert as very annoying.	Robert	
Priti carefully hung her clothes up in the wardrobe, making sure that all the same colours were placed next to each other.	Priti	
'I really don't want to do the washing-up, even if it is my turn,' said Adana.	Adana	
The problem with Josef was that he found it difficult to socialise.	Josef	
Thomas said, 'I feel really sorry for people who struggle in their lessons at school.'	Thomas	

b Based on these sentences, what might we learn about the characters of Jane, Robert, Priti, Adana, Josef and Thomas? Share what you think with a partner.

c Now read the extract from *Hard Times*. As you read, think carefully about the methods Dickens uses to show us the characters of Mr Gradgrind, Sissy Jupe and Bitzer. Notice whether Dickens uses any further methods of his own to reveal character. Make notes as you read.

14.3 Finding evidence

Exercise 2

Dickens is a third-person omniscient narrator. This means that the reader is not left to work out what the characters in his novel are like. Dickens tells us what they are like. There is little or no room for any other judgement.

Did you notice that Dickens uses a few extra methods to show us what his characters are like? Discuss the following with a partner:

a What does the name 'Mr Gradgrind' make you think about the character?

b Another teacher, who doesn't appear in this extract, but appears a few lines later, is called Mr M'Choakumchild. Would you like to have this teacher as your teacher based on his name alone?

c Look at the description at the opening of the passage where Mr Gradgrind's forefinger is described as 'square'. Based on what you know of Mr Gradgrind already, why do you think Dickens gave him a 'square forefinger'?

d The chapter that this extract is taken from is called 'Murdering the Innocents'. What is your response to this?

Share your responses to these points with the class.

Exercise 3

Look at lines 1 to 27.

a Look back to the beginning of Exercise 1 and remind yourself of the three main ways that we find out about a character.
Which are the two main methods that Dickens is using here to portray the characters of Sissy and Mr Gradgrind?

   b Using a table like the ones below, record some of the things that we learn about either Sissy or Mr Gradgrind in this extract.
For each point, provide:
- a quotation from the text
- a short comment explaining it.

One point has been provided for you in each table.
When you have finished, share what you have written with the rest of the class.

Sissy		
What we learn	**Quotation**	**Comment**
She is very respectful to Mr Gradgrind	'standing up, and curtseying'	Her actions show that she recognises that she is his social inferior. She even curtseys a second time when Mr Gradgrind insults her name.

Mr Gradgrind		
What we learn	**Quotation**	**Comment**
He is rude and unkind	'I don't know that girl. Who is that girl?'	Repetition of 'that girl' is dismissive and sounds like a put-down. It takes away her individuality and sense of personal identity. Abrupt short sentences used. A kinder person would have simply directed their words to Sissy herself and asked her name politely.

Key term

Symbolism: The use of an idea, image or object to represent abstract ideas or qualities

Exercise 4

Reread lines 28 to 45. This paragraph is descriptive, mainly of Bitzer but also Sissy. Here Dickens is using yet further methods of revealing character:

» **symbolism**
» the children's physical appearances.

If you read the rest of the novel, you will learn that Sissy is a girl who is imaginative and compassionate. Bitzer is exactly the sort of pupil that Mr Gradgrind wants to produce in his school: rational, unfeeling and interested only in facts. He is another character, like Mr Gradgrind, whose name tells us about his character – he knows a lot of 'bits of' information / facts, but he has no ability to show compassion or imagination.

a Look at the way the ray of sunlight is described. Of course, a ray of sunlight would be usual to see in a room with windows, but it is also being used here symbolically. Make notes on the use of symbolism here.

b Pick out descriptions of Sissy and Bitzer that are in direct contrast with each other.

c Pick out descriptions of Bitzer that suggest his character.

Share your responses with the rest of the class. Remember to be ready to explain your ideas.

Exercise 5

Now look at the passage from line 46 until the end of the passage.

Bitzer's definition of a horse is exactly what Mr Gradgrind wanted to hear: factual and full of technical terms.

Write down what Sissy Jupe might have said about a horse, if Mr Gradgrind hadn't intimidated her. Bear in mind what you know of her character. Write two to three sentences. Read out your response and be ready to explain why you think she might have said this.

14.4 Writing practice

Exercise 6

Now that you have studied the extract in detail, look at this essay question:

How does Dickens vividly convey Mr Gradgrind's attitudes towards the pupils in his school at this moment in the novel?

a Copy out the question and highlight the key words.

b Write a brief plan of how you would answer the question – use a mind map, a planning table or a bullet-point list, not sentences. Pay close attention to the key words you have highlighted and make sure you address them (look at the Tip box for more help). Check that you have included relevant quotations and ideas from the work you have already done. Spend about 15 minutes on this.

TIP

The key words in this question are 'Mr Gradgrind's attitudes' and 'pupils'. Make sure you use these words and synonyms of them within your answer. This will help you to give a focused commentary. However, do not be afraid to develop your answer beyond these basic ideas. Focus on the question but make your answer a detailed and personal response.

Exercise 7

Read the student's first paragraph of a first draft of their response to the question. Then look at the feedback given by their teacher.

a Discuss the teacher's feedback with your partner or group. How would you improve the student's answer according to the teacher's advice?

b Share your ideas with the class.

Student's first paragraph

Mr Gradgrind's attitudes towards his pupils are illustrated by the way he speaks to Sissy and Bitzer. It is clear that he doesn't see children as individuals as he refers to Sissy as 'that girl' and 'girl number twenty'. He is rude to Sissy and doesn't address her personally or in a welcoming way. He intimidates her by telling her that 'Sissy is not a name' even though he must be able to see that she is 'blushing' and speaks in a 'trembling voice'. He obviously thinks there is no place for children to show their emotions and so his harsh tone is justified. When he asks her what her father's job is, she answers him honestly. Mr Gradgrind can't see the point of being a circus performer (a type of artist) because he is only interested in practical considerations not entertainment, so he focuses only on one side of the job. He is therefore belittling not just Sissy herself but her father's profession, and this shows a cruel attitude.

Teacher's annotations:

- A focused opening and it draws attention to how you are probably going to notice a difference between Mr Gradgrind's attitudes to Bitzer and Sissy as well as similarities.

- Good extension of the comments on 'that girl' and 'girl number twenty'. What does this show about what Mr Gradgrind believes his pupils should learn when dealing with other people?

- Good reference back to the question.

- Good quotations to illustrate that the children are not viewed as individuals. Can you comment further on the word 'that' (repeated) and 'girl number 20'?

- Can you integrate a quotation from the text to illustrate Mr Gradgrind's dismissive attitude towards circus performing?

c Rewrite this first paragraph, taking the teacher's advice into consideration. Allow yourself a further 30 minutes to finish the essay.

14.5 Set-text focus

Exercise 8

Consider the way characters are revealed in your prose set text.

a Choose an extract from your prose text where the writer focuses on revealing a character or characters.

b Look back to the beginning of Exercise 1. Decide which methods to reveal character that the writer is using in your prose text.

c Create a table for each character like you did in Exercise 3**b**.

d Does the writer use any other techniques, for example symbolism or physical appearance, to reveal character?

MAKING CONNECTIONS

Have a look at Units 13 and 15. Both contain extracts where the narrative voice is first person, and the narrator does not have the omniscient powers that Dickens has. Think about what is gained by having a third-person narrative and what is lost.

Key term

Working class: Poorer people who have manual jobs with a lower status in Victorian society

Take your learning further

Charles Dickens believed that education was very important for children. However, as you can see from this extract from *Hard Times*, he had concerns about some of the schools that were being set up and what they were actually teaching children.

1   Read more about what Dickens felt about education. Go to this website set up by the town in which he was born, Portsmouth in south England: **http://dickens.port.ac.uk/education**

2   Find out why Dickens felt education was important for children, especially **working-class** children.

3   Find out why he objected to schools like Mr Gradgrind's school.

Unit summary

In this unit, you have learned how to:
● Show detailed knowledge of the content of an extract from a prose text, supported by reference to the extract.
● Think about the ways in which characters are presented, beyond their surface appearances.
● Recognise and appreciate ways in which a writer uses language, structure and form to reveal character.
● Communicate a sensitive and informed personal response to the ways in which characters are described.

Think about how you have demonstrated each of these skills in the exercises in this unit. Think about the ways in which characters are presented in the other prose extracts in this book. Be sure to return to this unit and apply the skills you develop in the other units to *Hard Times*.

15 Annie John:
Focus on perspective

In this unit, you will:
- Show detailed knowledge of the content of an extract from a prose text supported by reference to the text.
- Demonstrate an understanding of the perspective from which a piece of fiction is told and think about the significance of what the narrator tells us and what is not included.
- Recognise and appreciate ways in which writers create and shape perspectives.
- Evaluate the effectiveness of different narrative perspectives.

In Unit 13 you learned about the impact of a first-person narrative on a text. The voice in *Nervous Conditions* is Tambu's voice and we had to infer the attitudes and feelings of other characters in the extract, for example Tambu's mother and father. In Unit 14 you learned that Charles Dickens is a third-person omniscient narrator. This means that the only perspective we receive on the characters is Dickens's. The reader does not have to work out what the characters are like because Dickens makes it very clear how we are meant to perceive them. *Annie John* is another first-person narrative; this extract will allow you to build on your skills and learn about the significance of the narrator in creating perspective.

Jamaica Kincaid was born in 1949 in Antigua, an island in the West Indies. She has written a number of semi-autobiographical novels. When a novel has a semi-autobiographical quality, it is often possible to judge that we are hearing the author's thoughts and perspectives through the narrator. Nowadays Kincaid lives mainly in Vermont, USA.

Annie John is set on the island of Antigua in the 1950s, when Antigua was a British colony. Annie and her friends attend a British school, where the curriculum includes such subjects as English literature, history and culture. Annie has to dress in British school clothes and is discouraged from engaging in traditional Antiguan culture. This attracts her to the Red Girl, who resists rules and acts as she pleases.

Glossary

Guava: A popular tropical fruit

Fresh from the mint: The mint is a place where notes and coins are made; Annie is telling us that the Red Girl has very bright orange or copper-coloured hair like a new penny

Corkscrews: Very tight curls that resemble the corkscrew used to open a bottle

Amphibian: A class of animal that includes frogs and toads

15.1 From *Annie John* by Jamaica Kincaid

One day, I was throwing stones at a guava tree, trying to knock down a ripe guava, when the Red Girl came along and said, "Which one do you want?" After I pointed it out, she climbed up the tree, picked the one I wanted off its branch, climbed down, and presented it to me. How my eyes did widen and my mouth form an "o" at this. I had never seen a girl do this before. All the boys climbed trees for the fruit they wanted, and all the girls threw stones to knock the fruit off the trees. But look at the way she climbed that tree: better than any boy.

5

Polishing off the delicious ripe-to-perfection guava in two bites, I took a good look at the Red Girl. How right I had been to take some special notice of her the first time I had seen her. She was holding on to her mother's skirt and I was holding on to my mother's skirt. Our mothers waved to each other as they passed, calling out the usual greetings, making the usual inquiries. I noticed that the girl's hair was the color of a penny fresh from the mint, and that it was so unruly it had to be forcibly twisted into corkscrews, the ends tied tightly with white thread. The corkscrews didn't lie flat on her head, they stood straight up, and when she walked they bounced up and down as if they were something amphibian and alive. Right away to myself I called her the Red Girl. For as she passed, in my mind's eye I could see her surrounded by flames, the house she lived in on fire, and she could not escape. I rescued her, and after that she followed me around worshipfully and took with great forbearance any and every abuse I heaped on her. I would have gone on like that for a while, but my mother tugged at me, claiming my attention; I heard her say, "Such a nice woman, to keep that girl so dirty."

10

15

20

25

The Red Girl and I stood under the guava tree looking each other up and down. What a beautiful thing I saw standing before me. Her face was big and round and red, like a moon – a red moon. She had big, broad, flat feet, and they were naked to the bare ground; her dress was dirty, the skirt and blouse tearing away from each other at one side; the red hair that I had first seen standing up on her head was matted and tangled; her hands were big and fat, and her fingernails held at least ten anthills of dirt under them. And on top of that, she had such an unbelievable, wonderful smell, as if she had never taken a bath in her whole life.

30

35

15.2 First impressions

Exercise 1

a Think of three people in your life who might know different sides of you as a person. Examples might be your teacher, your best friend, a grandparent. Write down the names of these people and write a few sentences for each person to show what they might say about you. Your sentences could start 'I think of Paul as...' Share your sentences with the class.

b Now read the extract from *Annie John*. As you read, think carefully about the perspectives on the Red Girl. The narrative is mostly from the perspective of Annie John. However, if you read closely you will be aware of more than one perspective on the Red Girl. Who else has a perspective on the Red Girl? Is it the same as Annie John's?

15.3 Finding evidence

Exercise 2

Now that you have read the extract, you should be aware of the benefit of a first-person narrative. As readers, we are allowed direct access to the narrator's thoughts, feelings, perceptions and memories. However, using a first-person narrative also enables an author to expose the character's blind spots, flaws or, as is the case here, naivety and innocence.

a Reread paragraph 1. Why is Annie impressed by the Red Girl? What does that suggest to you about the attitudes towards boys and girls and the way they are expected to behave in the time and place this novel is set?

b The narrative uses the technique of flashback. Identify the point at which the technique of flashback is used. How is the technique of flashback effective here?

c Look closely at the descriptions of the Red Girl's hair in lines 14 to 19. How do Kincaid's vivid descriptions convey Annie's fascination with the Red Girl's hair?

d Look at how Annie imagines her relationship starting and progressing with the Red Girl in lines 20 to 24. What sort of relationship does she want with her? How is this childlike?

e Write down the adjective that Annie's mother uses to describe the Red Girl. Look back to what you wrote about Annie's perspective in part c above. Answer the following questions:
  i What did Annie either not notice or not care about when she first saw the Red Girl?
  ii What might Annie's mother have said about the Red Girl's hair? Write this down. Start with the words 'I think...'
  iii What does this show about the differences between an adult perspective and a child's perspective?

f Now look at the last paragraph. Annie calls the Red Girl 'a beautiful thing'. Pick out details about the Red Girl that Annie uses to support her idea that the Red Girl is 'a beautiful thing'. Write them down. What does the word 'thing' tell us about how Annie perceives the Red Girl? Write down your thoughts on this. Share your ideas with the class.

Exercise 3

Look at what some students wrote about this extract.

Student A

The effect of writing from Annie's perspective here is both humorous and ironic. We find it humorous because of the childlike adoration of the Red Girl for no other reasons than the things she does and the way she looks. We find it ironic because the reader would probably not agree that a girl who was allowed to get so dirty, smells so badly and goes barefoot is someone 'wonderful'.

Student B

I liked how the Red Girl was described from Annie's perspective because it gives the reader an insight into the important things we should judge other people on. Annie's mother is conditioned by social and cultural expectation not to see past the Red Girl's 'dirtiness' and she judges her mother for it. Annie on the other hand sees only wonder in a girl who looks and is so different from other girls she knows.

Student C

By writing from Annie's perspective, the author gives us an effective insight into the innocence of childhood. We have Annie imagining a grand scenario where, like a super-hero, she boldly rescues the Red Girl from a house fire. This is juxtaposed on either side with the **bathos** of her mother's words about the Red Girl's dirtiness and the little detail that Annie is in reality not a super-hero at all: she is very young and timid, clinging to her mother's skirt for protection.

Discuss in a small group or with a partner the views of the students and consider how far you agree with their comments. Share your ideas with the class.

Key term

Bathos: A device used in literature; it is like an anti-climax and its effect is often humorous because it involves a mood change from something serious to something trivial

Exercise 4

Reread the section in the middle of the extract where Annie recalls the first time she saw the Red Girl.

a   Imagine that, instead of Annie, Annie's mother is the narrator at this point. Think about what Annie's mother would say about the Red Girl. Would she, for example, refer to her as the Red Girl? Would she know what Annie's thoughts were? Write a few sentences in which you, as Annie's mother, describe the Red Girl's appearance and your thoughts about her. Your sentences could start 'When I first saw the child…'.

b   Imagine that, instead of Annie, there is a third-person narrator at this point. Think about what a third-person narrator would say about Annie and the Red Girl. Again, would a third-person narrator be likely to use the phrase 'the Red Girl'? Write a few sentences as a third-person narrator describing the two girls, their appearances and actions. Your sentences could start 'The two children were both holding their mother's skirts…'.

c   Share what you have written with a partner. What has been gained by using different narratorial perspectives? What has been lost?

15.4 Writing practice

Exercise 5

Now that you have looked at the extract in detail, look at this essay question:

Explore the ways in which Kincaid convincingly conveys a child's perspective in this part of the novel.

a   Copy out the question and highlight the key words.
b   Look through the work you have done in this unit on Annie's perspective. Use bullet points or a planning table to plan your essay and organise your points effectively. Remember to use quotations and to comment meaningfully on your quotations.

Exercise 6

Read this annotated paragraph taken from a student response to the essay set in Exercise 5.

Student's paragraph

Another way in which Kincaid convincingly conveys Annie's perspective as childlike is through her fascination with the Red Girl's behaviour. Annie tells us 'How my eyes did widen and my mouth form an "o"' when she saw the Red Girl climb the guava tree. The word 'How' placed at the beginning of the sentence emphasises her exclamatory tone. Also, Annie's inability to conceal her wonderment here is very childlike: an older or more worldly person might have been less inclined to reveal their feelings so overtly. Furthermore, 'I had never seen a girl do this before' is a strong declarative sentence that demonstrates an innocence and a narrow range of experience that we might associate with children. It seems that Annie is a young girl living within certain constraints and so to see another girl breaking rules is exciting for her.

Strong focus on the question throughout.

Knowledge and quotations from the text.

A convincing analysis of an information point.

Close analysis of a technique that creates a strong impression of Annie's pleasure and amazement.

Another close analysis of how sentence structure contributes to the effect and very clearly pulled together to address the question.

Development of ideas with informed personal response..

Now, using your planning table or bullet points, and using the annotated paragraph above as additional help, write your own response to the essay set in Exercise 5.

15.5 Set-text focus

Exercise 7

Consider perspectives in your prose set text.
a Choose an extract from your prose set text where there is more than one perspective on a person, event or object (your teacher may help you find this).
b Write down what the different perspectives are, plus supporting evidence from the text. Explain the supporting evidence and how it shows the perspective.

Exercise 8

Annie John is a novel about a young girl growing up. If relevant, consider the theme of growing up in your prose set text.

a Choose an extract from your prose text where a character or characters learn or discover something as part of growing up.

b Use a table like the one below to record as many instances as you can think of.

Character / characters	What they learn / discover	Quotation	Comment

---

MAKING CONNECTIONS

For more about perspective, look at Unit 8 'Elegy For My Father's Father': Focus on character and perspective. Think about the differences in how we approach the question of perspective in poetry and prose.

Take your learning further

At the beginning of *Annie John*, Annie is very close to her mother. In fact, she fears separation from her. We see this in the extract at the beginning of this unit, where Annie holds her mother's skirt.

However, later in the novel Annie begins to resent and even hate her mother, largely because of the rules by which her mother expects her to live, as a girl growing up in a British colony. Because the novel is written from Annie's perspective, the reader has to read between the lines to understand that the mother's intentions for her daughter are probably good ones, and that Annie is trying to make her mother sound much worse than she is.

Jamaica Kincaid wrote a humorous **prose-poem** called 'Girl' in 1978, in which a mother gives her daughter advice on how a girl should behave and scolds her for not conforming to her expectations. You can watch and listen to Jamaica Kincaid read 'Girl' on YouTube.

Key term

Prose-poem: A text that is half poem, half prose – as the name sounds; it lacks such features as rhyme, lines and traditional forms of poetry, as well as the narrative structure of conventional fiction

Unit summary

In this unit, you have learned how to:
- Show detailed knowledge of the content of an extract from a prose text supported by reference to the text.
- Demonstrate an understanding of the perspective from which a piece of fiction is told and think about the significance of what the narrator tells us and what is not included.
- Recognise and appreciate ways in which writers create and shape perspectives.
- Evaluate the effectiveness of different narrative perspectives.

Think about how you have demonstrated each of these skills in the exercises in this unit. Consider the perspectives from which the other prose pieces in this book are told. Can you imagine them being told from an alternative perspective?

16

The Sorrow of War:
Focus on setting and mood

In this unit, you will:
- Use quotations and indirect references to support your views or argument when exploring setting and mood in an extract from a novel.
- Think about an author's description of setting beyond its surface meaning and discuss the mood that it helps to create.
- Explore the techniques by which an author creates mood.
- Communicate and explain your personal feelings about the mood of a piece of writing.

In Unit 12 on 'The Gold-Legged Frog', you explored how Khamsing Srinawk uses setting at the opening of his short story to create mood and to enable a reader to understand Nark's frame of mind. The setting was hot and oppressive and reflected Nark's own feelings of how his life was full of trial and difficulty. The whirlwind as a portent of death also foreshadowed the tragic event that we learn about at the end of the short story.

Setting in a novel often serves a far greater purpose than merely creating a word-picture of a scene. It helps a reader to understand the context of their novel, and to explore beyond surface meanings. Setting in a novel will often help a reader to determine mood.

The Sorrow of War is an award-winning novel by Vietnamese author Bảo Ninh. It was translated into English in 1994, and tells the story of Kien, a North Vietnamese soldier who participated in the Vietnam War (1955 to 1975).

This extract is from the start of the novel, and shows Kien in 1976 on a post-war mission to collect the remains of his fallen comrades of Battalion 27. Nearly all his comrades were eliminated in a fierce battle here in the Jungle of Screaming Souls in 1969. Kien was one of just ten survivors. The setting and mood at the start of the novel are important in helping the reader to understand Kien's experience and how he feels about the past.

Glossary

Tailgate: A flap at the back of a truck

Somnambulantly: In a way that resembles someone sleepwalking

Napalm: Used in the weapons of US troops in the Vietnam War; napalm filled the area with carbon dioxide, causing asphyxiation and extreme burns

16.1 From *The Sorrow of War* by Bảo Ninh

On the banks of the Ya Crong Poco River, on the northern flank of the B3
battlefield in the Central Highlands, the Missing in Action body-collecting
team awaits the dry season of 1976.

The mountains and jungles are water-soaked and dull. Wet trees. Quiet
jungles. All day and all night the water steams. A sea of greenish vapour   5
over the jungle's carpet of rotting leaves.

September and October drag by, then November passes, but still the
weather is unpredictable and the night rains are relentless. Sunny days but
rainy nights.

Even into early December, weeks after the end of the normal rainy season,   10
the jungles this year are still as muddy as all hell. They are forgotten by
peace, damaged or impassable, all tracks disappearing, bit by bit, day by
day, into the embrace of the coarse undergrowth and wild grasses.

Travelling in such conditions is brutally tough. To get from Crocodile Lake
east of the Sa Thay river, across District 67 to the crossroads of Cross Hill   15
on the west bank of the Poco river – a mere fifty kilometres – the powerful
Russian truck has to lumber along all day. And still they fall short of
their destination.

Not until after dusk does the MIA Zil truck reach the Jungle of Screaming
Souls, where they park beside a wide creek clogged with rotting branches.   20

The driver stays in the cabin and goes straight to sleep. Kien climbs wearily
into the rear of the truck to sleep alone in a hammock strung high from
cab to tailgate. At midnight the rains start again, this time a smooth drizzle,
falling silently.

The old tarpaulin covering the truck is torn, full of holes, letting the water   25
drip, drip, drip through onto the plastic sheets covering the remains of
soldiers laid out in rows below Kien's hammock.

The humid atmosphere condenses, its long, moist, chilly fingers sliding in
and around the hammock where Kien lies shivering, half awake, half asleep,
as though drifting along on a stream. He is floating, sadly, endlessly,   30
sometimes as if on a lorry driving silently, robot-like, somnambulantly
through the lonely jungle tracks. The stream moans, a desperate complaint
mixing with distant faint jungle sounds, like an echo from another world.
The eerie sounds come from somewhere in a remote past, arriving softly
like featherweight leaves falling on the grass of times long, long ago.   35

Kien knows the area well. It was here, at the end of the dry season of 1969,
that his Battalion 27 was surrounded and almost totally wiped out. Ten men
survived from the Unlucky Battalion, after fierce, horrible, barbarous fighting.

That was the dry season when the sun burned harshly, the wind blew fiercely,
and the enemy sent napalm spraying through the jungle and a sea of fire   40
enveloped them, spreading like the fires of hell.

16.2 First impressions

Exercise 1

When writing about setting in a prose text, we consider the following:

» place
» time.

In a prose text the mood is the atmosphere or feeling created in the writing by the author through such features as:

» setting
» description
» attitudes of characters.

Read the first three paragraphs (lines 1 to 9) of the extract.

a Which of the following pictures would you choose as an illustration to accompany the first three paragraphs and why?

Try to think of reasons why you might not choose them as well as why you might choose them. Discuss your ideas with a partner or the class.

b Write your own preparatory notes to help an artist to sketch your ideal illustration to accompany the extract. Discuss your ideas.

Exercise 2

Very often, writers use descriptions of the weather and the natural world to create mood, using a literary device known as the **pathetic fallacy**. Look at sentences 1, 2 and 3 below. What mood is created in each sentence and how has the pathetic fallacy contributed to the mood?

1 The sky began to turn dark and thunder growled dangerously as the army advanced menacingly on the enemy.
2 Rain fell heavily and the soaked tree branches bowed in defeat as I travelled home, worried about what I would find.
3 The sun lit up the sky and little rays of light danced on the waves as we enjoyed our picnic on the beach.

Read the extract from *The Sorrow of War* carefully, paying close attention to what you learn about the setting and the mood of the extract and how the pathetic fallacy helps you to understand the mood. Identify any words or phrases that you don't understand and share them with your teacher and the class.

16.3 Finding evidence

Exercise 3

a Most of what we can deduce about the mood of the first three paragraphs is achieved through the setting and description, though if you read closely you may be able to work out the narrator's attitude.
Which of the words below do you think best describe(s) the mood of the first three paragraphs?
 – Hopeless
 – Depressing
 – Tense
 – Resentful
 – Resigned
Discuss your choices with a partner or with the class.

b In pairs or small groups, look at the quotations from the first three paragraphs in one of the three tables on the following page (your teacher may assign each group one of the tables). Discuss how the structural devices and language choices contribute to the mood. The first quotation in each table has been done for you.
Share your ideas with the rest of the class.

A

Quotation	Comments
'[The mountains and jungles are] water-soaked and dull.'	The entire landscape is drenched in rain. The word 'dull' has a few meanings here. It suggests how the landscape is sombre and lacks colour. It also suggests lifelessness and sadness.
'Wet trees. Quiet jungles.'	
'All day and all night the water steams.'	

B

Quotation	Comments
'A sea of greenish vapour'	The metaphor 'sea' suggests a vast covering and 'greenish' colour suggests a mystical quality to the escaping water vapour. Both convey how the secrets of the jungle are concealed by its natural elements.
'over the jungle's carpet of rotting leaves'	
'[September and October] drag by'	
'[the night rains] are relentless'	

C

Quotation	Comments
'[the jungles this year are still] as muddy as all hell'	'… as (all) hell' is a colloquialism, often used to convey extreme feeling or make a comment more forceful. You can detect the narrator's tone of extreme annoyance here. '[H]ell' also takes on the meaning of a place of great suffering and death. The effect is dramatic.
'forgotten by peace'	
'[all tracks disappearing,] bit by bit, day by day'	
'[into the] embrace of the coarse undergrowth and wild grasses'	

c Reread the fourth paragraph (lines 10 to 13). What pieces of information are we given that help us to understand how the mission is very difficult?

Key term

Colloquialism: An informal, chatty or slang word or phrase, which we tend to use more in speech than in writing

Exercise 4

a Reread paragraphs 6 to 8 (lines 19 to 27). To bring the night-setting to life, Ninh makes less use of visual images and greater use of the senses of touch and hearing.

In pairs, copy and complete either Table X or Table Y, adding your own examples and explanations of the effect created. One example is done for you in each table.

X

Sense of touch	
Example	**Effect**
'as though drifting along on a stream'	Kien is half asleep. The image suggests he feels powerless on this mission and merely carried with the flow.

Y

Sense of hearing	
Example	**Effect**
'letting the water drip, drip, drip'	The use of the repeated verb 'drip' is effective as not only does it suggest the endless rainfall, but the repeated sounds /d/ and /p/ mimic the sound of the continual droplets of rain, thus recreating the whole moment for the reader.

b Look again at lines 26 to 27. The narrator tells us that 'the remains of soldiers [are] laid out in rows below Kien's hammock'. This piece of information is slipped, almost unnoticed, into the narrative, and is the first reference to the party having already retrieved some bodies.

Discuss with a partner why you think Bảo Ninh does this and whether you think this is an effective narrative technique.

c In the last section of the extract, the technique of flashback is used. Kien is taken back to the time in 1969 when his battalion were nearly all brutally murdered. The structure of the novel is **non-chronological**.

Discuss with a partner how the setting and mood of the opening of the novel prepares a reader for this flashback to the same place at a different time.

> **Key term**
>
> **Non-chronological:** When a narrative is chronological it relates events in the sequence that they happened; the narrative in the extract from *The Sorrow of War* does not follow events in the order that they happened, so it is non-chronological

16.4 Writing practice

Exercise 5

Now that you have looked at the extract in detail, look at this essay question:

How does Ninh vividly convey Kien's experience in the Jungle of Screaming Souls at this point in the novel?

a Copy the question and highlight the key words.
b Write a brief plan of how you would answer the question; use a mind map or a planning table – not sentences. Pay close attention to the key words you have highlighted and make sure you address them. Check that you have included relevant quotations and ideas from the work you have already done.

Exercise 6

Read below the student's first paragraph of their response to the question. Then look at the feedback given by their teacher.

Student's first paragraph

Ninh shows Kien's experience on his return to the Jungle of the Screaming Souls to be miserable and in many ways traumatising. He does this through a detailed description of the setting, which creates a sombre and hopeless mood. He tells us that the landscape is 'water-soaked and dull'. He also uses the word 'hell' several times in the passage and by referring to the name 'the Jungle of the Screaming Souls' it makes the reader feel the horror that Kien is feeling. The word 'eerie' is used to describe the sounds that Kien can here while he is sleeping in the truck.

This is a good focused opening to the question – well done!

How does the phrase 'water-soaked and dull' contribute to what you have described as a 'sombre and hopeless mood'?

What does 'eerie' mean here and what does it suggest about Kien's experience of the night in the truck?

The word 'horror' here is good – well done. However, you need to do more to explore the use of 'hell' in the extract. It appears once near the beginning and again at the end. What are the meanings of 'hell' here and how does the repetition of the idea that this jungle is 'hell' add to the what the reader is learning about Kien's experience?

a Discuss the teacher's feedback with your partner or group.
b Is there any further feedback you would wish to give this student?
c Write an improved paragraph based on your discussions.

16.5 Set-text focus

Exercise 7

Consider the mood and settings of your prose set text.

a Choose an extract from your prose set text where the setting and mood are important.

b Which of your five senses does the extract most appeal to? Create a table like the ones used in Exercise 3 and try to find an example for each sense that you think is being used.

c Consider how you think the author has used the setting to help tell the story. In what significant ways has the author used language and other literary devices to create the setting and mood? How are the mood and setting important?

Take your learning further

A number of people have written about the Vietnam War, from both the American and the Vietnamese perspective.

1   The poem 'What Were They Like?' was written in 1971 by Denise Levertov in protest against the Vietnam War. The poem is available online, and there are a number of versions of 'What Were They Like?' performed on YouTube.

2   Look at the way the poem is structured, with **stanza** 1 formed by a series of questions and stanza 2 giving the answers to those questions. Why do you think the poet has structured the poem in this way?

3   What is the mood of the poem and how does it compare with the mood of the extract you have read from *The Sorrow of War*? Compare and contrast the methods that the authors have used to create mood.

Key term

Stanza: A group of lines in a poem, similar to a paragraph in a prose text; common stanza lengths are two, three, four, six or eight lines – in popular music, we often call stanzas 'verses'

Unit summary

In this unit, you have learned how to:

● Use quotations and indirect references to support your views or argument when exploring setting and mood in an extract from a novel.

● Think about an author's description of setting beyond its surface meaning and discuss the mood that it helps to create.

● Explore the techniques by which an author creates mood.

● Communicate and explain your personal feelings about the mood of a piece of writing.

Think about how you have demonstrated each of these skills in the exercises in this unit. What is the mood of the other prose extracts you have studied in this section of the book? Think also about how you have used the skills you developed in the previous units in exploring the setting and mood of the extract from *The Sorrow of War*.

17 *Villette:* Focus on developing a personal response

In this unit, you will:
- Read an extract from a novel and demonstrate your knowledge of it in developing a personal response.
- Think about the context of a literary work and consider the ways this contributes to its deeper meanings.
- Explain how an author uses language, as well as structural devices, to explore themes, create mood and present characters.
- Use the skills you have gained in the previous units to develop a sensitive and informed personal response to a piece of prose fiction.

Now that you have considered a number of different aspects of prose fiction, you are in a position to develop an informed and sensitive response of your own to a short extract. Usually, we need to read and reread texts to develop an informed personal response. Class and group discussions of what has been read, and reading other opinions online or in books, can all help you to form your own personal response to a text. A good personal response will include your own reactions and thoughts about characters and events but also the way in which the writer presents them. The more you can comment on how the writing informs your response, the better.

Villette (1853) is a novel by Charlotte Brontë (1816 to 1855), an English novelist and poet. Many critics consider *Villette*, her last novel, her most sophisticated and convincing work. The novel's main character, Lucy Snowe, is a young woman who, after her parents' deaths, decides to go abroad to find new work and opportunities. She travels to the French-speaking town of Villette in Labassecour (Brontë's fictitious names for Brussels and Belgium). On arriving in Villette, she is followed by two men and, in trying to escape them, gets lost. By luck, she finds herself outside the Pensionnat de Demoiselles, a girls' boarding school, an establishment she remembers being mentioned on the boat on which she left England.

Glossary

Flight: A set of steps (as in the phrase 'flight of stairs')

Loftier by a story: Higher / taller (than other buildings) by a floor level

Porte-cochère: A large grand entrance

Pensionnat de Demoiselles: A boarding school for girls

Providence: God's protective care

Fate: Events or forces outside a person's control

Bonne: A French woman servant

Salon: A large living room

Pendule: An ornate clock with a pendulum

Gilt mouldings: Intricate gold designs, often using flowers or birds

Ayre Engliss: 'Are English' – spelt in this way to indicate Madame Beck's French accent and how she pronounces the words

Merely: Only

Prelude: Introduction

Shod with the shoes of silence: Madame Beck walked very quietly into the room; 'shod' means wearing shoes

Insular: Uninterested in experiences or cultures other than one's own, or relating to an island

Volubly: Fluently and / or incessantly

Hitherto: Previously / before now

Ere: Before

Maîtresse: Young female teacher

Adept: A very skilled person

17.1 From *Villette* by Charlotte Brontë

I came at last to an old and worn flight, and, taking it for granted that this must be the one indicated, I descended them. The street into which they led was indeed narrow, but it contained no inn. On I wandered. In a very quiet and comparatively clean and well-paved street, I saw a light burning over the door of a rather large house, loftier by a story than those round it. *This* might be the inn at last. I hastened on: my knees now trembled under me: I was getting quite exhausted.

No inn was this. A brass-plate embellished the great porte-cochère: "Pensionnat de Demoiselles" was the inscription; and beneath, a name, "Madame Beck."

I started. About a hundred thoughts volleyed through my mind in a moment. Yet I planned nothing, and considered nothing: I had not time. Providence said, "Stop here; this is *your* inn." Fate took me in her strong hand; mastered my will; directed my actions: I rang the door-bell.

While I waited, I would not reflect. I fixedly looked at the street-stones, where the door-lamp shone, and counted them and noted their shapes, and the glitter of wet on their angles. I rang again. They opened at last. A bonne in a smart cap stood before me.

"May I see Madame Beck?" I inquired.

I believe if I had spoken French she would not have admitted me; but, as I spoke English, she concluded I was a foreign teacher come on business connected with the pensionnat, and, even at that late hour, she let me in, without a word of reluctance, or a moment of hesitation.

The next moment I sat in a cold, glittering salon, with porcelain stove, unlit, and gilded ornaments, and polished floor. A pendule on the mantel-piece struck nine o'clock.

A quarter of an hour passed. How fast beat every pulse in my frame! How I turned cold and hot by turns! I sat with my eyes fixed on the door – a great white folding-door, with gilt mouldings: I watched to see a leaf move and open. All had been quiet: not a mouse had stirred; the white doors were closed and motionless.

"You ayre Engliss?" said a voice at my elbow. I almost bounded, so unexpected was the sound; so certain had I been of solitude.

[It was] merely a motherly, dumpy little woman, in a large shawl, a wrapping-gown, and a clean, trim nightcap.

I said I was English, and immediately, without further prelude, we fell to a most remarkable conversation. Madame Beck (for Madame Beck it was – she had entered by a little door behind me, and, being shod with the shoes of silence, I had heard neither her entrance nor approach) – Madame Beck had exhausted her command of insular speech when she said, "You ayre Engliss," and she now proceeded to work away volubly in her own tongue. I answered in mine. She partly understood me, but as I did not at all understand her – though we made together an awful clamour (anything like Madame's gift of utterance I had not hitherto heard or imagined) – we achieved little progress. She rang, ere long, for aid; which arrived in the shape of a "maîtresse," who had been partly educated in an Irish convent, and was esteemed a perfect adept in the English language.

40
45
50

17.2 First impressions

Exercise 1

A starting point for an informed personal response to your prose set text is an understanding of its context.

When Charlotte and her sisters, Emily and Anne, sent their poetry and prose works for publication, they used the **pen names** Currer, Ellis and Acton Bell because these names had a 'male' sound about them.

a Take a quick look at those names. What do you notice about the initials to the names the women chose?

Villette was published in 1853, during the reign of Queen Victoria in the United Kingdom. Charlotte Brontë was a contemporary of Charles Dickens, an extract from whose novel, *Hard Times*, is featured in Unit 14. In Brontë's day, young, single women would be protected and provided for by their families. The role of protecting and providing for a woman was transferred to her husband when she married. Although many women were not expected to work at all, certain types of employment could be considered appropriate for a young woman, like Lucy, who has lost her parents and has no other means of providing for herself. Such roles might include being a governess to young children in a household or a nurse-companion to an older or disabled lady.

b With a partner, discuss why you think the jobs referred to above might have been considered acceptable for a young woman at the time.

Furthermore, in the mid-19th century, many people would have considered it socially unacceptable for a young woman to travel abroad on her own.

c Reread the opening paragraphs of the extract and look for clues that tell you what time of day it is. Note down these clues and the time of day they suggest.

d How does this contextual information and knowledge of the time of day that Lucy was travelling add to the tension in the passage?

Key term

Pen name: A false name used by a writer instead of their real name

17.3 Finding evidence

Exercise 2

In Unit 16, we look at how Bảo Ninh creates setting and mood in the extract from his novel *The Sorrow of War*. You might wish to read about the methods that Ninh uses to create setting and mood before you complete the following exercises on *Villette*.

Bearing in mind what you now know about the social and historical context of *Villette*, and the experience of being a young single woman in Victorian times, you can probably appreciate how scared and vulnerable Lucy Snowe felt while looking for a place to stay in Villette.

a Reread the first four paragraphs of the extract. With a partner, consider:
 - how Brontë creates a setting that would be frightening to a young woman on her own in a foreign city
 - how Brontë creates mood and enables us to understand Lucy's feelings both before she finds a place to stay and when she is standing outside the 'Pensionnat de Demoiselles'.

b Reread the seventh and eighth paragraphs (from 'The next moment...' to '... closed and motionless').
 With a partner, discuss:
 - how Brontë makes the salon in which Lucy is sitting sound quite formidable
 - what this tells us about the way that Lucy is feeling at this point.

Exercise 3

In the work on *Hard Times* in Unit 14, we look at how we learn about character in a prose text. You may wish to read about the methods that Dickens uses to reveal character in his writing before completing this exercise.

Using a table like the one below, write down a quotation for any of the methods used to reveal the character of Madame Beck and explain what that method reveals of her character.

	Quotation	What is revealed of Madame Beck
What Madame Beck says		
What Madame Beck does		
What the narrator (Lucy) tells us about Madame Beck		

Exercise 4

In the work on *Annie John* in Unit 15, we look at what is meant by 'perspective' and how different kinds of narrator (first person and third person) can impact on the perspective offered to the reader. You might wish to read about how different types of narrator can create different perspectives by looking at Unit 15.

Villette is a first-person narrative written from the perspective of Lucy Snowe. As you may have gathered already from her description of Madame Beck, Lucy is not always a kind narrator and she very often makes quick assessments of people based on appearances, prejudice and previous experience.

a Write down three short descriptions and / or judgements that Lucy makes regarding Madame Beck that you think could be unnecessarily unkind.

b Explain your ideas about why they could be interpreted as unkind.

c Imagine you are Madame Beck. Write two or three sentences giving your first impressions of Lucy Snowe. Your sentences will be in English of course, so this will be a translation of what Madame Beck would say, since she doesn't speak English.

d Compare with a partner or other people in the class what you wrote as Madame Beck. There are likely to be differences in what Madame Beck wrote about Lucy. Why might that be?

> **MAKING CONNECTIONS**
>
> To further your understanding of how a writer reveals character and perspectives in a prose text, have a look at your work on *Nervous Conditions* in Unit 13.

Exercise 5

In the 'Take your learning further' section of Unit 12 you are encouraged to create a storyboard for Khamsing Srinawk's short story 'The Gold-Legged Frog.' You might need to refer to that unit to remind yourself what a storyboard is. A storyboard often helps a reader to see the movements in a text in terms of mood, setting and action. It also gives a reader an overview of the text and its structure. This extract from *Villette* lends itself to a storyboard comprising four frames:

1 Lucy running down the steps into the street
2 Lucy standing outside the Pensionnat de Demoiselles
3 Lucy sitting alone in the salon
4 Lucy talking to Madame Beck

a Create the storyboard including the frames suggested above. For each frame, choose a quotation from the text that you think best suits your picture. Remember to read the text closely to make sure that you get the details right for each frame.

b Swap your storyboard with a partner and together consider your use of pictures and captions.
 – In what ways are your storyboards similar and in what ways are they different?
 – How have the storyboards helped you to consider the structure of the extract in terms of changes in mood, setting and action?

> **MAKING CONNECTIONS**
>
> To further your understanding of how a writer uses setting and mood in a prose text, have another look at the opening paragraph of 'The Gold-legged Frog' in Unit 12.
> ● Consider how Srinawk's use of setting here helps us to understand the mood at the opening of this short story.
> ● In turn, how is the mood established at the beginning of the story important to a reader's understanding of the rest of the text?

17.4 Writing practice

Exercise 6

Look at the following essay question.

> **Explore the ways in which Brontë convincingly conveys Lucy Snowe's feelings in this extract.**

a Write down the question. Your key words are 'Lucy Snowe's feelings', so highlight them.
b Look back to the work you have done on this extract. You will find it useful in preparing you for this essay. Spend 15 minutes planning your essay by using bullet points, notes or a planning grid.

Exercise 7

a Three students have made a start on the essay question from Exercise 6 and written their first paragraph. Read these first attempts and rank them in order of merit. Compare your rankings with a partner and explain why you put the responses in the order you did.

Student X

You can tell that there are a lot of strong feelings at this moment because the extract is about this poor girl called Lucy who is lost at night in a city she doesn't know. I can tell that it's night-time because there are references to lighting and it being very 'quiet'. Young women in those days would not have much worldly wisdom because they were used to being kept at home and looked after by their families.

Student Y

There is evidence that Lucy Snowe feels very scared and vulnerable in the beginning. In the opening sentence the phrase 'at last' tells us how long she has been looking for the inn and how pleased she is when she thinks she has found it. The word 'This' is italicised for emphasis and helps us to hear the relief in Lucy's voice. She doesn't directly tell the reader how scared she is but it is hinted at in 'I hastened on: my knees now trembled under me: I was getting quite exhausted.' She must be quite desperate.

Student Z

The whole passage shows Lucy's feelings as it is a first-person narrative. At the beginning she is very scared because she is lost in Villette, then she feels relieved when she sees what she thinks is the inn she was directed to. Her feelings change when she realises that the place she has arrived at is a girls' school and I think she feels hopeful that she might get given work. When she gets inside she feels a bit overawed by the salon because it is very ornate and rich looking, but also it seems cold which might reflect what she feels Madame Beck might be like. She seems to look down on Madame Beck when she sees her.

b The teacher of Students X, Y and Z has written a few comments on each response. Match teacher responses A, B and C to the work of Students X, Y and Z.

Teacher response A

There is some understanding of context here and it is used appropriately. Rather than saying just 'strong feelings' it would be better to describe what Lucy's feelings are, for example 'frightened'. You need to find evidence to support your comments. Your point about it being dark and quiet is potentially a good one, but link it to the question and her feelings.

Teacher response B

It seems that your storyboard from earlier in this unit has helped you, as so far you have shown some overview and understanding of the passage, which is good. You are also very well focused on the question, which is about Lucy's feelings. There is some potentially very good interpretation of Lucy's feelings (for example, through her description of the salon as if it were a very cold and uninviting place). However, your ideas are not supported by close textual reference and explanation of these references. I suggest that your paragraph is further broken down to four paragraphs for the different sections you have identified in the text.

Teacher response C

There is some very good attention to language and sentence-level structure here – well done. The final quotation is a very long one – did you need it all to make your point? You are right that the narrator does not tell us directly how she feels, but lets the reader infer this by her language choices. Could you shorten the quotation or choose the important words from it to quote? The word 'trembled' is interesting because although it is used here to describe Lucy's tired legs, it also suggests her feelings. Can you improve what you have written here to cover these ideas and any other ideas suggested in that quotation?

c Now that you have matched the teacher's comments with the students' responses, discuss with a partner what the teacher has said to check that you understand the points being made. Can you add any further advice?

d Rewrite one of the paragraphs, using the teacher's advice and your own ideas to improve it.

17.5 Set-text focus

Exercise 8

Find an extract in your set prose text where there is evidence of a character feeling fear or anticipation. You need to choose only one of these emotions.

Answer the following question.

> **In what ways does [author's name] convincingly convey fear or anticipation at this moment in the novel?**

» Remember to make a planning grid, or to use bullet points or notes to plan your essay. Spend 15 minutes on this.

» Look at the work you did on setting, mood, characterisation, perspective and structure in this unit to help you find evidence for your response to this question.

» Spend about 30 minutes writing up your response.

Take your learning further

All three Brontë sisters worked as governesses in real life and Charlotte and Ann reflected their own experiences in their writing. Several other famous Victorian novels also prominently feature governesses.

You might like to carry out some research into the role of Victorian governesses, the real-life experiences of the Brontë sisters and other novels that feature governesses. Why might governesses be such compelling figures for novelists? Think about the unique perspective they might offer, and the themes that they allow a writer to explore.

Unit summary

In this unit, you have learned how to:
● Read an extract from a novel and demonstrate your knowledge of it in developing a personal response.
● Think about the context of a literary work and consider the ways this contributes to its deeper meanings.
● Explain how an author uses language, as well as structural devices, to explore themes, create mood and present characters.
● Use the skills you have gained in the previous units to develop a sensitive and informed personal response to a piece of prose fiction.

Think about how you have demonstrated each of these skills in the exercises in this unit. Now that we have reached the end of the Prose section, be sure to look back to the texts you have studied and think about how the different skills you have developed can be combined to create a sensitive and informed personal response to each.

DRAMA

Units

18 Top Girls: Focus on drama

Key terms

Form: The text type a writer chooses to communicate in; the three main forms in English literature are poetry, prose and drama – within those main forms are other forms; for example, a sonnet is a poetic form and a short story is a prose form

Protagonist: A main character in a literary text

Folklore: The traditional beliefs, customs and stories within a community

Patriarchal: A society ruled or controlled by men

In this unit, you will:
- Identify choices made by a dramatist to support your arguments.
- Think about how the various elements of a dramatic performance combine to create meaning.
- Develop an awareness of drama as a literary form and understand that a script is a text to be performed, rather than just read.
- Demonstrate a sensitive and empathic response to a play by writing from one of the character's perspectives.

When you are studying a drama text, you need to be mindful that drama is a different **form** from prose and poetry. This unit will introduce you to a range of these differences. Plays are meant for performance. They are not meant to be read silently, as a short story or a novel might be, or read aloud as a poem might be. A playscript is interpreted by a director and by actors so that it can be turned into a performance. When you read a play in class, look for opportunities to perform the script and always try to imagine what the play might look and sound like. Sketches of characters and scenes can help you to visualise moments in the play.

Top Girls (1982) is a play written by the English dramatist Caryl Churchill. The **protagonist** of the play is Marlene, a very successful businesswoman. *Top Girls* was written at a time when Britain had elected its first female prime minister, Margaret Thatcher. Caryl Churchill wanted to explore ideas about what it meant for a woman to be successful at that point in history.

The play opens with a dinner in a restaurant where Marlene is celebrating her success. Five women from history and **folklore** are at the dinner to celebrate with her. We hear how these women have suffered in their **patriarchal** societies. The extract is from near the end of Act One when the final guest, Griselda, arrives.

Glossary

Anorexic: A person who lives with an eating disorder called 'anorexia nervosa', a condition characterised by a refusal to eat

Concubine: A woman who, in some societies, lives and sleeps with a man but who has lower status than his wife or wives

Brueghel: A 16th-century Flemish painter known for his depictions of landscapes and scenes from everyday life

Boccaccio: A 14th-century Italian poet and scholar who wrote the most famous version of the Griselda story, having taken it from a French source

Petrarch: A 14th-century Italian scholar and poet; he translated Boccaccio's Griselda story into Latin, presenting her as model woman because of her loyalty to her husband

Chaucer: A 14th-century English poet who wrote *The Canterbury Tales*, one of the greatest poetic works in English, which includes a retelling of the Griselda story

Profiteroles: Small balls of soft cream-filled pastry covered with chocolate sauce, usually served in a pile

Zabaglione: An Italian dessert made of egg yolks, sugar and Marsala wine

Marquis: A European nobleman

Mr Nugent: A guide in the Rocky Mountains with a reputation for drinking and fighting, befriended by Isabella Bird on her travels

Procession: A line of people travelling the same way, here during a public celebration

Heir: A person who will legally receive money, property or a title when another person dies

Walter: The marquis in the story who marries Griselda

John: Isabella Bird's husband

Bonkers: An informal word meaning 'silly' or 'crazy'

Bastard: An unpleasant person

18.1 From Act One of *Top Girls* by Caryl Churchill

[MARLENE notices GRISELDA.]

MARLENE: Griselda! / There you are. Do you want to eat?

GRISELDA: I'm sorry I'm so late. No, no, don't bother.

MARLENE: Of course it's no bother. / Have you eaten?

GRISELDA: No really, I'm not hungry.   5

MARLENE: Well have some pudding.

GRISELDA: I never eat pudding.

MARLENE: Griselda, I hope you're not anorexic. We're having pudding, I am, and getting nice and fat.

GRISELDA: Oh if everyone is. I don't mind.   10

MARLENE: Now who do you know? This is Joan who was Pope in the ninth century, and Isabella Bird, the Victorian traveller, and Lady Nijo from Japan, Emperor's concubine and Buddhist nun, thirteenth century, nearer your own time, and Gret who was painted by Brueghel. Griselda's in Boccaccio and   15 Petrarch and Chaucer because of her extraordinary marriage. I'd like profiteroles because they're disgusting.

JOAN: Zabaglione, please.

ISABELLA: Apple pie / and cream.

NIJO: What's this?   20

MARLENE: Zabaglione, it's Italian, it's what Joan's having, / it's delicious.

NIJO: A Roman Catholic / dessert? Yes please.

MARLENE: Gret?

GRET: Cake.

GRISELDA: Just cheese and biscuits, thank you.   25

MARLENE: Yes, Griselda's life is like a fairy-story, except it starts with marrying the prince.

GRISELDA: He's only a marquis, Marlene.

MARLENE: Well everyone for miles around is his liege and he's absolute lord of life and death and you were the poor but beautiful   30 peasant girl and he whisked you off. / Near enough a prince.

NIJO: How old were you?

GRISELDA: Fifteen.

NIJO: I was brought up in court circles and it was still a shock. Had you ever seen him before?   35

GRISELDA: I'd seen him riding by, we all had. And he'd seen me in the fields with the sheep.*

ISABELLA: I would have been well suited to minding sheep.

NIJO: And Mr Nugent riding by.

ISABELLA: Of course not, Nijo, I mean a healthy life in the open air.   40

JOAN: *He just rode up while you were minding the sheep and asked you to marry him?

GRISELDA: No, no, it was on the wedding day. I was waiting outside the door to see the procession. Everyone wanted him to get married so there'd be an heir to look after us when he died, /   45
and at last he announced a day for the wedding but

MARLENE: I don't think Walter wanted to get married. It is Walter? Yes.

GRISELDA: nobody knew who the bride was, we thought it must be a foreign princess, we were longing to see her. Then the carriage stopped outside our cottage and we couldn't see the   50
bride anywhere. And he came and spoke to my father.

NIJO: And your father told you to serve the Prince.

GRISELDA: My father could hardly speak. The Marquis said it wasn't an order, I could say no, but if I said yes I must always obey him in everything.   55

MARLENE: That's when you should have suspected.

GRISELDA: But of course a wife must obey her husband. / And of course I must obey the Marquis.*

ISABELLA: I swore to obey dear John, of course, but it didn't seem to arise. Naturally I wouldn't have wanted to go abroad while I   60
was married.

MARLENE: *Then why bother to mention it at all? He'd got a thing about it, that's why.

GRISELDA: I'd rather obey the Marquis than a boy from the village.

MARLENE: Yes, that's a point.   65

JOAN: I never obeyed anyone. They all obeyed me.

NIJO: And what did you wear? He didn't make you get married in your own clothes? That would be perverse.*

MARLENE: Oh, you wait.

GRISELDA: *He had ladies with him who undressed me and they had a   70
white silk dress and jewels for my hair.

MARLENE: And at first he seemed perfectly normal?

GRISELDA: Marlene, you're always so critical of him. / Of course he was normal, he was very kind.

MARLENE: But Griselda, come on, he took your baby.   75

GRISELDA: Walter found it hard to believe I loved him. He couldn't believe I would always obey him. He had to prove it.

MARLENE: I don't think Walter likes women.

GRISELDA: I'm sure he loved me, Marlene, all the time.

MARLENE: He just had a funny way / of showing it.   80

GRISELDA: It was hard for him too.

JOAN: How do you mean he took away your baby?

NIJO: Was it a boy?

GRISELDA: No, the first one was a girl.

NIJO: Even so it's hard when they take it away. Did you see it at all?   85

GRISELDA: Oh yes, she was six weeks old.

NIJO: Much better to do it straight away.

ISABELLA: But why did your husband take the child?

GRISELDA: He said all the people hated me because I was just one of them. And now I had a child they were restless. So he had   90
to get rid of the child to keep them quiet. But he said he wouldn't snatch her, I had to agree and obey and give her up. So when I was feeding her a man came in and took her away. I thought he was going to kill her even before he was out of the room.   95

MARLENE: But you let him take her? You didn't struggle?

GRISELDA: I asked him to give her back so I could kiss her. And I asked him to bury her where no animals could dig her up. / It

ISABELLA: Oh my dear.

GRISELDA: was Walter's child to do what he liked with.*   100

MARLENE: Walter was bonkers.

GRET: Bastard.

ISABELLA: *But surely, murder.

GRISELDA: I had promised.

MARLENE: I can't stand this. I'm going for a pee.   105

[MARLENE goes out.]

18.2 First impressions

Exercise 1

Let's start to imagine what *Top Girls* might look like. There are many different features we could imagine: the characters' actions, movements, gestures, reactions to what is said, entrances and exits or the design of the set; but let us begin with the characters' appearance.

a Look again at the passage in which Marlene introduces the other diners to Griselda:

> Now who do you know? This is Joan who was Pope in the ninth century, and Isabella Bird, the Victorian traveller, and Lady Nijo from Japan, Emperor's concubine and Buddhist nun, thirteenth century, nearer your own time, and Gret who was painted by Brueghel. Griselda's in Boccaccio and Petrarch and Chaucer because of her extraordinary marriage.

What strikes you as strange about the group of characters that Churchill presents on stage together?

b The tables below include details about the characters in Act One: the table on the left shows their names, their historical time and place and information about their lives; the table on the right includes some of the costume designer's ideas about how the different characters should be dressed. With a partner, match the character to the costume.

Name	Time and place	Character notes	Costume ideas
Joan	9th century, Italy	Disguised as a man, she was rumoured for many centuries to have been Pope 854–856; most modern historians regard her story as fictional	• Armour worn over an apron • Soldier's helmet • Armed with a sword of the period • Basket • Greasy hair, generally unkempt
Nijo	13th century, Japan	An emperor's concubine and later a Buddhist nun who travelled on foot through Japan for 20 years	• Close-fitting white skull cap • Long, elaborately embroidered gown featuring Christian crosses • Holding a staff shaped as a shepherd's crook
Griselda	Middle Ages, Italy	The obedient wife whose story is told by Chaucer in 'The Clerk's Tale' of *The Canterbury Tales*	• Dress jacket with many buttons from top to bottom, high neck, long sleeves • White blouse underneath with a ruffle stand-up collar • Long dress in the same material as the jacket, reaching the floor • Hat of the period decorated with feathers from exotic birds

Gret	Middle Ages, Flanders (modern Belgium)	The subject of the Brueghel painting, *Dulle Griet*, in which a woman in an apron and armour leads a crowd of women charging through hell and fighting the devils	• Business suit with padded shoulders in a blue material • Jewellery • High heels • Overall impression of glamour
Isabella	19th century, Victorian England	Lived in Edinburgh, travelled extensively between the ages of 40 and 70, despite her poor health	• A long gown of luxurious fabrics, including silk • Overall visual impression of luxury in her dress but simplicity too, suggestive of her peasant roots • Long plaits in hair coiled into buns, or... • A headdress in the shape of a cone
Marlene	20th century, England	The protagonist of the play; she is the very successful boss of a London employment agency – at a time when businesswomen were usually overshadowed by businessmen	• A beautiful silk kimono • Multiple thin layers • Make up: whitened face, red lips

c Look at the costume designer's notes for each character. Use these ideas – or ideas based on your own research about the characters – to create a sketch of one or more of the characters. Share your sketch with the rest of the class.

d How do you think the audience will feel on seeing such varied costumes at the start of the play? Is it something they will have seen on stage before? Do you think a similar effect could be created through poetry or prose?

18.3 Finding evidence

Exercise 2

We have begun to think about what the extract might look like in performance. What about the sound of the performance? **Stage directions**, if present in the playscript, will give clues about how the lines might be delivered by the actors. There are no such stage directions in the extract here, but there are a few small clues, if you know what you are looking for.

a In a group of five, act out the following short extract from the middle of the extract.

GRISELDA:	But of course a wife must obey her husband. / And of course I must obey the Marquis.*
ISABELLA:	I swore to obey dear John, of course, but it didn't seem to arise. Naturally I wouldn't have wanted to go abroad while I was married.
MARLENE:	*Then why bother to mention it at all? He'd got a thing about it, that's why.
GRISELDA:	I'd rather obey the Marquis than a boy from the village.
MARLENE:	Yes, that's a point.
JOAN:	I never obeyed anyone. They all obeyed me.
NIJO:	And what did you wear? He didn't make you get married in your own clothes? That would be perverse.*
MARLENE:	Oh, you wait.
GRISELDA:	*He had ladies with him who undressed me and they had a white silk dress and jewels for my hair.

What do you think is the purpose of the asterisks (*) and forward slashes (/) in the text?

A notable feature that Churchill included in this play is **overlapping**. This overlapping is carefully noted in the script.

b With a partner, read the lines below for Marlene and Griselda. The **/** you see in the first line is the cue for Griselda to start her line. She is overlapping Marlene by talking at the same time. Griselda overlaps with Marlene again in the third line.

MARLENE:	Griselda! / There you are. Do you want to eat?
GRISELDA:	I'm sorry I'm so late. No, no, don't bother.
MARLENE:	Of course it's no bother. / Have you eaten?
GRISELDA:	No really, I'm not hungry.

And sometimes a character replies to a character who wasn't the last one to speak.

c   With your partner, join another pair and read the lines for the characters in the passage below. Here, Isabella replies to Griselda, but so too does Joan. This is shown by the *****.

> GRISELDA: I'd seen him riding by, we all had. And he'd seen me in the fields
>
> with the sheep.*
> ISABELLA: I would have been well suited to minding sheep.
> NIJO: And Mr Nugent riding by.
> ISABELLA: Of course not, Nijo, I mean a healthy life in the open air.
> JOAN: *He just rode up while you were minding the sheep and asked you to marry him?

d   Now return to the original passage from part **a** and perform it again. How was it different?

e   As a class, discuss the following questions:

   i   Do conversations in real life involve people waiting for the other person to finish speaking? How often do people interrupt each other? Why do they do this? Would a script based wholly on natural and realistic speech be practical to stage in a theatre?

   ii   Churchill is not copying natural speech completely, but the overlapping is a realistic feature. Overall, what do you think the effect of this overlapping will be on the audience? Will it be an advantage or a disadvantage – think about how carefully they will have to listen. How might the actors, led by the director, help the audience to follow the **dialogue**?

   iii   Which is the best explanation for the overlapping that you have seen in the extract, in your opinion? Are different explanations possible? What different effects will these explanations have on the audience? How would your chosen explanation affect the way the lines were said?
   - The characters are in competition with one another.
   - The characters are self-centred and not interested in what the others are saying.
   - The characters are enthusiastic and supportive of each other.
   - The characters have become more excitable throughout the meal.

While the overlapping in this playscript is quite an unusual feature, it highlights how, in all plays, the action of the play continues while the lines are delivered. Try to imagine how the lines in a script sound as they are delivered but also try to visualise the reaction of the characters to the lines.

Key terms

Stage directions: Instructions in a play script that give details about where a character is and how they move and speak, as well as giving descriptions of set and sound and light effects

Overlapping: Dialogue in which two or more characters speak at the same time

Dialogue: A conversation between two or more people that is presented in a text; in prose texts, dialogue is often written as direct speech

Exercise 3

When a play is staged, there are many decisions for the director to make about how the play will be presented to the audience that affect the way the play will look and sound.

You have imagined what the individual characters within the story might look like and how their dialogue might sound. Now, consider the overall effect of having all of these diverse characters on stage. Think about the following questions with a partner and then discuss your thoughts with the rest of your class.

a How many of the characters have you heard of before? Generally, whose stories do we hear about in history – the stories of men or the stories of women? Why do you think that the dramatist has Marlene dining with such a wide range of women?

b There are 16 female characters in the play. Usually directors choose to use far fewer actors (seven in the original production), with these actors playing more than one character. If the actors are playing multiple roles, what message does this convey about the capabilities of women? Must a woman's role necessarily be **stereotypical** and fixed?

c There is a nameless waitress in Act One who brings the characters their food and drink – desserts in this extract. She has no lines in the extract and none in the whole act, making her practically invisible in the playscript. She does, however, have a very important **dramatic function**. What do you think this is? Think about how she is **juxtaposed** with Marlene. How might a director make the most of the character through the way she is presented on stage?

d The rest of the play makes the audience question whether or not Marlene has actually been successful. By the end, it is clear that she has acted in a stereotypically male way to achieve what society thinks of as 'success': she has put her career ahead of care for her family. Her child is being brought up by her sister so that she can succeed.

   i Look again at the extract and the character notes from Exercise 1. Which characters behave in stereotypically male ways and which individual character behaves in a stereotypically obedient female way? Is there anything about the way this character is presented in the extract that might single her out as different? How might the director and the cast emphasise this difference?

   ii Marlene has chosen to invite these women out of all the women in history. What do you think that each of them represents to her? Think about why it was important for her to invite characters who behave in stereotypically male ways, as well as a character who behaves in a stereotypically obedient female way. What **internal conflict** does Marlene seem to have? What problem within society does this internal conflict reveal?

Key terms

Stereotype: An idea or belief people have about an object or group that is based upon how they look on the outside; it may be completely untrue or only partly true

Dramatic function: The reason that an element, such as a character, is within a text

Juxtapose: Putting two images or ideas that are not similar close together to create a contrasting effect

Internal conflict: A conflict within a character's own mind, creating a psychological struggle

---

18.4 Writing practice

Exercise 4

> **Key term**
>
> **Tone (of voice):** A character's personality conveyed by language choices for speech and thoughts; it can change over the course of a text

Imagine that you are one of the women at the dinner party who has heard Griselda's story. What would you think of her 'extraordinary marriage'? Write a short empathic response that creates a suitable **voice** for that character.

If you are doing Cambridge IGCSE World Literature (0408), one of your coursework assignments must be an empathic response; if you are doing Cambridge IGCSE Literature in English (0475/0992) and are following the coursework route, you have the option of submitting an empathic response as one of your two assignments.

Below, you will find work from a student who has started to respond to this task:

You are Isabella, alone, at the end of the dinner party, thinking about Griselda's story. Write your thoughts.

Use the teacher's comments on it to support you as you write your own response.

Sample empathic response

How my spine aches this evening! I had forgotten it for a while at the party. It is lovely to see Marlene doing so well and I am so grateful she thought to invite me. But the stories I have heard this evening… The cruelty… How can the hearts of men beat so cold? Griselda, for instance. What a woman!

I did not notice her arrive, not until Marlene called out her name. It is funny how I did not place her sooner. It was not until Marlene mentioned Chaucer that I remembered who she was. Griselda from 'The Clerk's Tale'! I read her story to dear Henny when she was small. Dear, dear Henny. How I miss her!

Well done for choosing these details from the text to set the scene.

Really, Griselda and Henny are quite alike. So mild, so sweet… But yet, Griselda is something else entirely. How on earth could she tolerate Wal—? I can't imagine! To have to leave the freedom of the fields; to live in thrall to him; to be subject to his selfish whims; to be confined by him. I can scarcely use the barbarian's name. What manner of man would test a woman's love by taking her children from her? I thank Heaven for Doctor Bishop… He made life at home less dreary… I miss him so.

Your voice for Isabella is really convincing here: she valued 'freedom' and hated 'confinement'.

An effective echo of language from the text: 'barbaric'.

You have shown a detailed personal understanding of the character. Her love for Henrietta, John Bishop and travel is very clear, as is her distaste for Walter.

> Marlene was outraged by Griselda's story but I wonder if she has thought about her own child. What made Marlene give her up? My word! I do believe I know now why Griselda was invited. Marlene and she are the same! Walters, Walters everywhere! That's the problem.

— You have come to your own understanding of Marlene's situation

---

MAKING CONNECTIONS

There is more in-depth guidance about how to write an empathic response in Unit 26.

18.5 Set-text focus

Exercise 5

» The most helpful exercise you can do when studying a drama text is to see a performance of the play. If this is not possible for your drama set texts, see if you can find an audio-visual recording, an audio recording or still photographs on the internet.

» Using the resources that you have found, make notes about the choices that have been made about the appearance of the set and the characters.

» How have stage directions – or the lack of stage directions – affected the performance? What choices have been made about aspects of performance, such as how the characters enter and exit, and how they move and speak, listen and react to one another?

Take your learning further

1   A television adaptation of *Top Girls* can be found online. If you have time to do so, you might enjoy watching the part showing the extract, or watching the whole of Act One to find out more about the stories of the women who feature in it. As you watch, think again about what the juxtaposition of characters shows us about Marlene and about the place of women in English society in the 1980s.

2   In *Top Girls*, Churchill chose women from myth, history and art for the dinner party in the opening scene with the purpose of highlighting women's suffering in societies dominated by men. If you were the host of such a fantastical party, who would you invite? How many continents can you represent in your choices? Write a short passage in the form of a script depicting the dinner party. What stage directions do you think are necessary, and where do you think the director and actors can make their own choices? Think about the set, the characters' appearances, costumes and how the characters move and speak, listen and react to each other.

Unit summary

In this unit, you have learned how to:
- Identify choices made by a dramatist to support your arguments.
- Think about how the various elements of a dramatic performance combine to create meaning.
- Develop an awareness of drama as a literary form and understand that a script is a text to be performed, rather than just read.
- Demonstrate a sensitive and empathic response to a play by writing from one of the character's **perspectives**.

Think about how you have demonstrated each of these skills in the exercises in this unit. The skills and knowledge you have developed in this unit will be helpful when studying the remaining dramatic texts in this section. Be sure to return to this unit and apply the skills you develop in the remainder of the Drama section to *Top Girls*.

Key term

Perspective: Like a lens through which readers view characters and events in a text; the perspective of a text is created by the speaker: we interpret the characters and events based on what the speaker shows and tells us

A Doll's House: Focus on language

> **In this unit, you will:**
> - Select appropriate quotations to demonstrate the ways that a dramatist uses language.
> - Think about how writers use language to convey the deeper meanings of a play.
> - Explore how dramatists use language to create effects.
> - Give personal opinions about the themes explored by a writer, based on their presentation of characters and situations.

In the previous unit, we considered the various tools that dramatists can use to create an effect on stage. Many of these – costume, stage directions, even **setting** – may be interpreted by directors and actors in different ways, but one thing that will remain largely constant between different productions of the same play is language. In the majority of dramatic texts, this will be limited to the dialogue that characters speak to each other, or perhaps to themselves or the audience. Studying the way a dramatist uses language can help us to understand the characters and their feelings or motivations, as well as the **themes** and ideas that the writer is exploring.

A Doll's House is a three-act play written by Henrik Ibsen in 1879. Ibsen is thought of as the father of modern drama: his plays were the first **problem plays**; realistic plays that turned the theatre into a forum for exposing problems that existed within society.

A Doll's House exposes how restrictive late 19th-century Norwegian society was for women. Women were not allowed to vote or manage their own money and it was not socially acceptable for a **middle-class** woman to work. Therefore, women had to depend upon their husbands.

The play's protagonist is Nora: she is married to a banker named Torvald Helmer and they have two children. Typically for the time, Nora's identity is defined by her marriage and her motherhood. At the end of the play, Nora realises the unsatisfying nature of her marriage. At the end of Act Three, in the following extract, she decides to leave Torvald and her children, to discover her own separate identity.

The play caused great controversy at the time of its first performances because of Nora's decision. Audiences could not understand how a woman could leave not only her husband but also her children. This decision was thought to be one that no woman would take.

MAKING CONNECTIONS

Realism in the theatre was a style that began in the 1870s. Performances in this style were designed to be as true to life as possible. Compare the realistic characters and dialogue in this extract with the fantastic situation Caryl Churchill creates in Act One of *Top Girls*, featured in Unit 18. Also, compare the authentic dialogue within this extract with the verse used in *The Merchant of Venice* in Unit 22.

Key terms

Setting: The time, place and culture in which a text takes place

Theme: A key idea or subject that is repeated throughout a text

Problem play: A type of drama that developed in the 19th century; problem plays are staged in a realistic way to expose problems within society so that the audience will reflect on those issues

Middle class: Professional people, who are not poor but are not very rich

Realism: A movement in theatre that started in about the 1870s; plays in this genre seek to imitate real life on the stage in the way that characters, events and settings are shown

Glossary

A settling of accounts: A metaphorical phrase meaning a final resolution to a conflict, or an act of revenge or repayment for previous wrongdoing; it comes from the financial process of paying or claiming money that is owed

Acquaintance: A familiar relationship; the term can also be used to describe someone you know, but whom you wouldn't describe as a friend

Bear: Take responsibility for

In earnest: In a serious and determined way

Merely: Only

Committed a great sin: Done something morally wrong

Merry: Showing enjoyment

Strained: Stretched, forced

Pay... heed: Pay attention

Undertake: Do or begin to do something, especially something difficult

19.1 From Act Three of *A Doll's House* by Henrik Ibsen

HELMER:	Nora – what is this? – this cold, set face?	
NORA:	Sit down. It will take some time; I have a lot to talk over with you.	
HELMER:	[sits down at the opposite side of the table] You alarm me, Nora! – and I don't understand you.	
NORA:	No, that is just it. You don't understand me, and I have never understood you either – before tonight. No, you mustn't interrupt me. You must simply listen to what I say. Torvald, this is a settling of accounts.	5
HELMER:	What do you mean by that?	
NORA:	[after a short silence] Isn't there one thing that strikes you as strange in our sitting here like this?	10
HELMER:	What is that?	
NORA:	We have been married now eight years. Does it not occur to you that this is the first time we two, you and I, husband and wife, have had a serious conversation?	
HELMER:	What do you mean by serious?	15
NORA:	In all these eight years – longer than that – from the very beginning of our acquaintance, we have never exchanged a word on any serious subject.	
HELMER:	Was it likely that I would be continually and forever telling you about worries that you could not help me to bear?	20
NORA:	I am not speaking about business matters. I say that we have never sat down in earnest together to try and get at the bottom of anything.	
HELMER:	But, dearest Nora, would it have been any good to you?	
NORA:	That is just it; you have never understood me. I have been greatly wronged, Torvald – first by papa and then by you.	25
HELMER:	What! By us two – by us two, who have loved you better than anyone else in the world?	
NORA:	[shaking her head] You have never loved me. You have only thought it pleasant to be in love with me.	
HELMER:	Nora, what do I hear you saying?	30
NORA:	It is perfectly true, Torvald. When I was at home with papa, he told me his opinion about everything, and so I had the same opinions; and if I differed from him I concealed the fact, because he would not have liked it. He called me his doll-child, and he played with me just as I used to play with my dolls. And when I came to live with you –	35

HELMER: What sort of an expression is that to use about our marriage?

NORA: [undisturbed] I mean that I was simply transferred from papa's hands into yours. You arranged everything according to your own taste, and so I got the same tastes as you – or else I pretended to, I am really not quite sure which – I think sometimes the one and sometimes the other. When I look back on it, it seems to me as if I had been living here like a poor woman – just from hand to mouth. I have existed merely to perform tricks for you, Torvald. But you would have it so. You and papa have committed a great sin against me. It is your fault that I have made nothing of my life. 45

40

HELMER: How unreasonable and how ungrateful you are, Nora! Have you not been happy here?

NORA: No, I have never been happy. I thought I was, but it has never really been so.

HELMER: Not – not happy! 50

NORA: No, only merry. And you have always been so kind to me. But our home has been nothing but a playroom. I have been your doll-wife, just as at home I was papa's doll-child; and here the children have been my dolls. I thought it great fun when you played with me, just as they thought it great fun when I played with them. That is what our marriage has been, Torvald. 55

HELMER: There is some truth in what you say – exaggerated and strained as your view of it is. But for the future it shall be different. Playtime shall be over, and lesson-time shall begin.

NORA: Whose lessons? Mine, or the children's? 60

HELMER: Both yours and the children's, my darling Nora.

NORA: Alas, Torvald, you are not the man to educate me into being a proper wife for you.

HELMER: And you can say that!

NORA: And I – how am I fitted to bring up the children? 65

HELMER: Nora!

NORA: Didn't you say so yourself a little while ago – that you dare not trust me to bring them up?

HELMER: In a moment of anger! Why do you pay any heed to that?

NORA: Indeed, you were perfectly right. I am not fit for the task. There is another task I must undertake first. I must try and educate myself – you are not the man to help me in that. I must do that for myself. And that is why I am going to leave you now. 70

19.2 First impressions

Exercise 1

a Look closely at these pictures of Nora and Torvald taken from different parts of the play. What dialogue do you imagine between the two characters in each image? Discuss your ideas with a partner and share them with the class.

b With a partner, discuss the nature of the relationship between the couple as it appears to you from the images.

  i What is happening in each image and why do you think it is happening?

  ii How equal does their relationship seem?

  iii Who seems to have control in the relationship?

  iv What appears to be the attitude of the woman to the man?

  v What appears to be the attitude of the man to the woman?

  vi Does the relationship seem to be a happy one?

c Now, read the extract from the play as a class activity. After you have read it, talk with a partner about how the images prepared you for the ideas in the extract. What has the characters' marriage been like? Find quotations that support your view and share your ideas with the class.

19.3 Finding evidence

Exercise 2

a With a partner, read the extract a second time. Discuss the shifting balance of power that you see in the script.

  i Who dominates?

  ii Look at the moments when that dominance is challenged. What methods does Ibsen use to show these challenges?

  iii How successful (long-lived) are these challenges?

  iv Overall, who does Ibsen present as holding the balance of power?

b Share your ideas with the class. Refer to line numbers and quotations from the passage and explain the significance of the language the characters use.

c Now that you better understand how power is balanced in the extract, you will rehearse the extract with your partner in a way that draws attention to the power of the characters at different moments in the extract. You will need a sheet of paper on the floor for this. Whenever the power shifts, the person who is dominating should step onto the paper to highlight the shift.

d Of course, a realistic play would never actually use the device that you used to highlight a shift in power. What more natural ways of showing the shifts in power could be used in a realistic play? Think about the way that voices might be used, body language, gesture and movement. Write some suitable stage directions.

e Perform the section again using the more natural methods of demonstrating shifts in power.

f If possible, repeat your performance for the class and seek feedback:

  i What power shifts did the class notice?

  ii How were these power shifts shown?

  iii Overall, how successful was the performance in showing who holds the balance of power?

Exercise 3

The power relationships in a script are created by the stage directions and the **language choices** in the script. Language choices can refer to the words that are chosen but can also refer to the types of sentences that are used.

a There are four main types of sentences: declarative, interrogative, exclamative and imperative. Match each sentence type with a definition from the list below:

  i Sentences that ask a question. They end with a question mark.

  ii Sentences used to make a statement or give information. They end with a full stop. These are the most common type of sentence.

  iii Sentences used to give an order.

  iv Sentences used to make an exclamation – something said or shouted suddenly as an emotional reaction. They end with an exclamation mark.

> **Key term**
>
> **Language choices:** The specific words that a writer chooses to use to convey particular ideas

b Now you will analyse how the sentence types chosen by the dramatist help to shape the way that the audience will respond to the characters. Create a table similar to the one below and complete it by noting the sentence type and then writing a sentence or two discussing how you imagine the audience will respond to that moment in the extract. Add four quotations of your own to the bottom of your table and complete the whole table accordingly.

Quotation	Sentence type	Audience response
'HELMER: Nora – what is this? – this cold, set face?'	Interrogative	The audience might detect a nervousness here as Helmer pauses after saying Nora's name. He asks 'what is this?' but avoids saying what troubles him directly, preferring to follow up with a fragmented second question '– this cold, set face?' It seems that he has never seen this side of Nora before.
'NORA: Sit down.'	Imperative	
'NORA: Torvald, this is a settling of accounts.'		
'NORA: Does it not occur to you that this is the first time we two, you and I, husband and wife, have had a serious conversation?'		
'NORA: [shaking her head] You have never loved me.'		

c Who uses more interrogative sentences in the extract? What does this suggest about the changed nature of the relationship?

MAKING CONNECTIONS

Metaphors are encountered in several units, including Unit 6 in the poem 'Thistles', Unit 11 in *The Secret River* and in Unit 14, which features an extract from the novel *Hard Times*.

Exercise 4

a What is meant by the terms **metaphor** and **simile**? Share your ideas with a partner before checking your answers in the key terms box on this page.

b Work with a partner to identify where Ibsen has used metaphors and similes in the extract. Make a list of those you find. Analyse the effect of each metaphor and simile.

c The play's title *A Doll's House* is metaphorical. In the extract, Nora explains why she feels that she was first a 'doll-child' and then a 'doll-wife'. In what ways do children play with dolls? What does Ibsen's metaphor suggest about the way that Nora was treated by her father, and then by Torvald?

d Nora clearly feels that her relationships with her father and Torvald have been unsatisfactory. Find quotations to support the following interpretations of the extract. Use a table like the one below.

Interpretation	Quotation
The relationship between Nora and Helmer has been superficial.	
Nora believes that Helmer has not loved her.	
As a child, Nora kept her personal ideas and opinions to herself.	
Nora sees herself as Helmer's property.	
Nora's identity seems to have merged with her husband's.	
Nora feels that her role has been to entertain her husband.	
Nora realises that she has not been truly happy in the relationship.	
Nora wants to break out of her confining marriage and find her own identity.	

MAKING CONNECTIONS

In the title of his play, Ibsen highlights the way that Nora is denied her own identity: she is treated like a doll. Metaphor is used again when Torvald says to Nora 'Playtime shall be over, and lesson-time shall begin'. This infantilises Nora: it makes her seem like a child. Compare this to the title of Churchill's play *Top Girls*. Do you think Churchill is highlighting a similar tendency within British society in the 1980s?

Key terms

Metaphor: A description of one thing as another thing that is mostly unrelated to make a comparison that highlights the similarity between the two things

Simile: A comparison of one thing to another, using the word 'as' or 'like' – 'They are *like* pale hair' is an example of a simile; the comparison gives emphasis to a description or makes it more vivid, but similes are generally thought of as less powerful than metaphors

Exercise 5

In *A Doll's House,* the highest point of **dramatic tension** comes just before Torvald opens a letter from a man who is blackmailing Nora. When Torvald opens the letter, this is the **climax** of the play. The letter will reveal that Nora illegally borrowed money by forging her father's signature – women in Norway at the time could not borrow money without permission from their husbands. (Nora did this so that she and Torvald could make a trip to Italy to improve his health, which was dangerously poor. Since then, Nora has been secretly working to repay this borrowed money – it was not socially acceptable for women of her **class** to work as their husbands provided for them.)

Ibsen uses language and stage directions to heighten the dramatic tension before the climax. As Torvald goes to read his letters, the stage directions tell us that Nora 'seizes' Torvald's coat and 'throws it round her', showing the urgency with which she wants to leave the house. She speaks in 'quick, hoarse, spasmodic whispers' as if she is in a state of great desperation. Ibsen shows this feeling of desperation through her repeated exclamatives: 'Never! Never! Never to see my children again either – never again. Never! Never! –' It is as if she is steeling herself to carry out the suicide that she has planned.

a With a partner, choose five key quotations to show moments when the level of dramatic tension in the extract changes. Plot these on a graph. Compare your answers with another pair of students and discuss any differences that you find.

b Analyse Ibsen's use of language at these key moments. Think about the word choices and the types of sentences that are used.

> **Key terms**
>
> **Dramatic tension:** The feeling of anticipation and excitement that builds within a text or a drama performance
>
> **Climax:** The most exciting point in a text or performance when dramatic tension has increased to its highest point
>
> **Class:** The way society can be divided into groups of people who have similar levels of wealth and status

Exercise 6

> **Key term**
>
> **Resolution:** The final part of a story, in which everything is explained or resolved; sometimes called the 'denouement'

The **resolution** that you have read was hugely controversial at the time of the play's first performance – as you have read in the introduction to the unit. Ibsen was even forced to write an alternative ending when the play was performed in Germany; an ending he viewed as a 'barbaric outrage'.

In the alternative ending, Torvald seizes Nora's arm and shows her their sleeping children. To Torvald's joy, Nora realises that she cannot leave them.

Discuss the following questions with a partner and feed back to the class.

a Why do you think that the revised ending would have been more acceptable to the audiences of the time? Does current society – nearly 150 years later – still expect women to fulfil the role of wife and mother above all else?

b What was Ibsen's original ending saying to audiences about the importance of individual freedom? How important is it for somebody to fulfil their potential rather than be trapped in an unjust situation? How harmful is it for somebody to trap someone else within an unjust situation? Use evidence from the extract to support your ideas. Look at the word choices Nora uses to describe the relationships she has been in.

Key term

Characterisation: The ways in which a writer presents a character to an audience

c   Do you think the alternative ending fits with the **characterisation** of Nora in the extract that you read? Why or why not? Use evidence from the extract to support your ideas.

d   Ibsen's alternative ending was just eight lines long. Have a go at writing your own alternative ending of equivalent length and using similar ideas. Mind map the language and stage directions that might feature in the ending – you might like to include a number of exclamative sentences in such an emotionally charged scene.

e   Draft the imagined alternative ending. If you can, perform it to another pair or the class.

19.4 Writing practice

Exercise 7

The extract shows how Nora confronts Torvald with the uncomfortable truths that have lain hidden behind their relationship. It is a memorable moment in the play because Nora takes control of her life in a way that Torvald – and the audience – could not have anticipated.

Imagine you were asked the following question about the extract:

In what ways does Ibsen memorably convey the relationship between Nora and Torvald at this moment in the play?

TIP

Remember always to underline the key words in any questions that you are asked about a text.

Think back to the work that you have done already in this unit. Copy and complete the mind map below to create a plan that you might use to answer the question. Add at least one short quotation to each part of the mind map.

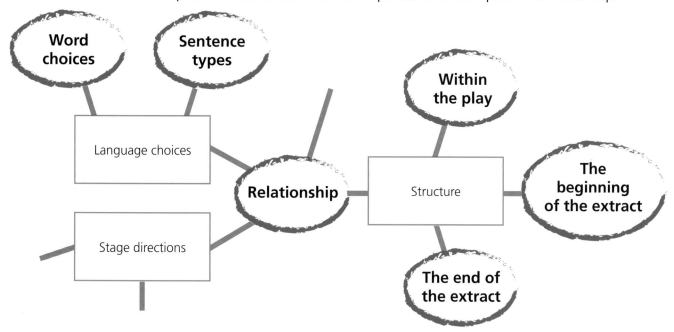

Exercise 8

Now that you have mind mapped your ideas, write a paragraph for each oval in your mind map. An example paragraph is provided below:

Example paragraph

The word choices that Ibsen makes in the extract make the relationship memorable. Nora is described as having a 'cold, set face'. These lines would likely be delivered in a tone that suggests Torvald's astonishment because he has only seen Nora acting in a 'merry' way. He has never realised that truly she is unhappy. This description of Nora at the start of the extract foreshadows the metaphor she uses later when she describes herself as a 'doll-child'. The two images combine to show the audience that Nora is living a life that she would not choose for herself; her passive doll-like life brings her no joy ('cold') and leaves her no freedom ('set'). The only identity she has is the identity that society gives her as wife and mother.

You are showing an awareness of **form** – that this a drama text that would be performed on the stage.

Cross-referencing two quotations like this helps to show that you have your own sensitive and personal response to the text.

You are showing a deeper awareness of ideas here.

Key terms

Foreshadowing: Hinting at something to come in the future

Image / Imagery: A word or phrase that prompts the reader to imagine the way that something looks, sounds, smells, feels or tastes

Form: The text type a writer chooses to communicate in; the three main forms in English literature are poetry, prose and drama – within those main forms are other forms; for example, a sonnet is a poetic form and a short story is a prose form

Cross-referencing: Referring to another text or another part of the same text to draw attention to a similarity or difference

19.5 Set-text focus

Exercise 9

a   Review your notes on your drama set text, looking carefully at key quotations that you have recorded. What sentence types have been chosen by the dramatist? Does the choice of sentence type create any specific effect on the audience? Discuss your ideas with a partner.

b   Choose one of your key quotations. Write a paragraph analysing the language choices made in that quotation. Include a comment about the effect of choosing that sentence type.

Exercise 10

Think carefully about the title of one of your set texts. Think about the choice that the dramatist has made in using that particular title. Ibsen, for example, chose *A Doll's House* rather than, say, *Nora* (which has been the title of some adaptations). Why do you think that the writer of your drama set text chose the title they did? How effectively does the title relate to the main ideas within the text? If the title is metaphorical, how is that metaphor developed through the text, if at all?

Exercise 11

a   Evaluate the dramatic tension in the resolution of your drama set text. Do this using a graph (as you did in Exercise 5). Is the ending expected or unexpected? How will the audience react?

b   Note moments during the resolution of your drama set text that increase the dramatic tension within it. Record the quotations associated with these changes in tension and analyse the language choices made within them.

Take your learning further

1   You have thought a great deal about how the language in the extract from *A Doll's House* shapes the audience's understanding of the characters and situations they find themselves in. Watch a performance of the play or an adaptation of it. Make notes on how the cast perform the quotations that you have focused on during this unit. Are they performed as you imagined they would be? How does the way that the lines are performed affect your understanding of the words, the characters and the situation that the characters are in.

2   Watch the short film *Nora*. In it you will see a woman trying to balance the demands of family and work. How much freer is this protagonist than the original Nora in *A Doll's House*? What has changed? What has remained the same?

Unit summary

In this unit, you have learned how to:

● Select appropriate quotations to demonstrate the ways that a dramatist uses language.
● Think about how writers use language to convey the deeper meanings of a play.
● Explore how dramatists use language to create effects.
● Give personal opinions about the themes explored by a writer, based on their presentation of characters and situations.

Think about how you have demonstrated each of these skills in the exercises in this unit. The skills and knowledge you have developed in this unit will be helpful when studying the other dramatic texts in this section. Be sure to return to this unit and apply to *A Doll's House* the skills you develop in the remainder of the Drama section.

20

The Lion and the Jewel: Focus on characters and characterisation

> In this unit, you will:
> - Use textual evidence to support your opinions about different characters.
> - Examine the actions, attitudes and motivations of different characters, and think about what they represent beyond surface meanings.
> - Explore how writers use language, structure and dramatic devices to present characters and their character arcs.
> - Demonstrate your personal opinions about characters and their relationship using references to the text.

Characterisation is the process by which writers present their characters; how they tell the audience about a character's thoughts, feelings and personality. There are several tools a dramatist can use to contribute to an audience's overall impression of a character: what the character says, what they do, how they move and how they look and sound. In some instances, writers will use characters to represent a broader theme or idea; the way that they change throughout the course of a play can tell us a lot about the dramatist's intentions and the deeper meanings that they wish to convey.

The Lion and the Jewel (1959) tells the story of Sidi, a beautiful young woman, who receives marriage proposals from two men: Lakunle, a westernised schoolteacher, and Baroka, the chief of her village. Some people have interpreted the play as an **allegory** in which Sidi represents Nigeria (in the 1950s); Lakunle represents the idea of progress and Baroka represents tradition.

The play describes the events of one day and is divided into three parts, titled 'Morning', 'Noon' and 'Night'. The extract below is taken from the from the first part, 'Morning', near the beginning of the play, and shows Lakunle asking Sidi to marry him. She is willing to marry him but insists that he must pay money to her family, as is traditional.

> **Key term**
>
> **Allegory:** A story that can be read as having a hidden meaning because the characters and events represent particular qualities, ideas or real-life historical events

---

Glossary

Bush: Wild countryside

Cockatoo: A type of parrot

Bride-price: Money or goods that a groom or his family give to a bride's family

Laughing-stock: A person mocked by others

Heritage: Cultural traditions from the past

Gross: Twelve dozen; 144

Pulpit: A platform in a church from which a preacher gives a sermon

Declamatory: A style of speaking that is full of passion

Engrossed in: Paying complete attention to

Heifer: A young cow, usually one that has not yet given birth to a calf

Chattel: A legal word meaning 'property'

Tethered: Tied

Lagos: A city in Nigeria that was the capital city when the play was written

Waltz / foxtrot: Ballroom dances

Ibadan: A large city in Nigeria

Grandeur: Impressiveness due to size and beauty

20.1 From *The Lion and the Jewel* by Wole Soyinka, 'Morning'

SIDI: [shakes her head in bafflement]
                 If the snail finds splinters in his shell
                 He changes house. Why do you stay?

LAKUNLE: Faith. Because I have faith.
                 Oh Sidi, vow to me your own undying love   5
                 And I will scorn the jibes of these bush minds
                 Who know no better. Swear, Sidi,
                 Swear you will be my wife and I will
                 Stand against earth, heaven, and the nine
                 Hells…   10

SIDI: Now there you go again.
                 One little thing
                 And you must chirrup like a cockatoo.
                 You talk and talk and deafen me
                 With words which always sound the same   15
                 And make no meaning.
                 I've told you, and I say it again
                 I shall marry you today, next week
                 Or any day you name.
                 But my bride-price must first be paid.   20
                 Aha, now you turn away.
                 But I tell you, Lakunle, I must have
                 The full bride-price.
                 Will you make me
                 A laughing-stock?   25
                 Well, do as you please.
                 But Sidi will not make herself
                 A cheap bowl for the village spit.

LAKUNLE: On my head let fall their scorn.

SIDI: They will say I was no virgin   30
                 That I was forced to sell my shame
                 And marry you without a price.

LAKUNLE: A savage custom, barbaric, out-dated.
                 Rejected, denounced, accursed,   35
                 Excommunicated, archaic, degrading,
                 Humiliating, unspeakable, redundant.
                 Retrogressive, remarkable, unpalatable.

SIDI: Is the bag empty? Why did you stop?

LAKUNLE: I own only the Shorter Companion   40
                 Dictionary, but I have ordered
                 The Longer One – you wait!

SIDI: Just pay the price.

LAKUNLE:	[with a sudden shout]	
	An ignoble custom, infamous, ignominious.	45
	Shaming our heritage before the world.	
	Sidi, I do not seek a wife	
	To fetch and carry,	
	To cook and scrub,	
	To bring forth children by the gross…	50

SIDI: Heaven forgive you! Do you now scorn
Child-bearing in a wife?

LAKUNLE: Of course I do not. I only mean…
Oh Sidi, I want to wed
Because I love,   55
I seek a life-companion…
[pulpit-declamatory]
'And the man shall take the woman
And the two shall be together
As one flesh.'   60
Sidi, I seek a friend in need.
An equal partner in my race of life.

SIDI: [attentive no more. Deeply engrossed in counting the beads on her neck]
Then pay the price.

LAKUNLE: Ignorant girl, can you not understand?   65
To pay the price would be
To buy a heifer off the market stall.
You'd be my chattel, my mere property.
No, Sidi! [very tenderly]
When we are wed, you shall not walk or sit   70
Tethered, as it were, to my dirtied heels.
Together we shall sit at table
– Not on the floor – and eat,
Not with fingers, but with knives
And forks, and breakable plates   75
Like civilized beings.
I will not have you wait on me
Till I have dined my fill.
No wife of mine, no lawful wedded wife
Shall eat the leavings off my plate –   80
That is for the children.
I want to walk beside you in the street.
Side by side and arm in arm
Just like the Lagos couples I have seen
High-heeled shoes for the lady, red paint   85
On her lips. And her hair is stretched
Like a magazine photo. I will teach you
The waltz and we'll both learn the foxtrot
And we'll spend the week-end in night-clubs at Ibadan.
Oh I must show you the grandeur of towns   90
We'll live there if you like or merely pay visits.
So choose. Be a modern wife, look me in the eye
And give me a little kiss – like this.

20.2 First impressions

Exercise 1

How might a dramatist present a romantic relationship in a dramatic text?

a Look closely at the image above. As a class, think of as many words as you can to describe the feelings you associate with the image.

b What impressions do you get of the couple? Think about the following ideas:
- Their feelings and attitudes towards each other
- The way they are likely to talk and listen to each other.

c Discuss your answers. How do you think a dramatist might show us, the audience, this scene through speech and action? Consider these issues:
- Language choices and ways of speaking
- Body language, movement and gesture
- Proximity to each other and touch.

Exercise 2

a Read the stage directions below, which introduce the characters Lakunle and Sidi.

[A clearing on the edge of the market, dominated by an immense 'odan' tree. It is the village centre. The wall of the bush school flanks the stage on the right, and a rude window opens on to the stage from the wall. There is a chant of the 'Arithmetic Times' issuing from this window. It begins a short while before the action begins. SIDI enters from left, carrying a small pail of water on her head. She is a slim girl with plaited hair. A true village belle. She balances the pail on her head with accustomed ease. Around her is wrapped the familiar broad cloth which is folded just above her breasts, leaving the shoulders bare.

TIP

If you are asked to explain how a dramatist creates a certain effect / presents a particular character, the stage directions may be just as important as the dialogue.

Almost as soon as she appears on the stage, the schoolmaster's face also appears at the window. (The chanting continues – 'Three times two are six', 'Three times three are nine', etc.) The teacher LAKUNLE, disappears. He is replaced by two of his pupils, aged roughly eleven, who make a buzzing noise at SIDI, repeatedly clapping their hands across the mouth. LAKUNLE now re-appears below the window and makes for SIDI, stopping only to give the boys admonitory whacks on the head before they can duck. They vanish with a howl and he shuts the window on them. The chanting dies away. The schoolmaster (LAKUNLE) is nearly twenty-three. He is dressed in an old-style English suit, threadbare but not ragged, clean but not ironed, obviously a size or two too small. His tie is done in a very small knot, disappearing beneath a shiny black waist-coat. He wears twenty-three-inch-bottom trousers, and blanco-white tennis shoes.]

b   Draw Sidi and Lakunle, using the information about them in these stage directions.

c   Share your drawings with a partner. Discuss your initial impressions of each character. Do you think that the characters are quite similar or quite different? Why? Share your ideas with the class.

d   Now read the extract from *The Lion and the Jewel* in 20.1. As you read, think carefully about the closeness of the relationship that the dramatist describes.

20.3 Finding evidence

Exercise 3

Look at lines 1 to 20 of the extract. Write a sentence or two about each of the following phrases, explaining what they show about Sidi's thoughts about Lakunle. The first sentence has been written for you.

a   If the snail finds splinters in his shell
He changes house. Why do you stay?

This quotation shows that Sidi is confused about why Lakunle stays in the village. If the village is making his life difficult, almost painful, like 'splinters' in a snail's shell would be, it would seem sensible for him to leave.

b   Now there you go again.
One little thing
And you must chirrup like a cockatoo.

c   You talk and talk and deafen me
With words which always sound the same
And make no meaning.

d   ... I say it again
I shall marry you today, next week
Or any day you name.
But my bride-price must first be paid.

Exercise 4

Look at lines 21 to 44. The dramatist's characterisation of the play's protagonists, Sidi and Lakunle, makes them **rounded** rather than **flat characters**. In other

Key terms

Rounded character: A believable character with a complex personality

Flat character: A character who is uncomplicated and undeveloped

words, they are believable individuals with different sides to their characters. This is achieved through the words the characters use as well as the stage directions that suggest how these words should be performed on-stage. Copy and complete the table below, giving an example quotation for each method that Soyinka uses to present the characters. Find quotations within the extract and the stage directions provided in Exercise 2.

Write a comment for each quotation to explain what it reveals about the character concerned. An example has been done for you.

Method of characterisation	Quotation	Effect
Vocabulary choices	'Rejected, denounced, accursed… unpalatable.'	Lakunle is verbose. He is educated but dull.
Manner of speaking (volume and tone)		
Movement		
Body language		
Costume choices		
Actions		

Exercise 5

Dramatists want their audiences to be engaged by the main characters, and an important part of this is making the characters' motivation clear. If two characters have opposing motivations, this **conflict** creates dramatic tension.

a In pairs, discuss what motivates Sidi and what motivates Lakunle. Write down what you think.

b Discuss how strong these motivations are for the characters and how this creates dramatic tension. Again, record your answers.

c Share your answers with the class.

Exercise 6

When a character conflicts with another character or with society, that is an **external conflict**. Characters can also be in a psychological struggle with themselves, and this is called an 'internal conflict'. Any type of conflict can create dramatic tension.

Now look at the following phrases taken from lines 45 to 63. Write a short paragraph about each of the phrases, explaining how they reveal conflict. Be sure to comment on language choices and other dramatic devices whenever possible. The first short paragraph has been written for you.

a Shaming our heritage before the world.

This quotation shows that Lakunle feels that the custom of a bride-price damages the village's reputation. His attitude is in conflict with the attitudes of all the other villagers. The verb 'shaming' shows the strength of his feeling on the topic: he is clearly outraged by the idea of a bride-price.

Key terms

Conflict: A situation in which there is an obstacle between a character and that character's goal; the conflict may be external or internal

External conflict: A conflict between a character and an outside force, such as another character, society, nature or fate

b	Heaven forgive you! Do you now scorn
	Child-bearing in a wife?
c	Of course I do not. I only mean...
d	Then pay the price.

Exercise 7

Dramatic irony is created when the audience knows something about a situation that a character in the play does not know.

a Read lines 64 to 90 again. Can you find evidence that Lakunle wants to present himself as modern and sophisticated? Can you find evidence that he is not these things? Working with a partner, complete a table like the one below. Write a sentence or two to explain how the pieces of evidence contrast.

Key term

Dramatic irony: A situation in which the audience knows something that a character in the play does not know

Lakunle claims he is modern and sophisticated	Lakunle is not modern and sophisticated	How the evidence contrasts
'To pay the price would be / To buy a heifer off the market stall. / You'd be my chattel, my mere property.'	'Ignorant girl, can you not understand?'	Lakunle claims that he does not want to treat Sidi poorly, like a dumb animal, yet he describes her as 'ignorant'.

b How does the way that Lakunle presents himself create dramatic irony? What effect does this have on the audience?

c Share your ideas with the class.

Exercise 8

Dramatists cannot describe a character's thoughts and feelings to us in the same way as a novelist might. Instead, dramatists depend upon the characters' speech (and the accompanying stage directions) so that we can **infer** these things. Dramatists mainly present characters' speech using dialogue, which is when two or more characters speak to each other. Sometimes, dramatists also choose to use a **soliloquy**, where a character reveals their thoughts and feelings by speaking alone on the stage. A **monologue** is when a character speaks at length, such as when Lakunle speaks from line 64 onwards.

Look back to the whole of the extract and think about **turn-taking**. Work with a partner to answer the following questions.

a Who takes the longest turns? What does this long turn-taking suggest about the character?

b What do the two shortest lines tell you about Sidi?

c Which character uses the most **interrogative sentences**? What does this suggest about the character? Look carefully at each interrogative and note its purpose.

d With a partner, choose a section of the extract where both characters speak at least once. Look carefully at the lines for each character. Agree on stage directions to accompany some of the lines. Read the lines out to each other following the stage directions.

TIP

When we communicate, meaning is created not just by words but also by **paralinguistic features** such as facial expression, eye contact, gestures, pitch, laughter, intonation, volume and stress. Consider these in your stage directions.

---

e Discuss how effective your stage directions were. Are there any that you would change?

Key terms

Infer: Reading between the lines of a text to find clues to understand more than is said directly

Soliloquy: A type of speech in which a character in a play reveals their thoughts and feelings by speaking alone on the stage

Monologue: A long speech by one of the characters in a play

Turn-taking: The way dialogue is shared so that the people in it take turns speaking and listening

Interrogative sentence: A sentence that asks a question and ends in a question mark

Paralinguistic features: The methods of communication that accompany speech, such as facial expression, eye contact, gestures, pitch, laughter, intonation, volume and stress

---

Exercise 9

Sidi and Lakunle are **dynamic characters** rather than **static characters**. Dynamic characters have a **character arc**, whereas the personalities or perspectives of static characters do not change significantly.

Sidi is seen to change by the end of the play by deciding against marrying Lakunle and deciding to marry Baroka (who she previously thought was beneath her).

> Did you really think that you, and I...
> Why, did you think that after him,
> I could endure the touch of another man?
> I who have felt the strength,
> The perpetual youthful zest
> Of the panther of the trees?
> And would I choose a watered-down,
> A beardless version of unripened man?

Key terms

Dynamic character: A character whose personality or perspective changes because of the action of the plot

Static character: A character whose personality or perspective does not change as a result of the action of the plot

Character arc: The inner journey of a character in a text in which they gradually change personality or perspective as a result of the events in the play

Imagine you were Sidi at the end of the play looking back to the events in the extract from 20.1. Write a diary entry giving your thoughts and feelings about how you see Lakunle now. Remember that Sidi's feelings towards him will have changed dramatically. She is now certain that he is not the right husband for her!

20.4 Writing practice

Exercise 10

Now that you have looked in detail at the extract that starts this unit, look at this essay question:

How does Soyinka make this moment in the play so entertaining?

a   Think about what is meant by the key word 'entertaining'. Discuss your ideas with a partner.
b   Write a brief plan of how you would answer the question; use a mind map or a bullet-point list – not sentences. Think about which words in the key terms boxes for this unit will be useful.

> **TIP**
>
> It might help you to plan your response if you think about how each character is presented in an entertaining way. Also, the question asks you to look at a 'moment in the play', but if there are events outside the extract that are relevant to your ideas, do refer to them, but keep a tight focus on the question.

Exercise 11

Read below a student's first draft of their response to the question. Then look at the feedback given by their teacher.
a   Discuss the teacher's feedback with your partner or group. How would you improve the student's answer according to the teacher's advice?
b   Share your ideas with the class.

Student's first draft

Soyinka makes this moment in the play The Lion and the Jewel very entertaining. He does this in different ways.

Firstly, the audience will be entertained because Soyinka makes it clear that Sidi is very different from Lakunle. This is shown when she asks 'If the snail finds splinters in his shell / He changes house. Why do you stay?' The way she says this is clever and cheeky.

How can you make this introduction more focused and informed? How does making the characters and their relationship entertaining link with Soyinka's purpose for writing the play?

Which methods does Soyinka use?

Well done for a relevant quotation. Did you use any unnecessary words to introduce it?

You are starting to show an understanding of character. Now, extend your thinking with the conjunction 'because'.

Exercise 12

The student rewrote the response after feedback.
a What changes do you notice between the student's first draft and the second?
b Read the annotations to see the improvements. Are these the same changes you noticed?

Student's second draft

Soyinka makes this moment in the play The Lion and the Jewel very entertaining but it also contributes significantly to the dramatist's overall purpose. The play is an allegory where Sidi represents Nigeria and Lakunle represents the idea of progress. Therefore, the dialogue between them in the extract represents the conflict between tradition and progress for Nigeria.

Firstly, the audience will be entertained by Sidi's manner of speaking to Lakunle, which shows the comic gulf between them. She asks, 'If the snail finds splinters in his shell / He changes house. Why do you stay?' Soyinka gives Sidi monosyllabic language ('snail', 'shell', 'house'), which suggests that her approach to life is dramatically simpler than Lakunle's. Importantly, these earthy lexical choices also show the depth of her connectedness to her traditional, rural lifestyle in the village, which is another contrast between her and Lakunle. The frequent sibilance intensifies the noun 'snail', and this implied metaphor for Lakunle defines him as both fragile and somewhat repulsive; Lakunle's morality later proves to be both of these things as he turns his attention from Sidi to another girl just after Baroka 'wins' her. Her powerful and creative use of language is juxtaposed with her bluntness: her blunt interrogative 'Why do you stay?' might suggest a lack of affection for him.

You are showing an understanding of the deeper implications of the text here so the introduction is focused and informed.

This is a particularly good quotation to have chosen as there are various features to explore.

This is an insightful and original comment.

You have explored a range of techniques that Soyinka uses to have an effect on the audience.

Key term

Sibilance: The repetition of sibilant consonants such as 's', 'z' or 'sh'

Well done for showing an awareness of how the extract relates to the whole text.

20.5 Set-text focus

Exercise 13

Consider the characters in your drama set text.

a Choose three extracts from your drama set text where the dramatist shows conflict between characters or within a character. For each extract, make a note of the type of conflict involved. Is the conflict an internal one – a psychological struggle between the character and an 'inner demon' – or an external one? If it is an external one, think about what exactly the character is in conflict with. Is the character in conflict with another person, society, nature, supernatural forces or fate? How does that conflict affect the audience's feelings about the character?

b Select one of your three chosen extracts. Find quotations in the extract to explore how the character is presented by the words they are given and the stage directions that accompany those words. Use a table like the one in Exercise 4 to record your ideas.

c In Exercise 8 you thought about the types of speech in the extract. Are there soliloquies or monologues in your drama set text? If so, find some examples. What do you think was the dramatist's reason for selecting these forms? Explore your chosen extracts in terms of questions a to d in Exercise 8. What does this analysis reveal about the characters at that time?

d Consider whether dramatic irony is present in your drama set text. How? What is the effect on the audience?

e Which characters are rounded characters in your drama set text and which are flat characters? What do you think is the dramatic function of the minor characters in your drama set text (what purpose do they have within the play)?

f Create a mind map for each of the major characters, recording six or seven key quotations that best define the character at different points in the play. Try to commit these quotations to memory.

g Finally, consider the character arc of the major characters in the play. Make timelines to show how each character changes by the end of the play. Remember to think about changes in how they are acting and how they look, as well as in what the characters say. Choose one of the characters and write a soliloquy for them set near the end of the play reflecting on how the character feels now compared to before.

Take your learning further

You have now read the extract from *The Lion and the Jewel* and thought carefully about the choices Soyinka made in his characterisation.

1 Work in groups of three to prepare a final performance of the script with two actors and a director. The director needs to talk with the actors about an artistic vision for the performance: how should the characters be presented? Should Sidi be angry, amused, interested or disgusted? Is Lakunle just annoying or does he have any chance of success? Which of Soyinka's stage directions need changing? What directions need to be added? The actors need to think about how their performances can achieve this vision: how will they interpret the speech and stage directions using their voices, facial expressions, gestures and movements?

2 If possible, record the performance and obtain feedback from your peers. Was the vision behind the performance clear: how do you think the director wanted you to respond to the characters? How effectively did the actors' performances bring the characters to life? What was particularly effective in each of the performances and why? What improvements could be made to further improve the performance?

3 Make a one-minute or two-minute trailer to introduce the characters in one of your drama set texts. Include a voiceover that introduces the characters and include key quotations that give insights into each character.

Unit summary

In this unit, you have learned how to:

- Use textual evidence to support your opinions about different characters.
- Examine the actions, attitudes and motivations of different characters, and to think about what they represent beyond surface meanings.
- Explore how writers use language, **structure** and dramatic devices to present characters and their character arcs.
- Demonstrate your personal opinions about characters and their relationship using references to the text.

Think about how you have demonstrated each of these skills in the exercises in this unit. The skills and knowledge you have developed in this unit can be applied to the other dramatic texts in this section. Be sure to return to this unit and apply the skills you develop in the other units to *The Lion and the Jewel*.

Key term

Structure: The sequence of ideas in a text and how it is put together

21 *Pygmalion*: Focus on themes and ideas

In this unit, you will:
- Use quotations to support your views about the main ideas and themes of a play.
- Appreciate the deeper meanings of a script, reading between the lines to understand its main ideas and themes.
- Recognise how dramatists use language, structure and form to address themes in a play.
- Develop an informed response to the way a dramatist has addressed themes in a play.

Dramatists use techniques that are different from those used by poets and novelists to explore major themes and ideas within their work. They are reliant on how their play is performed: everything each character says and does on stage is significant in helping to develop and explore major issues. When you are considering themes, you will need to look closely at the characters and the words and actions the dramatist gives them too.

Pygmalion is a **comedy** written by the Irish dramatist George Bernard Shaw and first performed in 1913. It was very important for Shaw that his plays were more than just entertainment; he wanted his audiences to reflect on social issues. *Pygmalion* reflects on themes and ideas including the class system found in Edwardian England.

The play tells the story of how a flower-seller, Eliza (Liza) Doolittle, learns to 'talk like a lady' so that she can progress from selling flowers on the street to selling flowers from a shop (this is not possible for her because she appears **working class**). She takes her lessons from Professor Henry Higgins – an expert in **phonetics** – whose motivation is a bet with Colonel Pickering that she can pass as a duchess at an ambassador's garden party.

This extract is taken from Act Three of the play, some months after lessons have begun, and is set in an **upper-middle-class drawing room**. Higgins has taken Eliza to his mother's house on her 'at-home day' (her day for entertaining guests), only telling his mother about Eliza's background and the bet moments before. Mrs Higgins is alarmed to hear about this 'common flower girl' and thinks that her son is 'silly'.

Higgins wants to see whether Eliza can fool the guests into believing she is from their class with the way she speaks and the way she is dressed. The guests include the Eynsford Hills, who saw Eliza when she was selling flowers on the street (Freddy accidentally knocked over her flowers and Clara was mean to her), and Colonel Pickering, who is part of the plan and wants to witness her first test. Eliza presents herself as a perfect lady to begin with, but things soon start to go wrong.

Key terms

Comedy: A text in which there is humour and a happy ending

Working class: Poorer people who have manual jobs with a lower status in Edwardian society

Phonetics: The study of the sounds of human speech

Upper middle class: Wealthier, professional people with a higher status in Edwardian society

Drawing room: A room with comfortable furniture, used for entertaining guests

Glossary

Pedantic: Paying too much attention to small details

Tone: What a sound is like in terms of its length, pitch, intensity and quality

Cordially: In a friendly, but formal and polite, way

Ottoman: A long box with a soft top used both for storage and for sitting on

Impulsively: Doing something without thinking about it first

Infatuated: Being strongly attracted to someone

Divan: A long, low sofa with no back or arms, for more than one person to sit on

Extricating: Freeing

Imprecations: Curses, bad language

Depression: An area of low-pressure air, which creates unsettled weather

Barometrical: Relating to air pressure – a barometer is an instrument for measuring air pressure

Influenza: A highly contagious disease caused by a virus

Diphtheria: A dangerous infectious disease caused by bacteria

Startled: Surprised and alarmed

Indictment: Blame

21.1 From Act Three of *Pygmalion* by George Bernard Shaw

HIGGINS:	[rising hastily and running to MRS. HIGGINS] Here she is, mother. [He stands on tiptoe and makes signs over his mother's head to ELIZA to indicate to her which lady is her hostess.]	
	[ELIZA, who is exquisitely dressed, produces an impression of such remarkable distinction and beauty as she enters that they all rise, quite flustered. Guided by HIGGINS'S signals, she comes to MRS. HIGGINS with studied grace.]	5
ELIZA:	[speaking with pedantic correctness of pronunciation and great beauty of tone] How do you do, Mrs. Higgins? [She gasps slightly in making sure of the H in Higgins, but is quite successful.] Mr. Higgins told me I might come.	10
MRS. HIGGINS:	[cordially] Quite right: I'm very glad indeed to see you.	
PICKERING:	How do you do, Miss Doolittle?	
ELIZA:	[shaking hands with him] Colonel Pickering, is it not?	
MRS. EYNSFORD HILL:	I feel sure we have met before, Miss Doolittle. I remember your eyes.	15
ELIZA:	How do you do? [She sits down on the ottoman gracefully in the place just left vacant by Higgins.]	
MRS. EYNSFORD HILL:	[introducing] My daughter Clara.	
ELIZA:	How do you do?	
CLARA:	[impulsively] How do you do? [She sits down on the ottoman beside ELIZA, devouring her with her eyes.]	20
FREDDY:	[coming to their side of the ottoman] I've certainly had the pleasure.	
MRS. EYNSFORD HILL:	[introducing] My son Freddy.	
ELIZA:	How do you do? [FREDDY bows and sits down in the Elizabethan chair, infatuated.]	25
HIGGINS:	[suddenly] By George, yes: it all comes back to me! [They stare at him.] Covent Garden! [Lamentably] What a damned thing!	
MRS. HIGGINS:	Henry, please! [He is about to sit on the edge of the table.] Don't sit on my writing-table: you'll break it.	30
HIGGINS:	[sulkily] Sorry.	
	[He goes to the divan, stumbling into the fender and over the fire-irons on his way; extricating himself with muttered imprecations; and finishing his disastrous journey by throwing himself so impatiently on the divan that he almost breaks it. Mrs. Higgins looks at him, but controls herself and says nothing. A long and painful pause ensues.]	35

MRS. HIGGINS:	[at last, conversationally] Will it rain, do you think?	
ELIZA:	The shallow depression in the west of these islands is likely to move slowly in an easterly direction. There are no indications of any great change in the barometrical situation.	40
FREDDY:	Ha! ha! how awfully funny!	
ELIZA:	What is wrong with that, young man? I bet I got it right.	
FREDDY:	Killing!	
MRS. EYNSFORD HILL:	I'm sure I hope it won't turn cold. There's so much influenza about. It runs right through our whole family regularly every spring.	45
ELIZA:	[darkly] My aunt died of influenza: so they said.	
MRS. EYNSFORD HILL:	[clicks her tongue sympathetically]!!!	
ELIZA:	[in the same tragic tone] But it's my belief they done the old woman in.	50
MRS. HIGGINS:	[puzzled] Done her in?	
ELIZA:	Y-e-e-e-es, Lord love you! Why should she die of influenza? She come through diphtheria right enough the year before. I saw her with my own eyes. Fairly blue with it, she was. They all thought she was dead [...]	55
MRS. EYNSFORD HILL:	[startled] Dear me!	
ELIZA:	[piling up the indictment] What call would a woman with that strength in her have to die of influenza? What become of her new straw hat that should have come to me? Somebody pinched it; and what I say is, them as pinched it done her in.	60

21.2 First impressions

Exercise 1

We have seen that the British class system was an important theme that Shaw wanted to explore in *Pygmalion*. Make a mind map like the one below and add any other themes that you think are addressed by this extract. Give evidence for each theme or idea you identify. Share your findings with the rest of the class.

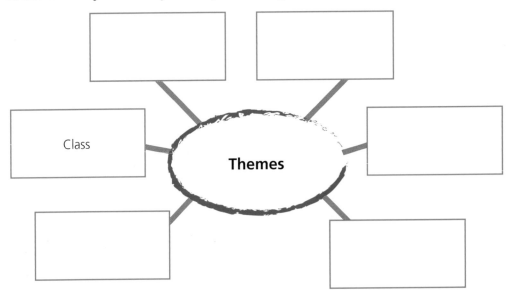

Key terms

Slang: A type of language that is very informal and that is usually spoken rather than written; it is used by particular groups of people

Dialect: A form of language that has some differences in vocabulary and grammar and that is spoken by people in a specific social group or from a specific place

Exercise 2

There are many **slang** and **dialect** terms in the extract. At the end of the extract, Eliza speaks in a working-class dialect, but Higgins and Freddy also employ some slang phrases more typical of upper-middle-class people.

a With a partner, read the list of slang phrases below and match them with their meanings. If you are not sure about any of them, look back to the extract to see how they are used. Two of the phrases have the same meaning.

Phrase
1 'What a damned thing!'
2 'how awfully funny!'
3 'Killing!'
4 'they done the old woman in'
5 'Lord love you!'
6 'them as pinched it'

Meaning
a An expression meaning 'those who stole it'
b A rude expression showing amazement
c An expression meaning 'they murdered her'
d An exclamation to emphasise the truth of what has just been said
e An exclamation showing amusement

b When Shaw gives these language choices to these characters, does it become easier to imagine the characters' personalities? What effect does it have on the likeability – or not – of the characters? Is there a direct relationship between a character's use of slang and their likeability?

c What do you think Shaw is showing by having characters who represent different classes all using non-standard language?

21.3 Finding evidence

Exercise 3

The exercises that follow in this unit will help you to understand how Shaw uses the characters' words and actions to explore some of the key themes in this passage.

Reread the extract from the start to line 44.

a Think about how the following quotations and stage directions are relevant to the play's themes and ideas. Make a director's note for each of them in a table like this. Use the examples to help you.

Quotation	Director's notes
'He stands on tiptoe and makes signs over his mother's head to indicate to her which lady is her hostess' [Higgins]	There is a great deal of visual comedy here. Higgins is behaving without any of the social etiquette that would be expected of a man of his class. By standing 'on tiptoe' and pointing 'over his mother's head' he presents a rather rude figure, ironically the exact reverse of how he is trying to present Eliza.
'speaking with pedantic correctness of pronunciation and great beauty of **tone**' [Eliza]	The use of 'pedantic correctness' suggests that Eliza is taking almost too much care in how she speaks, ensuring that every detail of her 'pronunciation', the tone of her delivery, is not only accurate but also attractive to listen to. She is trying to present herself as perfect and so does not really seem very likeable.
'How do you do?' [Eliza – repeated several times]	
'What a damned thing!' [Higgins]	
'MRS HIGGINS: Don't sit on my writing-table: you'll break it. HIGGINS: [sulkily] Sorry.'	
'extricating himself with muttered imprecations' [Higgins]	
'There are no indications of any great change in the barometrical situation.' [Eliza]	

> **Key term**
>
> **Tone (of voice):** A character's personality conveyed by language choices for speech and thoughts; it can change over the course of a text

b Swap your notes with a partner. Take turns to act the lines using both of your director's notes. Do you agree with your partner's notes? Do you have a better understanding of the characters based on these notes?

Exercise 4

Eliza is presented in a very memorable way in the second part of the extract, from line 45 onwards. Although she is dressed as an **upper-class** lady and her **accent** is that of an upper-class lady, she has not changed her **diction** or the content of her speech.

Eliza is expected to make 'small talk' in this situation. This means she should engage in polite conversation about general topics that will not offend or upset anybody, such as the weather. Of course, the topics would also need to match the expected interests of a well-brought-up lady.

Eliza is not able to make small talk successfully because of her class: she lacks education and her life experiences have been very different from those of the other guests.

a In your own words, explain what Eliza says about her aunt. Would her speech have been appropriate in upper-middle-class society in Edwardian England? Complete a table like the one below to explore the effect of Eliza's speech on the audience. Think about its content and **style**.

	Quotation	Effect
Detailed discussion of illness	'Fairly blue with it, she was.'	This is a very graphic description of her aunt, as her word choice creates a disturbing visual image of her aunt. 'Blue' has **connotations** of cold and death. It would be **taboo** to talk of illness and death in this blunt way.
Crime		
Use of slang		
Non-standard grammar		

b The content and style of what Eliza says might be inappropriate for the situation she is in, but how interesting does her life seem to be in comparison to the other characters'? What do you think Shaw is saying about the upper-middle-class idea of perfection?

Key terms

Style: The way in which an author writes, determined by the sort of language they tend to use, the way they structure sentences and by any other writing patterns that commonly appear in their text

Connotations: Feelings or ideas that are suggested by a word that are beyond its literal meaning

Taboo: A topic that custom prohibits or restricts speaking about

Key terms

Upper class: The people with the highest status in society and who are usually rich

Accent: How people in an area, country or social group pronounce words

Diction: The words and phrases chosen by a speaker or writer

Exercise 5

a There is dramatic irony in this scene. What does the audience and even some of the characters know about Eliza that the Eynsford Hills do not? Think back to what you learned about Eliza in the introduction to this unit. What is the effect of the dramatic irony on the audience?

b Shaw adds another layer of dramatic irony to the scene. In line 27, Higgins suddenly remembers that the Eynsford Hills met Eliza when she was a flower seller: Freddy accidentally knocked over her flowers and Clara was mean to her. How does Shaw's structural link between the two parts of the play increase dramatic tension?

c Read the extract carefully, thinking about how the characters in the scene might react to Eliza's lines. Try to picture their reactions in your head as clearly as you can. If you have a copy of the extract, highlight the quotations that give you ideas.

d Next, complete thought bubbles for each of the characters below to show their thoughts and feelings about Eliza as the action unfolds in the extract. A couple of examples have been done for you:
The characters who know about Eliza's background:

- Higgins (wants his experiment with Eliza to succeed)
- Pickering (has a bet with Mr Higgins that Eliza cannot fool people that she is a lady)
- Mrs Higgins (was alarmed to hear about Eliza's background moments before she arrived)

The characters who do not know about Eliza's background:
- Mrs Eynsford Hill
- Clara
- Freddy

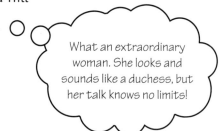

e As a small group, choose three key moments from the extract and rehearse a freeze frame for each of them. Try to maximise the comic potential of the scene through your choice of facial expression, gesture and body language.

f Show the class your favourite freeze frame from the three you have done. Invite them to guess which moment of the extract is being shown in each freeze frame.

g How does Shaw use dramatic irony to make his exploration of themes more powerful? How does it expose the superficial nature of the class system?

21.4 Writing practice

Exercise 6

Now that you have studied the extract in detail, look at this essay question:

How does Shaw make this such a powerful and memorable moment in the play?

a Copy out the question and highlight the key words.
b A student has begun to plan a response to this question. Make a mind map like the one below, adding your own ideas and quotations to it. Include quotations from the work you have done already in this unit.

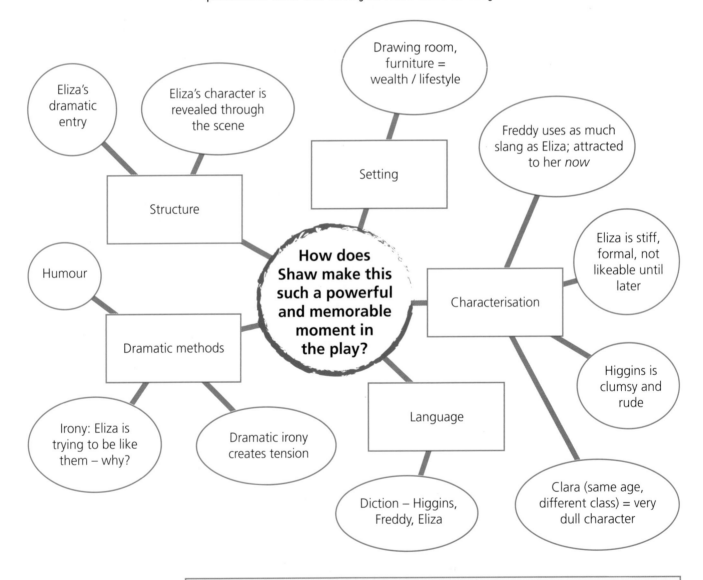

> **TIP**
>
> To answer essay questions effectively, you should always consider several areas of analysis at once and show that you understand how they combine to form a greater picture. This student is planning to analyse several aspects of Shaw's play.

c At the start of the unit, you thought about the themes and ideas that are present in the extract. Refer back to your notes on this and make any changes that you feel are necessary now that you have studied the extract in more detail.

d In your mind map in part **b**, you thought about how Shaw uses structure, dramatic methods, setting, characterisation and language to make the extract powerful and memorable. Add further notes to the mind map now, identifying how these dramatic aspects help Shaw to explore particular themes and ideas. For example, you might think that the contrasting impressions of Eliza at the start and end of the extract illustrate the idea that people in real life aren't perfect.

e After you have planned your essay, you need to think about the structure of your response. Number your mind map to show the order in which you will write about the different ideas. For instance, you might decide to explore the setting first. You might also choose to combine some ideas, especially if there is a link between them in terms of themes and ideas. In that case, draw an arrow to link ideas together.

Exercise 7

Read part of a student's first draft of their response to the question and the feedback that follows.

Student's first draft

Shaw wanted to make his audience think about how superficial and artificial the class system of Edwardian England was.

Perhaps you could also give a brief overview of the dramatic methods that Shaw uses. You can go into detail later on.

Eliza's entrance 'produces an impression of such remarkable distinction' that she immediately flusters everybody, almost as if she is more at home than everyone else in this carefully furnished upper-middle-class setting.

You have made a personal comment on the quotation. Perhaps you could be clear about the deeper meaning here; what theme / idea is Shaw suggesting?

You have made some useful comments here about the dramatic irony. Next, consider the effect of this moment on the dramatic tension in the scene. Think about the effect of Shaw's structure: why is Higgins shown remembering it at this precise moment?

Higgins suddenly remembers that the Eynsford Hills encountered Eliza when she was a flower girl. Of course, he then worries that the Eynsford Hills will see through Eliza's appearance and discover her real 'class'. This reinforces the dramatic irony as now it is not just the audience, Higgins, Pickering and Mrs Higgins who know Eliza is a flower girl; the other guests also know this but they just don't quite realise it.

Think carefully about the teacher's feedback. How would you improve the student's answer? Share your ideas with the class.

Exercise 8

The student rewrote the response following the feedback from their teacher.

Student's second draft

It was very important for Shaw that his audiences reflected on social issues, and Pygmalion encourages an audience to think about how superficial and artificial the class system of Edwardian England was. He confronted the audience with this important idea in an entertaining way using humour and irony.

Eliza's entrance 'produces an impression of such remarkable distinction' that she immediately flusters everybody, almost as if she is more at home than everyone else in this carefully furnished upper-middle-class setting. This powerful first impression is significant because it shows how quickly Edwardians judged people by their dress and their posture, before they even speak. The Eynsford Hills continue to be influenced by this impression even after Eliza starts to reveal her background.

Higgins suddenly remembers that the Eynsford Hills encountered Eliza when she was a flower girl. Of course, he then worries that the Eynsford Hills will see through Eliza's appearance and discover her real 'class'. This reinforces the dramatic irony as now it is not just the audience, Higgins, Pickering and Mrs Higgins who know Eliza is a flower girl; the other guests also know this but they just don't quite realise it. Shaw puts this dramatic moment halfway through the scene so that the dramatic tension is heightened – Eliza's test suddenly becomes more difficult just as she has to move beyond 'studied' introductions.

---

a Are these the same changes you suggested? What is the same and what is different? Think especially about whether the student has included comments about themes and ideas. Share your ideas with a partner and feed back to the class.

b What further ideas could you include? You could think about how and why Eliza becomes more interesting when the small talk finishes. What is the effect of that and what message is Shaw giving about class?

Key term

Irony: The use of words that are the opposite of what you mean; a situation or an event that seems deliberately opposite from what people would expect

21.5 Set-text focus

Exercise 9

a   With a partner, discuss your ideas about the main themes and ideas in your drama set text. Write each theme or idea on a sticky note or a sheet of paper and then arrange them into three groups: the most important theme or idea; the major themes or ideas; and the minor themes or ideas. Be sure to talk to one another about the reason for your ranking.

b   Present your ranking to another pair or the class. Do you agree on which is the most important theme or idea?

c   Make an attractive, illustrated poster for each theme or idea, including as many relevant quotations from the text as you can.

Take your learning further

The Pygmalion myth is a story from Greek mythology that is best known from Ovid's narrative poem *Metamorphoses*. The protagonist of the story is Pygmalion, a sculptor who is not interested in women because he cannot find one who meets his high standards. He decides to create one from ivory, but the statue is so beautiful that he falls in love with it and wishes that it would come to life. The goddess of love grants his wish and he and the living statue marry and live happily ever after.

Now that you have read a summary of the myth, you can start thinking about how the myth relates to the play. What ideas do you have at the moment? Share your ideas with a partner and then discuss the following questions together.

1   How might Higgins be compared to Pygmalion?
2   How might Eliza be compared to the statue in the myth? Think about how real she appears at first compared to the people around her.
3   Think about the impression that Eliza creates when she 'comes to life' in the second half of the extract. Why does she seem ridiculous? Think about the way that she looks compared to what she says.
4   What is Shaw showing in the extract about people of all classes? Think about whether it is possible, or desirable, to be as 'perfect' as a statue.

Unit summary

In this unit, you have learned how to:
● Use quotations to support your views about the main ideas and themes of a play.
● Appreciate the deeper meanings of a script, reading between the lines to understand its main ideas and themes.
● Recognise how dramatists use language, structure and form to address themes in a play.
● Develop an informed response to the way a dramatist has addressed themes in a play.

Think about how you have demonstrated each of these skills in the exercises in this unit. How do the skills and knowledge you have acquired in this unit apply to the extracts in the other drama units? And how can the skills developed in those units be used to explore further the extract from *Pygmalion*?

22 The Merchant of Venice: Focus on structure

In this unit, you will:
- Demonstrate knowledge of an extract and its relationship to the rest of the play from which it is taken.
- Think about characters' goals and motivations and the obstacles they face in trying to achieve those goals.
- Examine the structure of a speech, a scene and an entire play.
- Communicate a personal response about the presentation of different characters and their relationships.

'Dramatic structure' refers to the ways that the parts of a play have been arranged and the relationships between them. Although the events of a play may seem to follow a logical order dictated by the story being told, in reality the structure of a play will most likely have been carefully planned and plotted to maximise the dramatic tension that the audience feel, or to highlight certain thematic ideas that the dramatist wants them to think about. In this unit we will think about dramatic structure in three different ways: the structure of a speech, the structure of a scene and the overall structure of a play.

To begin our focus on structure, let's read an extract taken from the end of Act One of *The Merchant of Venice*, a 16th-century comedy written by the great English dramatist William Shakespeare.

The play opens in Venice where we meet Bassanio. He owes his friend Antonio money and would like to repay it. His plan is to marry a beautiful, rich heiress named Portia. He needs to appear suitably wealthy though, so first he must borrow some more money! Antonio is a successful merchant in Venice and is happy to help but unfortunately his merchant ships will still be at sea for two months, leaving him short of cash. The solution he suggests is for Bassanio to borrow from a moneylender, saying that Antonio will guarantee the loan.

A Jewish moneylender named Shylock agrees to lend Bassanio the money he needs for three months. Instead of the high interest he normally demands, he proposes that if the deadline passes, Antonio should forfeit a pound of his flesh. Antonio, confident that his ships will return in time, agrees to these unusual terms.

Glossary

Rated: Scolded, told off

Usances: Interest on a loan

Sufferance: Patience

Gaberdine: A loose upper garment

Void your rheum upon my beard: Spit on my beard

Foot me: Kick me

Cur: Dog

Suit: Formal request

Bondsman's key: Humble voice

When did friendship take / A breed for barren metal of his friend?: When did a friend ask interest for a loan?

No doit: Not even a small coin

Notary: A clerk who draws up contracts

In a merry sport: For fun

Forfeit: Penalty

Dwell in my necessity: Carry on without the money

Exaction of the forfeiture: Taking the penalty

Hie thee: You hurry

22.1 From Act One, Scene Three of *The Merchant of Venice* by William Shakespeare

SHYLOCK:	Signior Antonio, many a time and oft
	In the Rialto you have rated me
	About my moneys and my usances:
	Still have I borne it with a patient shrug,
	For sufferance is the badge of all our tribe. 5
	You call me misbeliever, cut-throat dog,
	And spit upon my Jewish gaberdine,
	And all for use of that which is mine own.
	Well then, it now appears you need my help:
	Go to, then; you come to me, and you say 10
	'Shylock, we would have moneys:' you say so;
	You, that did void your rheum upon my beard
	And foot me as you spurn a stranger cur
	Over your threshold: moneys is your suit
	What should I say to you? Should I not say 15
	'Hath a dog money? is it possible
	A cur can lend three thousand ducats?' Or
	Shall I bend low and in a bondman's key,
	With bated breath and whispering humbleness, Say this;
	'Fair sir, you spit on me on Wednesday last; 20
	You spurn'd me such a day; another time
	You call'd me dog; and for these courtesies
	I'll lend you thus much moneys'?
ANTONIO:	I am as like to call thee so again,
	To spit on thee again, to spurn thee too. 25
	If thou wilt lend this money, lend it not
	As to thy friends; for when did friendship take
	A breed for barren metal of his friend?
	But lend it rather to thine enemy,
	Who, if he break, thou mayst with better face 30
	Exact the penalty.
SHYLOCK:	Why, look you, how you storm!
	I would be friends with you and have your love,
	Forget the shames that you have stain'd me with,
	Supply your present wants and take no doit 35
	Of usance for my moneys, and you'll not hear me:
	This is kind I offer.
BASSANIO:	This were kindness.
SHYLOCK:	This kindness will I show.
	Go with me to a notary, seal me there 40

Your single bond; and, in a merry sport,
If you repay me not on such a day,
In such a place, such sum or sums as are
Express'd in the condition, let the forfeit
Be nominated for an equal pound   45
Of your fair flesh, to be cut off and taken
In what part of your body pleaseth me.

ANTONIO: Content, i' faith: I'll seal to such a bond
And say there is much kindness in the Jew.

BASSANIO: You shall not seal to such a bond for me: 50
I'll rather dwell in my necessity.

ANTONIO: Why, fear not, man; I will not forfeit it:
Within these two months, that's a month before
This bond expires, I do expect return
Of thrice three times the value of this bond.   55

SHYLOCK: O father Abram, what these Christians are,
Whose own hard dealings teaches them suspect
The thoughts of others! Pray you, tell me this;
If he should break his day, what should I gain
By the exaction of the forfeiture?   60
A pound of man's flesh taken from a man
Is not so estimable, profitable neither,
As flesh of muttons, beefs, or goats. I say,
To buy his favour, I extend this friendship:
If he will take it, so; if not, adieu;   65
And, for my love, I pray you wrong me not.

ANTONIO: Yes Shylock, I will seal unto this bond.

SHYLOCK: Then meet me forthwith at the notary's;
Give him direction for this merry bond,
And I will go and purse the ducats straight,   70
See to my house, left in the fearful guard
Of an unthrifty knave, and presently
I will be with you.

ANTONIO: Hie thee, gentle Jew.

[Exit Shylock]   75

The Hebrew will turn Christian: he grows kind.

BASSANIO: I like not fair terms and a villain's mind.

ANTONIO: Come on: in this there can be no dismay;
My ships come home a month before the day.

[Exeunt]   80

22.2 First impressions

Exercise 1

Read the extract in a group of three and discuss the following questions, ready to feed back to the class.

a What happens in the extract? Think about the beginning, middle and the end.

b Choose one word to describe each character in the scene. With which character or characters do you feel most sympathy? Why?

c The character of Shylock has been the subject of much debate since Shakespeare's time. Historically he has been presented as a villain, a product of the antisemitic prejudices of Shakespeare's time, but more recent interpretations have treated him more sympathetically as a result of the abuse he suffers. An actor playing Shylock could use different tones of voice in a performance of this extract depending on their interpretation of the character. Read the extract aloud in groups. Experiment with the following tones where they seem appropriate: hurt, conciliatory, **sarcastic**, angry, scheming, mocking.

d This extract is taken from near the beginning of the play. What themes and ideas are introduced here and what themes would you expect to be explored in the remainder of the play?

TIP

It is always a good idea to read a playscript aloud as this helps you to understand how lines can be delivered in various ways to create different effects. Shakespeare's plays can sometimes seem more challenging in this respect because some of the words on the page will be unfamiliar; however, when you read them aloud the overall meaning of the lines is usually clear.

MAKING CONNECTIONS

Themes are ideas that people can relate to because they reflect the overall experience of being human; therefore, you will often encounter similar themes in different texts. Which of the themes that you have encountered in this extract have you encountered in other texts (including texts in this book)? Were they treated as major themes or minor themes?

Key term

Sarcastic: Mocking somebody in an amusing but hurtful way

22.3 Finding evidence

Exercise 2

The first way we can look at structure is to think about how individual speeches are put together.

With a partner, read Shylock's speech at the start of the extract, recreated below with three sections highlighted in different colours. Swap the role of reader and listener each time there is a comma, semi-colon, colon, full stop or question mark.

Signior Antonio, many a time and oft
In the Rialto you have rated me
About my moneys and my usances:
Still have I borne it with a patient shrug,
For sufferance is the badge of all our tribe.   5
You call me misbeliever, cut-throat dog,
And spit upon my Jewish gaberdine,
And all for use of that which is mine own.

Well then, it now appears you need my help:
Go to, then; you come to me, and you say   10
'Shylock, we would have moneys:' you say so;
You, that did void your rheum upon my beard
And foot me as you spurn a stranger cur
Over your threshold: moneys is your suit.

What should I say to you? Should I not say   15
'Hath a dog money? is it possible
A cur can lend three thousand ducats?' Or
Shall I bend low and in a bondman's key,
With bated breath and whispering humbleness, Say this;
'Fair sir, you spit on me on Wednesday last;   20
You spurn'd me such a day; another time
You call'd me dog; and for these courtesies
I'll lend you thus much moneys'?

a In the first section of the speech, what do we quickly learn about how Antonio has previously treated Shylock? Choose four words or phrases that show how badly Shylock has been treated. Number them in order of seriousness and explain your choices. What do you notice about the order in which they are presented?

b In the second section of the speech, lines 9 to 14, Shylock rephrases and develops an idea he referred to in the first section. What is the effect of this? Shylock also reveals another of Antonio's actions. How significant is this new information and what is its dramatic effect? How is that effect intensified by the timing with which the information is revealed?

c Line 15 could be thought of as a **turning point** in the speech, introducing its final section. Now that Shylock has reminded Antonio of how he has been mistreated by him, who does he now ask for advice about how to respond? What is the effect of this? Which language methods are used in the line to create this effect? Think about the sentence type and the use of pronouns.

Key term

Turning point: A point in a literary text at which an idea or an attitude is changed or reversed

d What metaphor does Shakespeare repeat three times in Shylock's speech in lines 16 to 22? What is the effect of that pattern of language on the audience? Think about what this repetition suggests about Shylock's tone now compared to the start and the middle of the speech.

e Think about the pace with which the actor will deliver the lines. Shakespeare has not given stage directions to guide the actor's choice so we must look at the punctuation as a guide. Think back to your reading at the beginning of this exercise. How do you think the punctuation will affect the tone that the actor uses in different parts of the speech? Say why and give examples for your decisions. Think, for example, about the very long last sentence and its effect.

f In the second-to-last line of the speech, Shakespeare chooses to give the word 'courtesies' to Shylock. There is clear irony here. Does this give us a new perspective on how Shylock addresses Antonio at the start of the speech as 'Signior Antonio'? Do you think Shylock really respects Antonio? Why or why not? How might this affect the delivery of these opening words?

Exercise 3

A second way to consider structure in a dramatic text is to think about the structure of an individual scene (or, in our case, an extract from a particular scene). This requires us to think about the situation at the start of the scene; the situation at the end of the scene; and how the dramatist gets us from one to the other. Think about the following questions with a partner and discuss your answers with the rest of the class.

a A good way to think about the structure of a scene is to think about the goals of the different characters and the obstacles they face in achieving them. Think back to the introduction to this unit to help you with answering these questions:
  i What is Antonio's goal in this scene?
  ii What motivates him to achieve his goal?
  iii What obstacle does he need to overcome to achieve his goal?
  iv How does he overcome this obstacle?

b Try to answer the same questions in relation to Shylock. The extract will help you to do this, but the answers might not be as immediately obvious. Does thinking about the motivations of the two characters change your mind about which of them is sympathetic? Why?

c Bassanio has only a few lines in this extract, but he plays an important dramatic function.
  i What do you think he feels about the bond that Antonio has made with Shylock on his behalf? How do his opinions differ from Antonio's? Explain your answer with references to the text.
  ii How does Bassanio's presence in the scene increase the sense of danger that the audience might feel about the bond?
  iii Why do you think Shakespeare has Shylock exit when there are only four lines left in the scene, leaving Antonio and Bassanio alone on stage? What might these two characters discuss after the scene has finished?

MAKING CONNECTIONS

Entrances and exits are very important aspects of a scene to consider when studying drama texts. Nora's exit at the end of *A Doll's House*, when she leaves her husband and children, has enormous dramatic power. One critic described how 'that slammed door reverberated [echoed] across the roof of the world' because Nora was putting her own needs ahead of her role as wife and mother in a way that was unthinkable at the time.

---

d In Exercises 1 and 2, you considered the conflict between Antonio and Shylock, as described at the start of the extract. How has this changed by the end of the scene? What new tension has been introduced by the end of the scene?

TIP

Think about the purpose of key scenes in your drama set texts. How do these scenes build the audience's understanding of what they have seen before; how do these scenes help to set up the dramatic action that follows?

Exercise 4

A third way to consider structure is to look at how key moments work together to complete the overall structure of the play.

Study the list of key moments within the overall structure of the play that are given below. Think about how the key moments follow on from each other to affect the level of dramatic tension in the play.

1 **Bassanio approaches his friend Antonio for a loan** so that he can woo Portia, a wealthy heiress in Belmont. Antonio cannot help because his ships are at sea; he suggests that Bassanio borrows from a moneylender, saying that Antonio will guarantee the loan. (Act One, Scene One)

2 **Shylock agrees to loan Antonio three thousand ducats** without charging any interest – despite Antonio's abuse of him. However, 'in a merry sport' he sets a terrible penalty of a pound of Antonio's flesh. Bassanio does not trust Shylock's generosity but Antonio does; he also trusts his ships will return in good time. (Act One, Scene Three)

3 **Shylock's servant leaves Shylock to serve Bassanio instead.** (Act Two, Scene Two)

4 **Shylock's daughter runs away with Antonio's friend, Lorenzo.** She takes money and jewels with her. (Act Two, Scene Six)

5 **Shylock reveals more about how Antonio has mistreated him,** all because Shylock is Jewish. He points out their shared humanity. Jessica cannot be found but Shylock hears how she is spending his money. Antonio loses a ship. (Act Three, Scene One)

6 **In Belmont, Bassanio passes a test so that he can marry Portia.** Portia gives Bassanio a ring and he promises to keep it forever. After their marriage, a letter arrives from Antonio; his ships are lost and he is financially ruined. Shylock plans to take his pound of flesh. Portia says they should offer Shylock many times the original loan to save Antonio. Bassanio rushes back to Venice before the wedding celebrations take place. (Act Three, Scene Two)

7 **In court, Shylock demands the penalty from Antonio** and does not listen to appeals for mercy. Antonio prepares to die but a lawyer appears who is actually Portia in disguise. She advises Shylock to have mercy but then admits that the law allows the penalty. Shylock refuses Bassanio's offer of more money and insists on his pound of flesh. At the last moment, Portia tells him that the wording of the loan means he can only take a pound of flesh – exactly – and no blood. The tables turn and Shylock now faces execution for threatening a Venetian citizen. The Duke gives him mercy but Shylock must either lose his property to Antonio or convert to Christianity and agree to pass on his wealth to his daughter and Lorenzo when he dies. Still in disguise, Portia asks for Bassanio's ring as her only payment. Bassanio initially refuses but is persuaded to relent by Antonio. (Act Four, Scene One)

8 **There are celebrations on everyone's return to Belmont.** Portia returns her ring to her husband and explains her role in the courtroom. Antonio receives a letter saying that three of his ships have arrived safely home. (Act Five, Scene One)

a Make a graph like the one below. The vertical axis represents the dramatic tension within the play. The horizontal axis represents the play's five-act structure, typical of a Shakespearean play. Plot the rising dramatic tension that occurs during the play; the first point on the graph has been marked as an example.

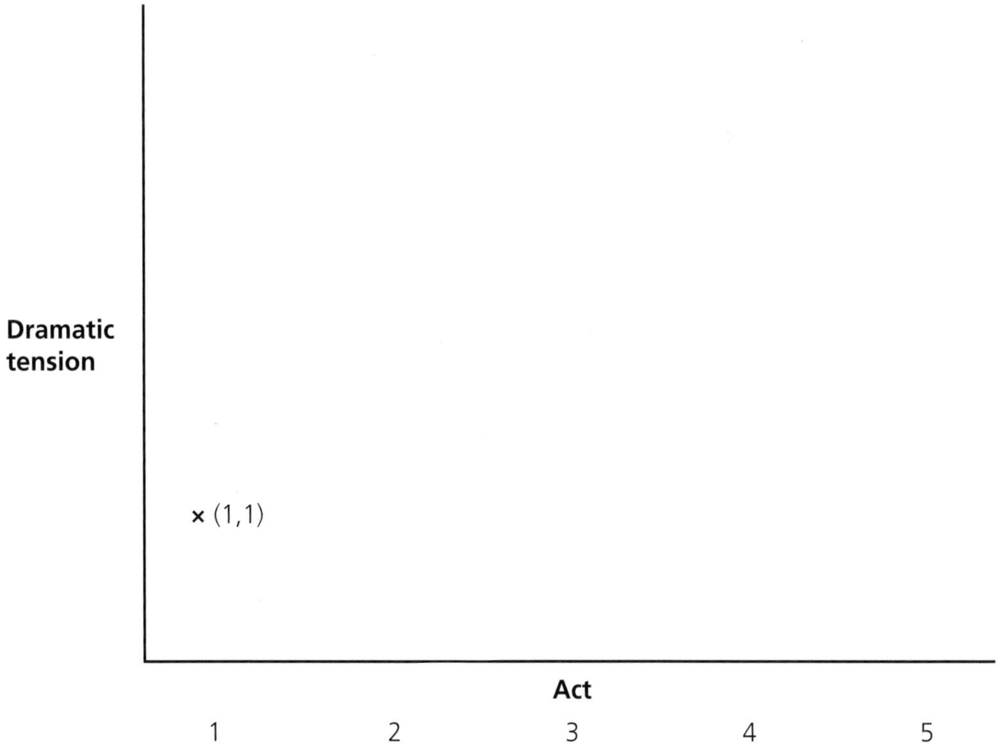

Dramatic tension

× (1,1)

Act

1   2   3   4   5

b Think about the dramatic effects created by the way that Shakespeare structures these key moments within the play. Answer the following questions with a partner.

i   What do you notice about the rise in dramatic tension in the play's **plot**?

ii How does Shakespeare increase dramatic tension in the first three acts? Think about how the **subplots** affect Shylock's attitude towards the loan.

iii Where is the dramatic tension in the play at its highest? Explain your opinion.

iv Portia's ring is a dramatic device Shakespeare uses to prolong the dramatic tension of the play. How does the device maintain the audience's interest? What would be the effect of removing this device from the play?

c Look at the lists below. The left-hand list contains several terms that are often used to describe the different parts of a play's structure in the order in which they occur. The right-hand list contains their definitions, but in an incorrect order.

1 Exposition	**a** The turning point in the story; the point at which the dramatic tension is at its highest
2 Inciting incident	**b** The conclusion of the plot; any unanswered questions are resolved
3 Rising action	**c** The events and actions of the characters that follow the climax
4 Climax	**d** Events that increase dramatic tension, building towards the climax
5 Falling action	**e** An event that sets the story in motion and introduces the central tension in the plot
6 Resolution	**f** The introduction of the setting, the mood and characters

i   Match the terms to their definitions.

ii Think about these terms in relation to the events of *The Merchant of Venice*. Label your graph with these terms and explanations for your decisions.

iii What is the structural importance of the scene we have studied in this unit in relation to the rest of the play?

> **TIP**
>
> The terms in part **c** can be useful when describing the structure of a play. However, if you just describe the structure of a play, perhaps with reference to some of these terms, you are not showing an understanding of the play as a text for performance. Instead, focus your attention on describing the dramatic effects of a play's structure. How will an audience watching a live performance respond to the developing action?

> **Key terms**
>
> **Plot:** The main events in a play or other text that interrelate to make the story
>
> **Subplot:** A part of the story in a play or other text that develops separately from the main story

22.4 Writing practice

Exercise 5

A student was asked to respond to this question:

Explore the ways in which Shakespeare makes the relationship between Shylock and Antonio so dramatically powerful.

a Read the beginning of a student's response and then look at the feedback given by their teacher.

Student response

Shakespeare maximises the drama of Shylock's first appearance, which takes place in Act One, Scene Three, by giving him an extended speech which effectively acts as a catalyst for the rest of the play. The speech establishes the character of Shylock and introduces the deep conflict between him and Antonio. The potential penalty which Shylock proposes, 'in a merry sport', can then create a sense of danger until the climax of the play.

Shylock begins his extended speech by addressing Antonio respectfully, 'Signior Antonio', and then shows the appalling history of mistreatment that he has suffered at the hands of Antonio: 'You call me misbeliever, cut-throat dog, / And spit upon my Jewish gaberdine'. This rule of three collection of insults is carefully structured so that they escalate, becoming more and more serious, creating sympathy for Shylock as well as characterising him as decent, rational, intelligent and articulate.

This characterisation of Shylock helps the audience to understand the injustice of Antonio's request for 'help' which follows in the middle part of the speech...

You are showing a good awareness of structure in the play by discussing how this moment contributes to the plot and dramatic tension. You could try to include some more textual references.

You have identified a literary device and then developed this to say how the words have been structured to maximise their dramatic effect.

There is evidence of a personal response here.

It seems that you will explore the structure of the speech (beginning, middle and end) and its dramatic effect.

b Now that you have read this part of the student's response and seen the feedback it received, write another paragraph or two to continue answering the question. Use the ideas from the exercises that you have done in this unit to help you make comments about structure as well as other **literary aspects**.

Key term

Literary aspect: An essential element within a text: the structure, the language, the themes and ideas, the character and perspective, the setting and the mood

22.5 Set-text focus

Exercise 6

a Explore how an extended speech given by a character in your drama set text is structured to have maximum impact. Use questions like these:
 i What happens at the beginning, the middle and the end?
 ii Is there a turning point in the speech, and how is it shown?
 iii What orders and patterns occur and how do they contribute to meanings?
 iv How does the ending relate back to the beginning to show a progression of ideas?

b Consider an individual scene in your drama set text in terms of the goals of the different characters and the obstacles they face in achieving them. This will help you to understand how the scene relates to the overall action of the play. Think about the following questions:
 i What goal does each character have in the scene?
 ii What motivates them to achieve their goal?
 iii What obstacles do they need to overcome to achieve their goal?
 iv How do they overcome this obstacle?

c Make a list of key moments within your drama set text. Plot them on a graph like the one shown in Exercise 4. Plot the rising dramatic tension that occurs during the play and label the resulting line with the following terminology: exposition, inciting incident, rising action, climax, falling action, resolution. Make notes for each key point about how it increases or decreases dramatic tension. It might help to think about how removing that moment from the overall structure of the play would affect the telling of the story.

Take your learning further

1 We have seen how conflict between characters can drive forward the action in the play. This is a key aspect that directors and actors need to consider when a play is staged. Look at the conflict and emotions of Antonio and Shylock in various performances as shown in online clips. What different decisions have the directors and actors made in their **staging** of this conflict? How effective do you think they have been?

2 Shakespearean comedies feature **conventions** including obstacles that are overcome, subplots, lovers being united and happy endings. Does *The Merchant of Venice* have all of these conventions? Are there any elements of the play that don't seem to fit its description as a comedy? You might like to carry out some research into definitions of Shakespearean **genres** to help you make a decision.

Key terms

Staging: The process of designing the performance space in which a play takes place, taking into account the set, the lighting and the costumes

Conventions: Typical features found within a literary genre

Genre: A category of literature

Unit summary

In this unit, you have learned how to:
- Demonstrate knowledge of an extract and its relationship to the rest of the play from which it is taken.
- Think about characters' goals and motivations and the obstacles they face in trying to achieve those goals.
- Examine the structure of a speech, a scene and an entire play.
- Communicate a personal response about the presentation of different characters and their relationships.

Think about how you have demonstrated each of these skills in the exercises in this unit. Also consider the structure of the other extracts you have examined in this section of the book, and the function of those scenes in the plays from which they are taken.

23 *The Dilemma of a Ghost:* Focus on staging and setting

> In this unit, you will:
> ● Use textual evidence to demonstrate an understanding of the way a play is staged.
> ● Think about the ways in which a play's setting can be used to explore deeper meanings.
> ● Recognise and appreciate the dramatic techniques that dramatists use to convey ideas about characters, relationships and settings.
> ● Present and explain your own ideas about the situations and settings in which characters find themselves.

When you are analysing a script, it is important to think about the impact a live stage performance would have on the audience. The way the stage is arranged and how the characters look on it can provide important visual clues for the audience about what they should think about the characters and their actions.

The Dilemma of a Ghost (1965) is written by the Ghanaian writer Ama Ata Aidoo. It is a problem play, which makes the audience think about the issues that can arise when people from different cultures get married. It tells the story of Ato, a Ghanaian who studied in America, and the woman he married there, Eulalie, a black American woman. Ato and Eulalie move to his home in Ghana where they come into conflict with traditional Ghanaian culture.

The extract is from early in Act One when Ato's grandmother brings the family together to hear news from his journey to America. Just before the extract begins, Ato's mother, Esi (or Maami), has said that she has sold a sheep to help pay the bride-price for when Ato decides to marry.

There are many different characters, all members of Ato's family, on stage at this moment in the play. A list of characters is included here, for reference:

» ATO YAWSON: A young Ghanaian graduate
» ESI KOM [Maami]: Ato's mother
» MONKA: His sister
» NANA: His grandmother
» AKYERE: His elder aunt
» MANSA: His younger aunt
» PETU: His elder uncle
» AKROMA: His younger uncle

Glossary

Dilemma: A situation in which somebody has to make a difficult choice between two (or more) different options, especially when the choices are equally undesirable

Overlapping: When two characters speak at the same time

Dissect: To cut something open to study its structure

Entrails: Intestines and other organs once they are outside the body

Hurere: Monka's first attempt to say Eulalie's name, repeated by the other women

Some of us did not hear the school bell: Some of Ato's relatives did not go to school

Fanti: A subgroup of the Akan ethnic group living in West Africa (also spelled 'Fante')

Contemptuously: In a way that shows a lack of respect for someone or something

23.1 From Act One of *The Dilemma of a Ghost* by Ama Ata Aidoo

ATO:	[Casually] But I am already married, Maami.
ALL:	You are married? Married! Married!
ESI:	[Overlapping] Who is your wife?
AKYERE:	[Overlapping] When did you marry?
MANSA:	Who is your wife?
MONKA:	[Overlapping] What is her name?
ESI:	Where does she come from?

[Everyone repeats her words to create confusion.]

PETU:	You must all be quiet. One must take time to dissect an ant in order to discover its entrails.
MONKA:	[Laughing wickedly] Ei, so I have a sister-in-law whom I do not know?
AKROMA:	Ei, Monka, keep quiet.
NANA:	[Who has been sleeping since she last spoke] What is all this noise about? Have you asked the child news from his journey?

[Silence while everyone stares at ATO]

PETU:	Ato, when did you marry?
ATO:	That is what I was going to tell you. One week ago.
NANA:	[Spitting] My grand-child, so you have married? Why did you never write to tell us?
ESI:	Ato my son, who is your wife?
ATO:	[Quite embarrassed] Eulalie.
ALL:	Eh!
ATO:	I said 'Eulalie'.

[By now all the women are standing.]

MONKA:	Hurere!
ESI:	Petu! Akyere! What does he say?
THE WOMEN:	Hurere!
MONKA:	Oh, let us say, let us say that some of the names that are coming into the world are fearful.
ESI:	Ato, you know that some of us did not hear the school bell when it rang. Therefore we will not be able to say this name. This Uhu-hu… I want her real name, my son.
ATO:	But Maami, this is her only name.
MANSA:	Our master, isn't your wife… eh… Fanti?
ATO:	No, aunt.

5

10

15

20

25

30

35

AKYERE: [Contemptuously] If so, what is her tribe?

ATO: She has no tribe. She does not come from…

NANA: [Looking up at him] She has no tribe? The story you are telling us is too sweet, my grand-child. Since I was born, I have not heard of a human being born out of the womb of a woman who has no tribe. Are there trees which never have any roots?   40

PETU: Ato, where does your wife come from?

[A short silence. All look at ATO.]

ATO: But no one is prepared to listen to me. My wife comes from… America.

ESI: [Putting her hands on her head] Oh Esi! You have an unkind soul. We always hear of other women's sons going to the white man's country. Why should my own go and marry a white woman?   45

MONKA: Amrika! My brother, you have arrived indeed.

AKYERE: But we thought that we too have found a treasure at last for our house. What have you done to us, my son? We do not know the ways of the white people. Will not people laugh at us?   50

ATO: [Very nervously] But who says I have married a white woman? Is everyone in America white? In that country there are white men and black men.

AKROMA: Nephew, you must tell us properly. We do not know.   55

ATO: But you will not listen to me.

[All quiet. Eyes are focused on ATO.]

           I say my wife is as black as we all are.

[Sighs of relaxation.]

ESI: But how is it, my child, that she comes from Amrika and she has this strange name?   60

[The old woman spits significantly.]

NANA: Is that what people call their children in the white man's country?

ATO: [Irritably] It is not the white man's country.

ALL: O… O… Oh!   65

ATO: Please, I beg you all, listen. Eulalie's ancestors were of our ancestors. But [warming up] as you all know, the white people came and took some away in ships to be slaves…

NANA: [Calmly] And so, my grand-child, all you want to tell us is that your wife is a slave?   70

[At this point even the men get up with shock from their seats. All the women break into violent weeping. ESI KOM is beside herself with grief. She walks round in all attitudes of mourning.]

ATO: [Wildly] But she is not a slave. It was her grandfathers and her grandmothers who were slaves.   75

NANA: Ato, do not talk with the foolishness of your generation.

23.2 First impressions
Exercise 1

a The play's settings are shown in these two modern images: the first shows a Ghanaian village and the second an American city. How might the experiences of living in these two places be different? Discuss your ideas as a class.

b What do you imagine it would be like to live in the village in the first image?

c What do you imagine it would be like to live in the city in the second image?

d If someone had grown up in the United States, what challenges might they face if moving to the village?

e Now read the extract from *The Dilemma of a Ghost*. As you read, think again about the additional challenge Eulalie will face when moving from America to the Ghanaian village.

23.3 Finding evidence

Exercise 2

Dramatists often include stage directions within their plays to help the director and actors bring the words in the script to life when the play is performed. These convey lots of different types of information.

a The mind map below shows the wide variety of information that Aidoo's stage directions give the director and the actors about the extract. These are just some examples of the types of information that stage directions can give. Copy the mind map and add quotations from the extract as examples of the different types of stage direction.

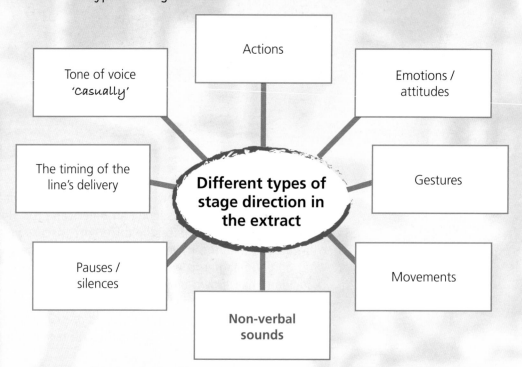

> **Key term**
>
> **Non-verbal sounds:** Sounds other than words that a person makes; for example: laughter, crying, groans or sighs

MAKING CONNECTIONS

In *The Merchant of Venice* (Unit 22) there are very few stage directions, and so it is up to the director to decide what every scene will look and sound like, and how the actors should say the lines. The director's and actors' decisions can make an audience think very differently about the events of the play.

TIP

When writing about a play, think about how stage directions affect meanings – often in dramatic ways that have a powerful effect on the audience. Consider, for example, how stage directions affect the way that words are spoken and how other characters react.

The extract contains a lot of stage directions, which help to develop the audience's understanding of characters, their relationships and the situation Ato has created for himself and his wife by marrying somebody who is not in his tribe.

Answer the following questions with a partner. Use short quotations from the stage directions and the characters' speech to support your answers.

b How does Ato reveal the news that he is married? What does this tell us about his character? (Think about the strength of his family's reaction to his news.)

c How does Ato's family react to the news that he is already married? What do you think this tells us about them as a family?

d The stage directions suggest that one of the family's questions is particularly important to them. Which question is this and how do the stage directions suggest its importance? Why do you think the question might be so important to the family?

e What do the stage directions reveal about the character of Monka? What do you think might be the reason for her reaction?

f What is Nana doing when Ato reveals the news that he is married? What do you think this will tell the audience about Nana?

g How does Nana react when she learns that Ato has married? What does this show us about her feelings? Look carefully at the character's speech and the stage directions too.

h How does Ato feel about revealing his wife's name? Why do you think he might feel this way?

i Look at the way that Mansa questions Ato about his wife's tribe. What does this suggest about her attitude?

j Look at the way that Akyere reacts when she learns that Ato's wife is not Fanti. What does this reveal about her attitude?

MAKING CONNECTIONS

Compare Aidoo's use of overlapping with the way Churchill's *Top Girls* features overlapping and a technique where the character replies to a character who wasn't the last one to speak. What impression does Aidoo create about the unity of the family? How does this compare with the unity of the characters at Marlene's dinner party?

Exercise 3

Within any text, there are quotations that are particularly significant because they are relevant to important themes and ideas within the text. An important idea that an audience might infer from *The Dilemma of a Ghost* is that the legacy of slavery still – like a ghost – haunts people of African heritage on both sides of the Atlantic. With a partner, look again at a key moment from the extract (below) and then discuss the questions; the final question focuses on how stage directions can help make a moment in a script dramatically powerful.

> NANA: [Looking up at Ato] She has no tribe? The story you are telling us is too sweet, my grand-child. Since I was born, I have not heard of a human being born out of the womb of a woman who has no tribe. Are there trees which never have any roots?
>
> PETU: Ato, where does your wife come from?
> [A short silence. All look at ATO.]

a What do you think Nana means when she calls Ato's story 'sweet'?
b What metaphor does Nana use? What comparison is she making? What is she suggesting about the importance of belonging to a tribe?
c Why does Eulalie not have 'roots' in the way that Nana expects?
d Why is Petu's question so poignant? ('Poignant' means causing a sharp feeling of sadness.)
e How do the two stage directions combine to create a powerful dramatic effect on this moment? Think about what the characters are doing (and not doing) and how this will make Ato feel.

Exercise 4

The stage directions below are found at the start of the play.

> [The action takes place in the courtyard of the newest wing of the Odumna Clan house. It is enclosed on the right by a wall of the old building and both at the centre and on the left by the walls of the new wing. At the right-hand corner a door links the courtyard with a passage that leads into the much bigger courtyard of the old house. In the middle of the left wall there is a door leading into the new rooms. A terrace runs round the two sides of the new sector. In the foreground is the path which links the roads leading to the river, the farm and the market.]

Later, Aidoo specifies the terrace as the location where the characters sit and talk during the events in the extract.

a With a partner, carefully read these stage directions about the setting. Discuss what they reveal about the following:
  – The family's wealth
  – The family's lifestyle
  – The family's status within the community
  – The ways of life that are traditional in the village

b You have thought about what this information about setting tells us about the family's status. Now, consider the character of Eulalie. With a partner, discuss how her arrival might be seen as a threat to the family's status and create conflict.

Act Two is the first time the audience see Eulalie, following a scene where two women were coming home from collecting firewood. This is how she is described by Aidoo:

> [Late afternoon of the next day. Everywhere is quiet. ATO is asleep in the inner room. EULALIE comes in with a packet of cigarettes, a lighter, an ash tray and a bottle of Coca-Cola. She sits on the terrace facing the audience.
>
> She begins sipping the Coca-Cola and soon the voice of her mind comes across the courtyard. Later her mother's voice is also heard. As the voices speak on, her body relaxes except for her mouth which breaks into a light smile or draws up tightly; and her eyes, which stare in front of her or dart left and right generally expressing the emotions that her thoughts arose in her.] [On the other hand the passage could be spoken as a soliloquy with the mother's voice interrupting from back stage.]

c Look at the visual clues in the stage directions and imagine how Eulalie appears in the set. With a partner, discuss whether Eulalie fits in or stands out against the set. Also, do you think she will fit in with the women of the village?
Think about:
   i   what she is doing
   ii the props she is holding
   iii how the timing of her entrance in the play, here in Act Two, might cause conflict in the story.

MAKING CONNECTIONS

Dramatists create strong impressions of their characters through the way that they are introduced. Eulalie is introduced in a way that clearly shows she does not fit well into the play's Ghanaian setting. In contrast, when Shaw introduces Eliza in Act One of *Pygmalion* (before the action of the extract in Unit 21), she fits so well into the setting of Covent Garden as a flower girl that she is knocked over by Freddy, who hasn't even seen her!

---

d Look at the stage directions, which relate to the sounds that the audience will hear. What different effects would be created if the actor spoke the words herself compared with the audience just hearing her voice? How do these stage directions affect the audience's understanding of the character's state of mind?
e The dramatist has not provided a description of Eulalie's costume. If you were a costume designer, how would you dress Eulalie to show the audience how she fits in (or doesn't) with the set and the other characters?
Draw a diagram of Eulalie's outfit to show the director of the play. Label it with reasons for each of your choices.

Exercise 5

Staging is the process of designing the performance space in which a play takes place, taking into account the set (the scenery and props), the lighting and the costumes. A director will consider the stage directions and a play's themes when making staging decisions.

Key term

Symbolism: The use of an idea, image or object to represent abstract ideas or qualities

For example, the stage directions for *The Dilemma of a Ghost* mention a path, and it is important that this path is a part of the scenery because of its **symbolism**. In Act Three, two children sing a song Ato used to sing about a ghost on the path not knowing whether to go left or right; either direction would have been bad because both Elmina and Cape Coast had forts from which slaves were transported to the New World. (This ghost's dilemma gives the play its title.) The path also represents the journey that Ato and Eulalie have taken, and furthermore it represents the ongoing traditional ways of life in the village as it connects the river, the farm and the market. Therefore, the path relates to several of the themes in the play:

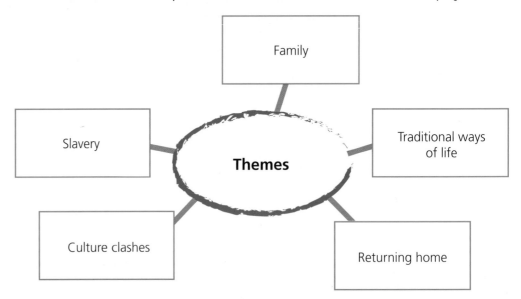

a Imagine that you are a director thinking about the staging of a performance of the extract in a theatre. What scenery; props; lighting and sound effects; and costumes would you need? Think about the themes of the play as you do this. Discuss your choices with a partner.

b Individually, draw the scene as you imagine it being staged within a theatre. Label the scene to explain the choices that you have made. Compare your drawing with your partner's or a different partner's.

23.4 Writing practice

Exercise 6

Now that you have looked at the extract in detail, look at this essay question:

Explore the ways in which Aidoo stages conflict in this passage.

a Copy out the question and highlight the key words.

b Write a brief plan of how you would answer the question using a mind map or a bullet point list – not sentences. Which quotations in the extract will be the most useful in answering this question? Pay close attention to the key words you have highlighted and make sure you address them. Check that you have included relevant quotations and ideas from the work you have already done.

c Share your plan with a partner. Have you both selected similar quotations? Are there any useful quotations or ideas that might improve your own answer?

d Part of a student's response has been reproduced below. Read it and check the following success criteria:
  i Does the student have a detailed knowledge of the text?
  ii Does the student explore the text beyond its surface meaning?
  iii Is there an understanding of how the dramatist's choices have created dramatic effects?
  iv Is there a sense that the student is responding in a personal way to the question and to the task?

Student response

Aidoo stages conflict in the extract through the way that the characters interact. The stage directions instruct Ato to reveal his marriage 'casually'. However, Aidoo shows that the family reacts in an opposite way; they become very excited and all speak at once 'overlapping' and bombarding Ato with questions. The effect is comic, especially as his sister is shown 'laughing wickedly'. She is clearly delighted by the way he has broken conventions through his secrecy.

Aidoo shows us that Ato is in conflict with family and tribal conventions, represented on stage by the comic figure of Nana.

---

e Now write your response to the essay question.
f Swap your work with a partner. Give each other feedback using the success criteria in part **d**.

23.5 Set-text focus
Exercise 7

The Ghanaian setting of *The Dilemma of a Ghost* is central to the play. Eulalie has grown up in America, and moving to such a culturally different place proves to be very hard for her.

With a partner, consider the following questions in relation to one of your drama set texts.
a What are the main themes and ideas in your drama text? Make a mind map or list. Share your ideas with the class to ensure that you have remembered them all.
b What is the main setting of your drama text?
c Are there any other settings? Are any other places mentioned?
d How do the setting of the play and places mentioned help the dramatist present the themes and ideas that are explored in the play? The table over the page shows how *The Dilemma of a Ghost*'s settings relate to the central themes and ideas within that play. Create a similar table to explore the relationship between settings and themes and ideas within your drama set text.

Setting / place in the play	Key quotation(s) about the setting / place	Deeper meanings
Ghanaian village	In the foreground is the path which links the roads leading to the river, the farm and the market.	In addition to suggesting traditional ways of life, the path might evoke an image of enslaved Africans in the past on their way towards the New World. It might also suggest Ato's journey to and from the United States and Eulalie's journey from there.
New York	'Eulalie: My dear, did you see a single snail crawling on the streets of New York all the time you were in the States? And anyway, seeing snails and eating them are entirely different things!'	Eulalie is disgusted by the snails that her mother-in-law has given her to cook, which she cannot see as food, and throws this gift away. Again, this shows how it is hard for her to adapt to the place that was home for her ancestors.

You may find that once you have completed this table, it adds to your understanding of the characters in your set text, too. Go back to the work you did on your play's characters in Unit 20 and think about whether the new evidence you have found about how they act in different settings adds to your understanding of them. Do they act differently in different settings?

Exercise 8

a Look back to the essay question in Exercise 6. Adapt the question to your drama set text.

b Work with a partner to plan an answer to the question. Make notes about your ideas using bullet points or a mind map.

c Write an answer to the question, spending no more than 20 minutes.

d Swap your answer with a partner for marking. How well does it meet the success criteria in Exercise 6?

TIP

Include comments about the dramatic effect of stage directions in an answer to an essay question where possible. This helps to show that you understand that the form of the text is drama and that the text has been written to be performed live on a stage in front of an audience.

Take your learning further

1   If you can, watch on YouTube the interview about the play between Michael Walling, a director, and Ama Ata Aidoo and answer the questions below:
    a   How did Aidoo devise the idea for the play?
    b   Why did she choose to focus on the relationship between a Ghanaian man and an African American woman?
    c   How is her work unusual among that of African writers?
    d   Why is it important for people to engage with the issue of slavery?
2   Imagine the director of a performance is interviewing the dramatist who wrote one of your set texts to ask about the stage directions in the play. Role-play this in a hot-seating activity. The student playing the part of the director should choose particular stage directions to ask about. The student playing the part of the dramatist should explain what effect was intended for that stage direction.
3   If possible, find a video or film production of your drama set text. Look closely at the sets that are used. Make notes on what you see. How does the set relate to the themes and ideas in the play?

Unit summary

In this unit, you have learned how to:
●   Use textual evidence to demonstrate an understanding of the way a play is staged.
●   Think about the ways in which a play's setting can be used to explore deeper meanings.
●   Recognise and appreciate the dramatic techniques that dramatists use to convey ideas about characters, relationships and settings.
●   Present and explain your own ideas about the situations and settings in which characters find themselves.

Think about how you have demonstrated each of these skills in the exercises in this unit. The skills and knowledge you have developed in this unit will be helpful when studying the dramatic texts in the other units in this section. How can you apply the skills you have developed in the other drama units to the extract from *The Dilemma of a Ghost*?

The Post Office: Focus on developing a personal response

In this unit, you will:
- Identify quotations to help you explain your personal reaction to a play.
- Think about the deeper meanings of a play and the themes and ideas it explores.
- Examine a dramatist's use of language and discuss how it is used to present characters and ideas.
- Use the skills you have gained in the previous units to develop a sensitive and informed personal response to an extract from a play.

We have seen how dramatists use different tools to have certain effects on their audiences. Now that you have studied the various components of dramatic texts, you should be able to use your knowledge to support your personal opinions about a play and explain the effects that it has on you as a reader or as a member of the audience. This unit will help you to gain confidence in expressing those views.

The Post Office is a play by Rabindranath Tagore (1861 to 1941), the 'Bard of Bengal', who was awarded the Nobel Prize in Literature in 1913 in recognition of his poetry. He was the first non-European to receive this award.

This extract is from very near the start of the play. The audience has learned that Amal is an orphaned boy who has just been adopted by a man named Madhav. Amal is sick, and his doctor has advised that he must be kept inside, away from the autumn wind and sun. Madhav realises that there 'isn't much hope for his life'.

MAKING CONNECTIONS

A 'bard' was a professional poet in Celtic cultures. William Shakespeare (whose play *The Merchant of Venice* features in Unit 22) is often referred to as 'The Bard' in England to reflect his status as a dramatist and poet within that culture.

Glossary

Quirn: A device that uses a pair of heavy circular stones to grind seeds; it is usually spelt 'quern'

Wee: Little

Learned people: People with a lot of knowledge who have studied for a long time

Toil and moil: Work hard

24.1 From Act One of *The Post Office* by Rabindranath Tagore

[AMAL enters]

AMAL: Uncle, I say, Uncle!

MADHAV: Hullo! Is that you, Amal?

AMAL: Mayn't I be out of the courtyard at all?

MADHAV: No, my dear, no.   5

AMAL: See, there where Auntie grinds lentils in the quirn, the squirrel is sitting with his tail up and with his wee hands he's picking up the broken grains of lentils and crunching them. Can't I run up there?

MADHAV: No, my darling, no.   10

AMAL: Wish I were a squirrel! it would be lovely. Uncle, why won't you let me go about?

MADHAV: Doctor says it's bad for you to be out.

AMAL: How can the doctor know?

MADHAV: What a thing to say! The doctor can't know and he reads such huge books!   15

AMAL: Does his book-learning tell him everything?

MADHAV: Of course, don't you know!

AMAL: [With a sigh] Ah, I am so stupid! I don't read books.

MADHAV: Now, think of it; very, very learned people are all like you; they are never out of doors.   20

AMAL: Aren't they really?

MADHAV: No, how can they? Early and late they toil and moil at their books, and they've eyes for nothing else. Now, my little man, you are going to be learned when you grow up; and   25
          then you will stay at home and read such big books, and people will notice you and say, "he's a wonder."

AMAL:	No, no, Uncle; I beg of you by your dear feet I don't want to be learned, I won't.	
MADHAV:	Dear, dear; it would have been my saving if I could have been learned.	30
AMAL:	No, I would rather go about and see everything that there is.	
MADHAV:	Listen to that! See! What will you see, what is there so much to see?	
AMAL:	See that far-away hill from our window – I often long to go beyond those hills and right away.	35
MADHAV:	Oh, you silly! As if there's nothing more to be done but just get up to the top of that hill and away! Eh! You don't talk sense, my boy. Now listen, since that hill stands there upright as a barrier, it means you can't get beyond it. Else, what was the use in heaping up so many large stones to make such a big affair of it, eh!	40
AMAL:	Uncle, do you think it is meant to prevent your crossing over? It seems to me because the earth can't speak it raises its hands into the sky and beckons. And those who live far and sit alone by their windows can see the signal. But I suppose the learned people –	45
MADHAV:	No, they don't have time for that sort of nonsense. They are not crazy like you.	
AMAL:	Do you know, yesterday I met someone quite as crazy as I am.	50
MADHAV:	Gracious me, really, how so?	
AMAL:	He had a bamboo staff on his shoulder with a small bundle at the top, and a brass pot in his left hand, and an old pair of shoes on; he was making for those hills straight across that meadow there. I called out to him and asked, "Where are you going?" He answered, "I don't know, anywhere!" I asked again, "Why are you going?" He said, "I'm going out to seek work." Say, Uncle, have you to seek work?	55
MADHAV:	Of course I have to. There's many about looking for jobs.	
AMAL:	How lovely! I'll go about, like them too, finding things to do.	60
MADHAV:	Suppose you seek and don't find. Then –	
AMAL:	Wouldn't that be jolly? Then I should go farther! I watched that man slowly walking on with his pair of worn out shoes. And when he got to where the water flows under the fig tree, he stopped and washed his feet in the stream. Then he took out from his bundle some gram-flour, moistened it with water and began to eat. Then he tied up his bundle and shouldered it again; tucked up his cloth above his knees and crossed the stream. I've asked Auntie to let me go up to the stream, and eat my gram-flour just like him.	65
		70

MADHAV: And what did your Auntie say to that?

AMAL: Auntie said, "Get well and then I'll take you over there." Please, Uncle, when shall I get well?

MADHAV: It won't be long, dear.

AMAL: Really, but then I shall go right away the moment I'm well again. 75

MADHAV: And where will you go?

AMAL: Oh, I will walk on, crossing so many streams, wading through water. Everybody will be asleep with their doors shut in the heat of the day and I will tramp on and on seeking work far, very far. 80

MADHAV: I see! I think you had better be getting well first; then –

AMAL: But then you won't want me to be learned, will you, Uncle?

MADHAV: What would you rather be then?

AMAL: I can't think of anything just now; but I'll tell you later on. 85

MADHAV: Very well. But mind you, you aren't to call out and talk to strangers again.

AMAL: But I love to talk to strangers!

MADHAV: Suppose they had kidnapped you?

AMAL: That would have been splendid! But no one ever takes me away. They all want me to stay in here. 90

MADHAV: I am off to my work but, darling, you won't go out, will you?

AMAL: No, I won't. But, Uncle, you'll let me be in this room by the roadside.

[Exit MADHAV] 95

24.2 First impressions

Exercise 1

Read the extract as a class.

With a partner, discuss the reactions below, which were given by other students who had just read the extract. How far do you agree with their ideas?

> Amal's way of talking is convincingly childlike.

> Both characters are likeable, particularly Amal.

> The play seems to be a simple story but there seem to be some deeper ideas behind it.

> The opening of the play really gets the audience's attention.

> A performance on the stage would add a great deal to the meanings we see on the page.

Perhaps you have strong reactions to the extract yourself. The focus of this unit is to encourage you to support such opinions with evidence taken from the text.

24.3 Finding evidence

Exercise 2

a The first student made the comment that 'Amal's way of talking is convincingly childlike'. The student would need to support this thoughtful idea using quotations from the play. Some suitable quotations for this are listed in the table opposite. How do these quotations help to support the student's comment? Discuss the quotations with a partner, then copy the table and work individually to complete it – use the example to help you. Refer to any specific language techniques that help to achieve the effect of childishness in Amal's characterisation.

> **TIP**
>
> As you read the words in the script, remember to imagine the words being spoken by an actor on the stage. Think about how they would sound and the actions that might accompany them. This will help to bring the characters to life and make it easier to comment on the effect of the language in the quotations.

Quotation	Effect
'Uncle, I say, Uncle!'	As soon as the audience meets Amal, he appears to be energetic and excitable thanks to his repetition of 'Uncle' and the exclamative sentence type.
'the squirrel is sitting with his tail up and with his wee hands…'	
'Does his book-learning tell him everything?'	
'I beg of you by your dear feet I don't want to be learned, I won't.'	
'MADHAV: Suppose you seek and don't find. Then – AMAL: Wouldn't that be jolly? Then I should go farther!'	
'Please, Uncle, when shall I get well?'	
'MADHAV: Suppose they had kidnapped you? AMAL: That would have been splendid!'	

Key term

Pathos: A feeling of sadness or pity created by a writer through their use of language or other devices

TIP

When you comment on the quotation 'Please, Uncle, when shall I get well?', mention the effect of **pathos** that is created.

b Write a paragraph discussing how Tagore's language choices support his characterisation of Amal. Begin your paragraph as follows:

Tagore's language choices help to present Amal convincingly as a child…

Exercise 3

The second student made the comment that 'Both characters are likeable, particularly Amal.' We have seen that Amal is a convincingly childlike character and this helps to make him likeable. What about Madhav? How might the audience respond to him? This exercise will help you to develop the student's personal response into a sensitive and informed one.

a With a partner, look at the extract to identify quotations that you feel show the aspects of Madhav's character that might be considered positive and those that might be seen as less positive. Make a table like the one below to list your ideas.

Positive / negative aspects	Quotation
Madhav is protective of Amal and affectionate in the way that he talks to him.	'No, my dear, no.'

b Overall, what is *your* opinion of Madhav? Is he presented as a likeable character? Why or why not? Can you present your views to a partner, or the class, by talking for one minute without stopping?

c Choose a small section of the extract that you think best reveals the character of Amal and / or Madhav. Discuss the section with a partner. How could the section be performed so that the characterisation is as clear as possible? Think about how the words on the page could be given greater dramatic power through the actors' choices about voice, movement, body language, gesture and facial expressions. Perform the section to another pair of students.

d You have previously thought about conflict and how it is important for creating dramatic tension within literary texts. Look at the tables you have made about the personalities of Amal and Madhav. What conflict do you notice between their **viewpoints**? Do they value the same things? Discuss your ideas with a partner and then with the class.

> **Key term**
>
> **Viewpoint:** The thoughts and feelings that a character has towards a situation

---

MAKING CONNECTIONS

The conflict between Amal and Madhav is an external conflict. Compare this to the internal conflict that seems to exist in Marlene's mind in *Top Girls*. Marlene has invited to her dinner party women who have apparently been successful, but there is a dark side to their success, just as there is to Marlene's. The audience might interpret this as showing that Marlene is trying to come to terms with what she has had to sacrifice to succeed in a patriarchal society.

---

e Write a paragraph discussing the two sides of Madhav's character. Begin your paragraph as follows:

The audience will think of Madhav as a likeable character but his outlook on the world is very different from Amal's. He is likeable in that...

Exercise 4

Many people see Tagore's play as **allegorical**, with the simple story representing ideas that are far deeper. The third student commented: 'The play seems to be a simple story but there seem to be some deeper ideas behind it.' The student will need to develop a sensitive and informed response from this initial impression.

Some of the themes and ideas that are present in the play are listed below:

» The importance of lived experience versus book-learning
» Confinement and freedom
» The natural world
» Imagination
» Optimism and pessimism.

> **Key term**
>
> **Allegorical:** Having a hidden meaning, because the characters and events represent particular qualities, ideas or real-life historical events

a Look at the list below of quotations taken from the play. Work with a partner to discuss each one. Which theme / idea or themes / ideas do they seem to relate to? Take turns to lead the discussion. Make a note of your answers so that you can compare them with other students' answers later on.

i   AMAL: Mayn't I be out of the courtyard at all?

ii   MADHAV: No, my dear, no.

iii   the squirrel is sitting with his tail up

iv   very, very learned people are all like you; they are never out of doors

v   Early and late they toil and moil at their books, and they've eyes for nothing else.

vi   MADHAV: Dear, dear; it would have been my saving if I could have been learned.

vii   I would rather go about and see everything that there is

viii   It seems to me because the earth can't speak it raises its hands into the sky and beckons

ix   MADHAV: Suppose you seek and don't find. Then –

x   AMAL: Wouldn't that be jolly? Then I should go farther!

xi   I will walk on, crossing so many streams

b Write a paragraph that explores the central theme of book-learning versus lived experience. Begin your paragraph as follows:

Tagore engages the audience's interest through the opposite viewpoints of Madhav and Amal regarding book-learning and lived experience. Madhav admires 'learned people'...

Exercise 5

The fourth student commented that 'The opening of the play really gets the audience's attention' and the fifth student remarked that 'A performance on the stage would add a great deal to the meanings we see on the page'.

You will notice that there are very few stage directions in this extract, nor are there many in the rest of the play, so it is up to the director and the actors to work out how best to convey the meanings that they have found in the text. This is especially important at the beginning of the play where the plot, the characters and the themes are starting to be developed.

a Think about how you could reveal information about the two characters through choices regarding voice, movement, body language, gesture and facial expressions. Work with a partner to annotate a copy of the extract with appropriate stage directions. Keep the themes of the play in mind as you do this.

b Imagine you are a set designer, considering what scenery, stage furniture and props would suit a performance of the play and help to communicate the themes and ideas in the play. Discuss your ideas for the set with a partner and then write a report for the director that includes textual references. You might also like to draw the set, annotating the choices that you have made. Present your report to the class.

TIP

This exercise encourages you to think about staging and performance choices because imagining how the words on the page are actually performed can help you to understand drama texts.

24.4 Writing practice

Exercise 6

a In this exercise you will think deeply about how Tagore has made the extract so powerfully dramatic. Write each of the following headings onto sheets of paper:
  - Language
  - Setting
  - Events
  - Characters
  - Themes and ideas
  - Structure

b Work with a partner to find a suitable quotation to write under each heading. Choose quotations about which you have interesting ideas.

c Continue to work with your partner. Discuss different interpretations that can be made and additional layers of meaning that can be found, focusing on the idea of creating a sensitive and informed response. Record your best ideas, as shown by the example below for the heading 'Language':

Language

'the squirrel is sitting with his tail up and with his wee hands he's picking up the broken grains of lentils and crunching them'

- *Vivid imagery: What he sees is described in great detail; he imagines the sound too – he surely can't hear this! The audience will understand how imaginative Amal is and his desire to experience all the world has to offer.*
- *Adjectives: 'wee', 'broken' = appreciation of the smallest things. He loves nature... rather than books.*
- *Juxtaposition: Image of Auntie working hard / squirrel enjoying its freedom = symbolises Amal's love of nature and desire to be free.*

d Once you have made the fullest possible notes for each quotation, share your ideas with another pair of students, inviting them to suggest their own ideas where they can. Add these suggestions to your notes as you go.

e Work with your own partner to decide which ideas would create the most sensitive and informed responses. Individually, draft a paragraph on each quotation where you expand your notes into an extended comment on how the quotation is powerfully dramatic.

f Share your best paragraph with the class, who will listen to you carefully to suggest possible improvements. Make a note of these suggestions.

24.5 Set-text focus

Exercise 7

a Look back to the opening of your drama set text to find an extract that is about two pages long; perhaps an extract that presents a conflict, as you have seen in the extract from *The Post Office*.

The following exercises will prepare you to write a sensitive and informed personal response to an essay question based on your extract:

Explore the ways in which the dramatist makes your chosen extract such a powerfully dramatic moment.

b Working with a small group, make a mind map on a large sheet of paper. The mind map should look like the example below.

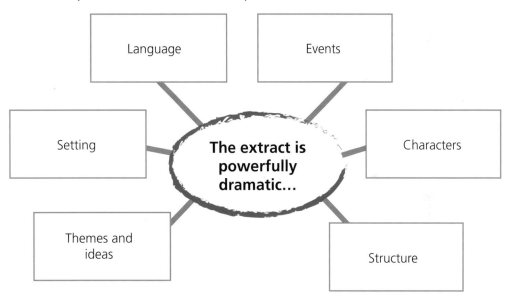

c Work with your group to select quotations from the extract for each topic. Choose quotations that will have a powerfully dramatic effect on the audience. Add the quotations to the mind map, together with notes about why each quotation is important. Look at Exercise 6 for an example quotation with notes, but remember you are working on your own drama set text now, not *The Post Office*.

d Finally, write your own answer to the essay question. Take no more than 40 minutes to do this. Concentrate on developing your personal response in a detailed, sensitive and informed way.

Take your learning further

1   *The Post Office* is only two acts long. Read it. Do you think the play is simply the story of a sick child who longs for freedom, or is the story allegorical, with a deeper spiritual meaning? If the latter, what meaning do *you* take from the play?

2   Create a poster of the quotations that seem to *you* to be the most powerful within your drama set texts. Put the poster in a place where you will see it often. As time passes, notice any additional layers of meaning that occur to you, and consider how that meaning could be conveyed on the stage.

Unit summary

In this unit, you have learned how to:
● Identify quotations to help you explain your personal reaction to a play.
● Think about the deeper meanings of a play and the themes and ideas it explores.
● Examine a dramatist's use of language and discuss how it is used to present characters and ideas.
● Use the skills you have gained in the previous units to develop a sensitive and informed personal response to an extract from a play.

Think about how you have demonstrated each of these skills in the exercises in this unit. Now that we have reached the end of the Drama section, be sure to look back to the plays you have studied and think about how the different skills you have developed can be combined to create a sensitive and informed personal response to each.

WRITING SKILLS

Writing an essay

In this unit, you will:
- Think about the different stages of planning and writing an essay: reading and understanding the question; identifying relevant information to include; writing an essay plan; writing your essay; and checking your essay.
- Assess the merits of passages taken from sample essay responses.
- Devise your own essay questions and plan and write a response to one of them.

Important notice: Please refer to Unit 1 'Making the most of your course' to understand which of the different types of essay you will need to write: essays about unseen texts; passage-based questions; general essay questions; coursework essays.

The text used in this unit is *Macbeth* by William Shakespeare, and the focus will be on Lady Macbeth, the wife of the **protagonist**, Macbeth. Lady Macbeth encourages Macbeth to kill the man on the throne, King Duncan, believing that this will lead to Macbeth being crowned king.

> **Key term**
>
> **Protagonist:** A main character in a literary text

Introduction to essay writing

When you write a Literature in English essay, you should aim to show the following skills:

» A **flair** for selecting and using suitable quotations that show your knowledge of the text
» Analysis that is **individual** and **insightful**
» A **sensitive** and **detailed** understanding of how the writer achieves effects for the reader or audience
» A **personal** and **evaluative** engagement with the task and the text.

The exercises in this unit will build on the work that you have done previously in the 'Writing practice' exercises throughout this book so that you can write a successful essay. They offer you an opportunity to test your skills and will help to get you ready for writing an essay, whether the question is extract based or a general question. The focus of this unit is mainly on the general questions, as the previous units have already given you a great deal of practice on extract-based questions.

Exercise 1

a What are the steps involved in writing an essay? Talk to a partner about this question. Think about the steps to follow before writing, during writing and after writing.

b Look at the list of steps below. Which steps are already strengths for you? Which do you find more challenging? Share your ideas with a partner.

1	Read and understand the question.
2	Identify relevant information to include.
3	Create an essay plan: • Include textual references and comments. • Decide on the best order for your ideas.
4	Write your essay: communicate clearly.
5	Reflect on and improve your essay.

The remainder of this unit explores each of these steps in turn, and contains advice and exercises designed to help you think about how to approach them.

Step 1: Read and understand the question

The first step of writing an essay is to read the question to work out what you need to write about. Take your time doing this because the success of your essay depends on this step. To make sure that you get this step right, underline the key words that you see in the question (as you have done in exercises in previous units).

Exercise 2

Look at the question below. Copy it and underline the key words that you find. Key words tell you what and / or who you need to write about, and where in the work you should focus your attention. A general question such as this one will not specify a particular part of the text because you are considering the whole work.

> **Does Shakespeare's writing make it possible for you to feel any sympathy for Lady Macbeth?**

General essay questions often begin with phrases such as the following:
» In what ways does [the writer]…
» How far does [the writer's] writing convince you that…
» To what extent do you think that [the writer]…
» Does [the writer's] writing make it possible for you to…
» Explore the ways in which [the writer]…

▲ A painting of famous Shakespearean actor Ellen Terry as Lady Macbeth

The questions then focus on the **literary aspects** that you have studied throughout this book. Note how each of the sentence starters in the questions above focus on what the writer has done. This is a clear reminder that you need to focus on the **choices** made by the writer in terms of **language**, **structure** and **form** when you respond to the question.

Key terms

Literary aspect: An essential element within a text: the structure, the language, the themes and ideas, the character and perspective, the setting and the mood

Language choices: The specific words that a writer chooses to use to convey particular ideas

Structure: The sequence of ideas in a text and how it is put together

Form: The text type a writer chooses to communicate in; the three main forms in English literature are poetry, prose and drama – within those main forms are other forms; for example, a sonnet is a poetic form and a short story is a prose form

Exercise 3

Use the sentence starters listed on the previous page to devise some general essay questions of your own. Check them with your teacher once you have finished.

Key term

Theme: A key idea or subject that is repeated throughout a text

> **TIP**
>
> Sometimes an essay question will have a similar – but not identical – focus to one you have answered previously, or be on a similar **theme** to something you have discussed in class. Do not be tempted to use the exact same ideas as you did on the previous occasion! Follow the steps in this unit so that your answer is fully relevant to the question.

Step 2: Identify relevant information to include

Once you have read and understood the question, you can think about which parts of the text you will refer to in the essay. You will need to be selective with this. You cannot include every possible point: you need to choose the most relevant ones. How you collect information depends on the type of question.

When you are responding to an unseen text, read it very carefully to ensure that you understand it properly – look at any definitions that have been provided for particularly difficult words. Carefully study the question and the bullet points that follow it and highlight key words. Next, reread the text, highlighting and annotating evidence that is relevant to the question. Be selective in your choices: ask yourself which pieces of evidence are most relevant. You can then plan your response (Step 3).

PASSAGE-BASED QUESTIONS

If the question refers to a passage, you will need to read the passage and then reread it, underlining or highlighting quotations that are relevant to the question. Annotate the highlighted quotations with very brief notes related to the question. You can expand your ideas in the plan you make later (Step 3), ready for their full expression in the essay itself.

GENERAL ESSAY QUESTIONS

Key terms

Indirect reference: Using some of the same words as the writer but in a different form; quotation marks are not required for an indirect reference

Setting: The time, place and culture in which a text takes place

When you are writing an answer to a general question (without a passage to look at), you will need to recall quotations from memory. If you cannot quite remember the quotation, you will need to recall the key words from it so that you can give an **indirect reference**.

It is worth reviewing the methods you can use to develop a knowledge of the whole text so that you are ready for questions of this type. By this stage in your Literature in English course, you should have a set of notes covering the characters, themes and **settings**. You might have recorded your notes in a variety of ways, including posters, lists, drawings, tables and mind maps. Do make sure that you have covered the whole of the text. Having a comprehensive knowledge of the whole text will benefit you when answering general questions, but it will enhance your answers to extract-based questions too, as you might need to refer to other parts of the text in these questions.

Exercise 4

Check that your notes are complete (as described above). If necessary, create further notes consisting of quotations, together with brief comments on the writer's use of language.

Exercise 5

a Write key quotations concerning character, theme and settings onto small sheets of paper or flash cards. Do this for each of your set texts. Write the most important key word from the quotation on the opposite side as a prompt. Use the prompt to test yourself on your recall of the quotations. As you do this, put the cards into piles: quotations that you know well and quotations that you struggle with.

Test yourself at regular intervals on the key quotations until you have memorised all of them. Concentrate on the quotations that you struggle with, but test yourself occasionally with the more familiar ones too so that you do not forget them.

> **TIP**
>
> Rather than a key word, you might prefer to draw an illustration on the opposite side of the flash card. This might help you to remember the quotation better and increase your enjoyment too. You might also include notes on the flash card to remind you of how the quotation is significant.

flower	*'Look like th' innocent flower,* *But be the serpent under 't.'*

b Play a game with a partner where you are shown the prompt on your flash card and recall the quotation as quickly as possible. Your objective is to recall as many quotations as possible in, say, two minutes. Award yourself a point for each quotation that you remember. As you become ever more proficient, you can adjust the difficulty of the game by penalising inaccuracies or hesitations. You might also comment on the significance of the quotation.

Step 3: Create an essay plan

If you were to begin writing immediately after you had read and understood the question, you would most likely encounter a problem: your essay would drift from one point to another and from one textual reference to another without a clear sense of direction.

The solution is to make an essay plan before you write. This need not be complicated, and it can take different forms. Some students use bulleted lists and some students use mind maps.

In the example that follows, note how the student has included textual references and brief comments recalled from study and revision notes. To save time, the student has not written out the whole textual reference in their plan but there is enough to prompt them when they write the essay. Also, note how the student has numbered the ideas in the plan to indicate the order in which they plan to include them in their essay.

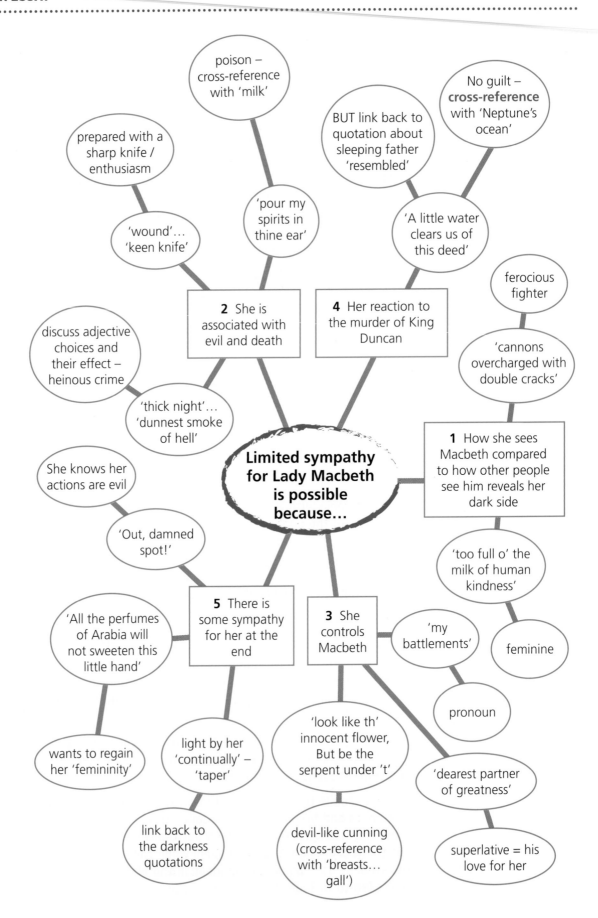

poison –
cross-reference
with 'milk'

prepared with a
sharp knife /
enthusiasm

BUT link back to
quotation about
sleeping father
'resembled'

No guilt –
cross-reference
with 'Neptune's
ocean'

'wound'…
'keen knife'

'pour my
spirits in
thine ear'

'A little water
clears us of
this deed'

ferocious
fighter

discuss adjective
choices and
their effect –
heinous crime

2 She is
associated with
evil and death

4 Her reaction to
the murder of King
Duncan

'cannons
overcharged with
double cracks'

'thick night'…
'dunnest smoke
of hell'

**Limited sympathy
for Lady Macbeth
is possible
because…**

1 How she sees
Macbeth compared
to how other people
see him reveals her
dark side

She knows her
actions are evil

'Out, damned
spot!'

'too full o' the
milk of human
kindness'

'All the perfumes
of Arabia will
not sweeten this
little hand'

5 There is
some sympathy
for her at the
end

3 She
controls
Macbeth

'my
battlements'

feminine

wants to regain
her 'femininity'

light by her
'continually' –
'taper'

'look like th'
innocent flower,
But be the
serpent under 't'

pronoun

'dearest partner
of greatness'

link back to
the darkness
quotations

devil-like cunning
(cross-reference
with 'breasts…
gall')

superlative = his
love for her

Key term

Cross-referencing: Referring to another text or another part of the same text to draw attention to a similarity or difference

TIP

If you cannot recall a full quotation when you are planning your essay, note its key words instead.

Planning using a mind map can make it easier to add further ideas before the writing starts and help you to see the connections between ideas. On the other hand, a bulleted list can encourage a very focused approach. Try different approaches and decide which works best for you. Whichever you use, ensure that you do not spend too much time on planning. The plan must be brief.

TIP

When you are answering an extract-based question, you will focus on the given extract, but you might refer briefly to the rest of the text where necessary to clarify a point, especially if the task asks you to consider how something in the extract is 'significant', or if you are discussing ideas such as **irony**. For general questions, you need to show a detailed overall knowledge of the text, so make sure that you have memorised key quotations and put them on your plan ready to include in your essay.

Key term

Irony: The use of words that are the opposite of what you mean; a situation or an event that seems deliberately opposite from what people would expect

Exercise 6

a Now that you have seen an example of an essay plan, write your own plan to answer one of the questions that you devised in Exercise 3. Give yourself about five minutes to do this.

b Compare your plan with a partner's. Can you read what you have written? Your planning needs to be quick but not rushed! Are the planned points relevant to the question? Have the points been numbered to put them in their best order? Are there textual references and brief comments about their effect? Is there an awareness of the form of the text? For example, if you are writing about a poem, will your comments refer to the sound of the words; if you are writing about a play, will your comments refer to the words being performed rather than read as a text?

Step 4: Write your essay: communicate clearly

Once your ideas are clear in your mind, you are ready to write your essay. You will need to communicate clearly with the reader so that they can see how much you know – and care – about the text.

Communicating clearly means:
» making appropriate word choices
» developing your ideas clearly
» ordering and linking your ideas clearly.

MAKING APPROPRIATE WORD CHOICES

A key part of clear communication is the language that you choose: the words and the phrases. Remember who your reader is and why they are reading your work. You are certainly not chatting casually about the text with a friend! Therefore, you need to write in a formal **register** so do not use **slang**; choose formal words instead of informal words, and do not use **contractions**.

> **Key terms**
>
> **Register:** The style of language, grammar and words used in a particular situation
>
> **Slang:** A type of language that is very informal and that is usually spoken rather than written; it is used by particular groups of people
>
> **Contraction:** When a word is shortened in informal writing, for example it is / it's, or he is / he's

Exercise 7

> **TIP**
>
> Writing in a formal register does not mean trying to use the most lengthy and difficult words or complicated sentence structures possible. Make the ideas in your essay as clear as you can.

Working with your partner, discuss how the sentences below should be redrafted without slang and without contractions.

a   Lady Macbeth said that King Duncan looked like her dear old dad.
b   Lady Macbeth is much tougher than Macbeth. He's a complete wimp!
c   The audience will feel sorry for Lady Macbeth cos of how she dies.

This book has listed key literary terms that are useful when writing about texts. You have seen students making good use of these throughout the examples of writing in the previous units. You should certainly use literary terms in your own writing, but only if they are linked with a textual reference. Use literary terms as a tool to help you comment on the effects that are created – and remember, it is the writer who chooses the language, not the character.

Exercise 8

> **Key term**
>
> **Superlative adjective:** The form of an adjective used to show the noun described is at an upper or lower limit; for example, the bravest character or the most cowardly character

With a partner, discuss the following versions of a student's sentence. Which version has used terminology most successfully? Why do you think this?

1   Macbeth uses **superlative adjectives** to show his love for Lady Macbeth.
2   Macbeth describes Lady Macbeth as his 'dearest partner of greatness'. Shakespeare uses a superlative adjective.
3   Macbeth describes Lady Macbeth as his 'dearest partner of greatness'. Shakespeare uses a superlative adjective to suggest the strength of affection that Macbeth has for her.

DEVELOPING YOUR IDEAS CLEARLY

> **Key term**
>
> **Assertion:** A strong statement of belief about something, often without evidence to support it

In everyday life, people quite often use **assertions** to express their views about things: the music or sports teams they like and don't like, for example. However, when you are writing an essay, assertions cannot be used at all and you must always give evidence to support your views. Typically, sentences in an essay about a literary text will build on one another in a certain way.

Point	• Focus on the question. • Relate your ideas to the key words in the question.
Evidence	• Focus on the text. • Use a quotation or indirect textual reference.
Exploration	• Focus on the reader. • Discuss the effect of the writer's choices.

Exercise 9

Look at the paragraph below, which has been taken from a student's response to the question about Lady Macbeth. Can you identify the point, the evidence and the exploration? What do you notice about the evidence that has been used?

> **Sample paragraph**
>
> The audience will feel growing sympathy for Lady Macbeth as her importance to Macbeth reduces: 'Be innocent of the knowledge, dearest chuck' he tells her in Act Three, as he secretly plots to kill Banquo. 'Chuck' highlights her lesser status and contrasts with the way he used to think of her as his 'partner' in Act One. The audience will sense Lady Macbeth's isolation and will feel sympathy towards her because of the hurt that these words will inevitably cause her.

ORDERING AND LINKING YOUR IDEAS CLEARLY

The introduction

TIP

The introduction (or conclusion) to your essay should not feature unnecessary **contextual** information as this will not help you to answer the question.

Key term

Context: The circumstances around a text; for example, the writer's life or the historical background

You should begin your essay with an introduction and end it with a conclusion. It is not a good idea to start an essay with 'In this essay, I am going to...' Instead, give a brief overview of the main ideas that you will present in your essay, making sure that you clearly relate these to the key words in the question. This approach creates a favourable impression in the reader's mind about what they are about to read as there is a clear sense of direction. Your positive start will also give you confidence as you write.

Exercise 10

Read the sample introduction below and work with a partner to discuss the questions that follow it.

> **Sample introduction**
>
> Lady Macbeth is a character who can attract some limited sympathy, despite her involvement in the murder of King Duncan, because of the way that her character develops over the course of the play. Her entrance in Act One reveals her potential for evil but by Act Five she is a broken figure and her sleepwalking and then her exit – throwing herself from the castle walls – reveals the extent of her guilt.

a How quickly does the student mention the key words from the question?

b Do the sentences in the introduction give detailed or general ideas?

c Is there any contextual information?

Exercise 11

a Now write an introduction to the essay you have planned.

b Compare your introduction with a partner's. Does it address the question directly? Does it avoid going into detail? Does it interest the reader in the essay to come?

The body paragraphs

After your introduction come the body paragraphs of your essay. Refer closely and regularly to the key words in the question at the start of each paragraph. Each body paragraph should contain a point relevant to the key words in the question, supported by textual reference (or textual references), and – crucially – feature developed and personal comments on language, structure or form.

Exercise 12

Read the body paragraphs below with a partner. Take turns to read the paragraphs aloud. Discuss the questions that follow.

Key terms
Soliloquy: A type of speech in which a character in a play reveals their thoughts and feelings by speaking alone on the stage
Metaphor: A description of one thing as another thing that is mostly unrelated to make a comparison that highlights the similarity between the two things
Juxtapose: Putting two images or ideas that are not similar close together to create a contrasting effect

Sample body paragraphs

In Act One Lady Macbeth is characterised as so evil that it would be difficult for an audience to feel sympathy for her. Shakespeare characterises Macbeth as war-like, masculine and strong, an 'eagle', yet in the **soliloquy** that Shakespeare gives Lady Macbeth (to give the character a dramatically powerful entrance), she describes him as being 'too full o' the milk of human kindness', a **metaphor** that shows how she sees his kindness as a feminine weakness. She wishes for him to hurry home so that she can 'pour' her 'spirits' in his ear; the noun suggests her connection with evil. Shakespeare **juxtaposes** good and evil in this way to characterise Lady Macbeth as a dangerous character who is capable of greater cruelty than her warrior husband and she attracts no sympathy.

She predicts how the 'raven' will croak itself 'hoarse' to announce King Duncan's entrance under 'my battlements'. Ravens are associated with carrion and death, so again the audience will think of Lady Macbeth as evil, and, moreover, Shakespeare's use of the pronoun 'my' shows that she is the dominant force in her relationship with Macbeth; he addressed her in the letter as his 'dearest partner of greatness', the superlative showing his love for her and therefore the power that she has over him. She talks of the 'wound' that her 'keen knife' will make, the adjective 'keen' suggesting both the extent of her preparation in making the knife sharp and her enthusiasm.

Key terms

Image / Imagery: A word or phrase that prompts the reader to imagine the way that something looks, sounds, smells, feels or tastes

Connotations: Feelings or ideas that are suggested by a word that are beyond its literal meaning

Foreshadowing: Hinting at something to come in the future

Stereotype: An idea or belief people have about an object or group that is based upon how they look on the outside; it may be completely untrue or only partly true

When Lady Macbeth meets with Macbeth she instructs him to 'look like th' innocent flower, But be the serpent under 't'; her casual juxtaposition of 'flower' with 'serpent' shows her devil-like cunning and capacity to deceive others, and the imperative verbs show her frightening ability to manipulate her husband to do the same. She is turning nature upside down, associating flowers with poison and the ability to kill, as she did earlier when she said 'Come to my woman's breasts, And take my milk for gall': a deeply disturbing **image** because the usual **connotations** of breasts with nursing and nurturing are replaced with ideas of poison and death.

In Act Two Lady Macbeth's 'mettle' is still evident. When Macbeth returns from the scene of King Duncan's murder, he is shaken by its 'sorry sight' but Lady Macbeth is chillingly calm and practical: she tells him to wash the blood, 'this filthy witness', from his hand, returns the bloodied daggers to Duncan's bedchambers, and reassures him that 'A little water clears us of this deed'. The audience will see that murder, regicide even, is of no consequence to her and merits no feelings of guilt. In contrast, Macbeth feels that 'Neptune's ocean' will not wash his hands clean, which shows his extreme guilt at his part in the plan – devised by Lady Macbeth. Lady Macbeth is thus, perhaps, characterised as a greater villain than her husband, who actually killed King Duncan! However, Shakespeare gives her character complexity by showing that compassion remains within her, **foreshadowing** her later guilt: she says that she could not kill King Duncan herself because he 'resembled' her father as he lay sleeping. This reveals her capacity to love as well as to destroy, balancing the audience's horror at her evil thoughts and actions with some – limited – sympathy.

The student could not quite recall the exact textual reference here ('Had he not resembled my father as he slept') but often one word is enough.

When Macbeth descends into a bloody cycle of violence to safeguard his throne, he does it independently. As his guilt diminishes, Lady Macbeth's increases, and so the audience's sympathy for her grows. In Act Five, it is Lady Macbeth – rather than Macbeth – who, sleepwalking in her madness, now fears that she cannot remove the moral stain of King Duncan's murder: 'Out, damned spot!' she exclaims, suggesting that she recognises the hellish ('damned') nature of her actions. When she mourns that 'All the perfumes of Arabia will not sweeten this little hand', the exaggerated image makes it seem that she is desperate to regain the femininity **stereotypically** associated with women and reminds the audience of how much she has changed from when 'a little water' would suffice to clear her guilt. She longed for the darkness of hell in Act One but Shakespeare now shows her longing for a light to be by her 'continually'; driven mad by her guilt she even sleepwalks with a candle in her hand. Perhaps she knows that the light of heaven is denied to her now and whatever she might do she is destined for hell.

a Are the ideas linked to the question?
b Where is there a textual reference?
c Where is there discussion of the effects that the writer's choices have created?
d Where is there an awareness of the form of the text?
e Where is there evidence of a personal response to the text?

Exercise 13

Now that you have read these body paragraphs, write your own, using the plan that you made earlier. If you think that you need to improve your plan first, do so.

The conclusion

Your conclusion should not use clumsy phrases such as 'I have shown how...' and you should not repeat the words from the question or your own introduction. Do not write a long conclusion that simply repeats ideas from the essay.

Round off your essay with an overview of the main ideas presented in the essay, making sure that you clearly relate these ideas to the key words in the question. The conclusion creates a space for you to give your personal views about the writer's purpose and choices and the effects created.

Exercise 14

Read the sample conclusion below.

> **Sample conclusion**
>
> Shakespeare makes it very hard to feel much sympathy for Lady Macbeth. Although she is driven mad by her guilt and ultimately throws herself from the castle walls, this is a consequence of her evil actions at the start of the play. Shakespeare is, however, very careful to keep her as a complex character who is immensely evil at the start but far less so later. This complexity enables Shakespeare to intensify the magnitude of Macbeth's downfall for the audience – Macbeth loses absolutely everything, including his wife.

Discuss the following questions with a partner:
a   Is there an overall statement that responds to the question?
b   Is the conclusion focused on details or main ideas?
c   Is there evidence of a personal response?

Exercise 15

Now write your own conclusion.

Step 5: Reflect on and improve your essay

When you are writing an essay for a coursework portfolio, you will have plenty of time to redraft it. In timed conditions, redrafting is not a good idea. If you feel the need to do this, it suggests you did not give enough time to your planning. You should, however, leave time to check your essay towards the end of the writing time.

The ABC tool below might be useful for you when you practise general essay questions. It can help you to ensure that you produce you best work possible.

A	Add	**Is anything missing?** Do I need to add a textual reference to support my point? Do I need to add a comment about the writer's choice of form, structure or language?
B	Build	**What can be improved?** Can I also include a less obvious textual reference? Are there alternative views on why the writer made a specific choice?
C	Challenge	**Is anything wrong?** Have I related everything to the key words in the question? Are my word choices appropriate (no slang or contractions)? Have I used the correct literary terms? Are there any errors of spelling, punctuation or grammar?

TIP

There is absolutely no need to count your words in a timed essay and no point in doing so. Remember that the quality of your ideas is the most important aspect, so use the time you have to write as well as you can.

Exercise 16

Use the ABC tool to check your work, or a partner's work. Use a different-coloured pen to make any improvements. With practice, you will find yourself 'adding', 'building' and 'challenging' as you write.

> MAKING CONNECTIONS
>
> The ABC tool can also help you when you are writing a response for your coursework portfolio. See Unit 26.

Exercise 17

At the start of this unit, you thought about the steps that you need to complete when writing an essay. Look back to this list now (Exercise 1). What progress have you made with these skills? What further steps can you take to improve your essay-writing skills? Write a reflection using the format shown below.

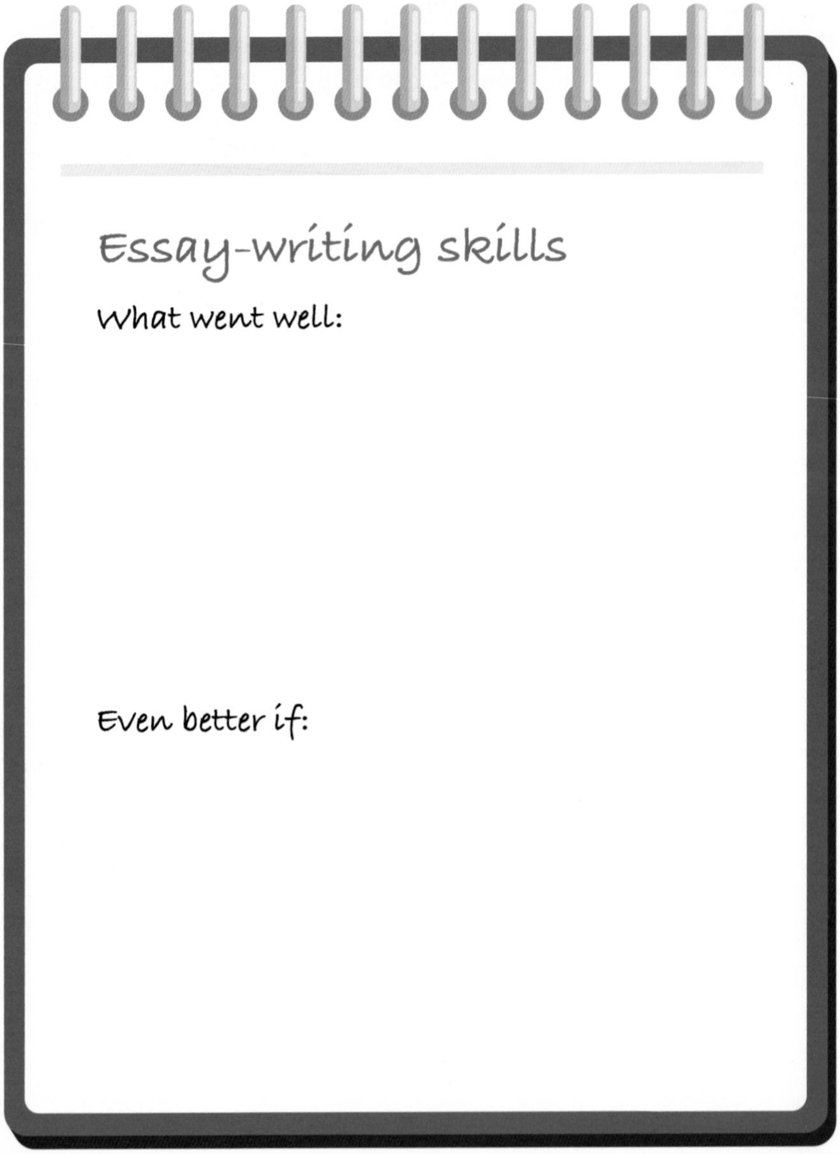

Essay-writing skills

What went well:

Even better if:

Unit summary

In this unit, you have learned how to:
● Think about the different stages of planning and writing an essay: reading and understanding the question; identifying relevant information to include; creating an essay plan; writing your essay; and reflecting on and improving your essay.
● Assess the merits of passages taken from sample essay responses.
● Devise your own essay questions and plan and write a response to one of them.

Think about how you have demonstrated each of these skills in the exercises in this unit. Be sure to spend more time on the skills you feel you need to improve.

Writing for a portfolio

In this unit, you will:
- Think about the approach required by coursework.
- Find out what is expected of you in the coursework portfolio.
- Improve your study skills through a thorough note-taking, drafting and redrafting process.

The information in this section is based on the Cambridge IGCSE Literature in English syllabuses (0475/0992) for examination from 2020, the Cambridge O Level Literature in English syllabus (2010) for examination from 2023 and the Cambridge IGCSE World Literature syllabus (0408) for examination from 2022. You should always refer to the appropriate syllabus document for the year of your examination to confirm the details and for more information. The syllabus document is available on the Cambridge International website at www.cambridgeinternational.org.

Important notice: This unit is relevant only for Cambridge IGCSE World Literature (0408) students and for Cambridge IGCSE Literature in English (0475/0992) students taking the coursework option. Students following the Cambridge O Level Literature in English (2010) syllabus do not need to submit coursework and this unit is not relevant to them.

> **Key term**
>
> **Secondary source:** A document or recording that interprets, analyses or evaluates a literary text

Thinking about your coursework portfolio

Coursework is an exciting way for you to improve your skills in Literature in English. Look at what students have said about their experience of completing coursework, below. What do you think is the main advantage of coursework? Do you have any concerns about coursework?

I used quite a few **secondary sources** when I wrote my essay. I think this will help me with my studies after my IGCSEs.

Coursework involved lots of useful study skills and these helped me in other subjects too.

We had time to explore the text really deeply and make up our own minds about it. I loved seeing how the same theme was treated in different texts.

I liked how it was our teachers who chose the texts. They chose texts that they were happy teaching and that we enjoyed studying.

In coursework, you have the chance to reflect on what you have written and improve it.

We got to discuss our ideas a lot and this helped me to make up my own mind about the text.

I absolutely loved using my imagination in my empathic response!

One of the students above mentioned how they had used secondary sources in their independent study. Reading secondary sources is another way for you to improve your understanding of the text. You might well find that study guides for your set texts are available in print or online. These might introduce you to interpretations that you had not thought of independently. Remember to explore these ideas in your coursework essay rather than just repeat them, as you need to show a sensitive and informed *personal* response to your set texts.

The requirements of the coursework portfolio are slightly different in the various syllabuses. The boxes below show a breakdown of the requirements for Cambridge IGCSE Literature in English (0475/0992) and Cambridge IGCSE World Literature (0408):

> **TIP**
>
> The Cambridge IGCSE Literature in English (0475/0992) syllabuses allow students to use poetry or short stories. Cambridge IGCSE World Literature (0408) does **not** allow poetry.

Cambridge IGCSE Literature in English (0475/0992) Component 5 (optional)	**Cambridge IGCSE World Literature (0408) Component 1 (compulsory)**
• Two assignments, both 600 to 1200 words (including quotations). • Assignment tasks must allow students to show that they have studied the whole text. • Students may write one empathic response, but it should be based on a drama or prose text. • They may write about one text from the set-text list. • If they choose poetry or short stories, they must use a minimum of two poems or stories, but they do not need to compare them. • Texts must have been originally written in English.	• Two assignments, one based on a prose text and one based on a drama text. • One assignment should be a critical essay of 800 to 1200 words. • One assignment should be an empathic response of 600 to 1000 words. • Texts must be drawn from two different countries or cultures. • Students must not write about texts from the set-text list. • If they choose to use short stories for their prose text assignment, they must cover at least two, but they do not need to compare them. • Texts do not have to have been originally written in English.

> **TIP**
>
> You may type your assignments or write them by hand. It might be a good idea to type your assignments if you feel that would improve the presentation of your work.

Essays

You have already practised the skills that you will need for writing an essay in the 'Writing practice' exercises of the other units in this book. Reading Unit 25 will have helped you to consolidate this knowledge, and this unit will help you with the specific requirements of coursework essays:

» Thinking about your assignment title
» Making targeted notes
» Writing your first draft
» Using references
» Redrafting.

THINKING ABOUT YOUR ASSIGNMENT TITLE

The assignment title that is chosen for your coursework is of vital importance. It must satisfy the following criteria:

» It must enable you to show the skills you have developed.
» It must enable you to consider the whole text.
» It must focus on a literary aspect, such as **characterisation**, themes, language or structure.
» In particular, the assignment title should guide you towards exploring how the writer's choices of form, structure and language achieve their effects.

> **TIP**
>
> One of the Cambridge IGCSE Literature in English (0475/0992) assignments can be based on a set text you are studying. Using an essay question that focuses on an extract is not permitted as you need to show knowledge of the whole text.

> **TIP**
>
> In your essay, you will explore the methods that the writer has used to achieve effects. Thinking of these methods as being a writer's **choices** can encourage you to explore fully the layers of meaning they create. Take every opportunity to discuss your ideas with other students so that you see how the text can be interpreted differently.

> **Key term**
>
> **Characterisation:** The ways in which a writer presents a character to an audience

Exercise 1

Match each essay title below with the comment that describes its suitability as a title for a coursework assignment.

> **Key term**
>
> **Plot:** The main events in a play or other text that interrelate to make the story

	Title		Comment on its suitability
1	A commentary on *Macbeth*	A	This title focuses on character but limits the student to only part of the text when the whole text should be considered.
2	The character of Lady Macbeth in *Macbeth*	B	This is far too general. The title is likely to lead the student into simply retelling the **plot**.
3	How does Shakespeare present Lady Macbeth in Act One, Scene Five of *Macbeth*?	C	This is an excellent assignment title. The mention of the writer helps the student to focus on the methods of characterisation that are used. The student is also guided towards considering the whole play.
4	How do you think Shakespeare makes Lady Macbeth's change during the course of the play so dramatic?	D	This title makes it seem as if Lady Macbeth is a real person! There is no mention of the writer so the student might not explore the writer's methods of characterisation.

MAKING NOTES

Coursework assignments give you the opportunity to reread parts of the text several times and become an expert on them. Make sure that early on you identify the parts of the text that are relevant to the assignment title so that your efforts are focused. Your rereading must be an active rather than a passive process. You will need to collect lots of textual references and record the ideas that you have about them. Again, make sure that you focus your mind on what you need before you start: set out your initial ideas in a mind map, a list or a table, and add notes to this.

TIP

Focus on the quality of the points that you make. Develop a range of points fully rather than giving brief attention to a greater number. This will result in a much more tightly focused response to your assignment title. Being selective in this way is also excellent practice for timed conditions when you will have far less time to plan.

Whenever you make notes from a secondary source, carefully note its details (author's name, title of the text, date of publication) to help you with your **referencing** and **bibliography**.

WRITING YOUR FIRST DRAFT

Once your note-taking is complete and you have an essay plan, you will be ready to write your first draft. Remember that you are writing a draft, so do not expect everything to fall into place straight away. First drafts are often rather messy!

Your introduction should engage immediately with the assignment title. Make a powerful point supported by a textual reference and comment on the choices made. Do not include background information about the writer or the setting of the text in the introduction as this will not help you to answer the question.

Here are some helpful pointers from students who are looking back to their coursework drafting:

TIP

Teachers cannot mark, correct or edit your draft(s); they can only give you brief general feedback about your first draft.

> Find a quiet place to work. The peace and quiet of the library was invaluable for me because home is sometimes a very busy place!

> I knew that I could not write the whole essay in one go. I set a timer for 25 minutes and then took a 5-minute break. I repeated that a few times and then came back to it the next day.

> Have the author's name on a sticky note right in front of you. This will remind you to focus on the writer's choices.

> I put my essay plan in front of me and kept referring to it so I didn't go off-track.

◀ Sticky notes can be really helpful when drafting an essay, but make sure you have somewhere you can work without being distracted!

REFERENCING YOUR ESSAY

Plagiarism is very serious academic misconduct. To avoid this, you must clearly show in your essay when an idea belongs to somebody else, whether you quote (copy) it directly or paraphrase it (put the idea into your own words). This is called 'referencing'.

Examples of referencing

There are different ways to reference. One approach is given below:

» Quoting: *Macbeth* has been described as having 'the most pronounced atmosphere of evil of any of [Shakespeare's] plays' (Clark, 2015).

» Paraphrasing: The atmosphere in *Macbeth* has been described as the most evil found in Shakespeare's plays (Clark, 2015).

A bibliography is a list of references at the end of your essay or, in some cases, your empathic response. An extract from a bibliography is given below; it gives details about two references the student used: one online source and one printed source.

Example entries in a bibliography

Brown, J. and Spencer, T. (2020). *William Shakespeare*. Online.
https://www.britannica.com/biography/William-Shakespeare
[Accessed 18 August 2020].

Shakespeare, W., Clark, S. & Mason, P. (2015). *Macbeth*. London, UK.

Exercise 2

Study the examples of referencing above and answer the following questions:

a What punctuation is used to show that the exact words of another writer have been copied?

b What do you think the square brackets show?

c What information is given in brackets when another writer has been quoted or paraphrased?

d Compare the quoted idea and the paraphrased idea. What changes and what remains the same? Think about the words that are used and how they are used, the punctuation that is used and how the source of the idea is indicated.

Study the extract from a bibliography above and answer the following questions:

e What extra information can the reader obtain from the bibliography compared to the reference within the essay? Why might this information be useful?

f Note that the reference to an online source includes the date the source was accessed. Why do you think this is?

> **Key term**
>
> **Plagiarism:** When somebody presents somebody else's ideas as their own

> **TIP**
>
> Referencing and a bibliography are required for essays. Bibliographies may also accompany empathic responses.

> **TIP**
>
> In the examples of referencing, you can see that the name of the play *Macbeth* is given in italic font. This is a convention that is used when typing the titles of plays and novels; when such titles are given in handwritten work, underlining is used instead. The titles of poems and short stories are shown in inverted commas whether you are typing or handwriting your essay.
>
> | novel | *Hard Times* / <u>Hard Times</u> |
> |---|---|
> | play | *Top Girls* / <u>Top Girls</u> |
> | poem | 'Phenomenal Woman' / 'Phenomenal Woman' |
> | short story | 'The Gold-legged Frog' / 'The Gold-legged Frog' |

Empathic writing

THINKING ABOUT YOUR ASSIGNMENT TITLE

Showing empathy means 'putting yourself in somebody else's shoes' so that you understand what it would be like to be that person in their situation. A good writer will bring characters to life so well that we can feel empathy for them: we feel that we know them inside out.

When you are asked to write an empathic response, you are being given the opportunity to show your deep understanding of the character from your study of details in the text. You imagine the character's thoughts and feelings about an experience and write about it from their point of view.

It is important that the assignment title focuses your attention on a specific character at a specific moment in the text and invites you to share the character's thoughts at that moment. The title must not simply invite you to retell the story.

Exercise 3

An assessment title such as the one below would allow you to write a successful empathic response:

> **You are Oliver. You have just been kidnapped by Nancy and Sikes during your errand to the book stall for Mr Brownlow. Write your thoughts.**
> **[Charles Dickens, *Oliver Twist*]**

a With a partner, look at the assignment title and identify the following features:
  - Where a specific character is identified
  - Where a specific moment in the text has been selected
  - Where the task invites you to share the character's thoughts (rather than retell the story)

b Now, check your own assignment title also has these features. If you have not yet been given a title, create your own using the template below:

> **You are [name of character]. You [what has just happened or is happening]. Write your thoughts. [author's name, title of the text]**

Key terms

Tone (of voice): A character's personality conveyed by language choices for speech and thoughts; it can change over the course of a text

Viewpoint: The thoughts and feelings that a character has towards a situation

Conventions: Typical features found within a literary genre

TIP

- Your assignment title should focus your attention on a significant character from the text for whom you can create a convincing **voice** and **viewpoint**. A minor character would not be suitable as there will not be enough detail in the text for you to work with to do this.
- The instruction 'Write your thoughts' at the end of a title reminds you to write from the viewpoint of the named character. This must be your focus. Avoid an assignment title that asks you to write in a particular format, such as a diary entry or a newspaper article, as you might start to concentrate on using the **conventions** of that format, or retelling the story, rather than creating an authentic voice and viewpoint for the character.
- Also, make sure that your assignment title does not move you away from the world created by the writer. Do not, for example, use an assignment title that asks you to write an alternative ending: focus on an actual moment that the writer creates within the text.

MAKING NOTES

A successful empathic response creates a completely believable voice for the character that has been chosen. This requires an excellent knowledge and understanding of the character at the specified moment and, by implication, of what happens before and after that moment.

The exercises that follow have been grouped into three key pieces of advice to help you make the notes you need to ensure you address the coursework requirements in your response.

Show a good knowledge of the character

When you 'write your thoughts', you need to convince your reader that the thoughts are really coming from the character. A suitable first step is to collect textual references concerning the character.

Exercise 4

Draw a large outline of your character on a sheet of paper. Inside the character, write textual references that relate to the character's own speech and thoughts; outside the character, write down textual references that relate to things that other characters have said or thought about the character. Aim to include ten or more textual references in total.

Exercise 5

Locate the part of the text that includes the moment specified in the assignment title and reread it.

a Make notes on the **inferences** that can be made about the character. What do we learn about the character's personality? How might they be feeling and what might they be thinking?

b Which of the text's themes are present in the extract? How does the character relate to those themes during the extract? Make notes of your ideas.

Key term

Infer: Reading between the lines of a text to find clues to understand more than is said directly

Key term

Perspective: Like a lens through which readers view characters and events in a text; the perspective of a text is created by the speaker: we interpret the characters and events based on what the speaker shows and tells us

Focus on the specified moment

When you write your empathic response, it is vital that you stay in the moment that you have chosen. Ensure the character's personality and **perspective** relates to the specified moment. Do not write as if later events had already happened! Your response has to be imaginative but you cannot alter the facts of the original text.

Exercise 6

a Make a flowchart showing the **character arc** of the character during the events of the whole text.

b Identify the key moments that reveal the most significant changes in the character's developing personality and perspective.

> **MAKING CONNECTIONS**
>
> The idea of **dynamic** and **static characters** and character arcs is discussed in Unit 20. Ensure that the character in your empathic response thinks as the reader would expect for that moment in the text.

> **Key terms**
>
> **Character arc:** The inner journey of a character in a text in which they gradually change personality or perspective
>
> **Dynamic character:** A character whose personality or perspective changes because of the action of the plot
>
> **Static character:** A character whose personality or perspective does not change as a result of the action of the plot

Exercise 7

Key term

Mood: In literature, the mood is the atmosphere or feeling created in the writing by the author through such features as setting, description or the attitudes of characters

It will help you to write your empathic response if you have a detailed image of the character and the moment in mind. Reread your extract, thinking about the following:

» The clues that the writer has given about the setting
» What the characters are doing, thinking and feeling
» What the characters look like at that moment (their facial expressions, gestures and body language)
» The overall **mood** of the moment.

Create a drawing or a mind map that includes all of this information. If you are drawing the moment, try to convey its overall mood through the choices you make about colour and composition.

Make sure that the voice and viewpoint of the character is authentic

The previous exercises have helped you to improve your knowledge and understanding of the character and the specified moment. To help you develop a really personal response to the text, now take your learning further with your classmates by hotseating (interviewing) your chosen character. This will reveal the character's viewpoint (their thoughts and feelings) in detail, which will help you to create a truly believable voice for the character when you write your response.

The interviewers need to ask questions that will probe the character's thoughts and feelings. Some sample questions are given below.

1 What has just happened and how do you feel about it?
2 What do you think will happen next and how do you feel about it?
3 What are your feelings towards the other characters involved, and why?
4 What is your main emotion right now, and why?

Exercise 8

a Work with a partner to devise further questions. Can you make the sample questions more specific to your text? Also, consider how the student in the hotseat might respond to these questions.

b As a class activity, take turns to role-play the parts of interviewer and character.

c At the end of the activity, reflect on what you have learned. Have your views about the character changed at all? If so, how?

WRITING YOUR FIRST DRAFT

Before you write your piece, you will need to make a plan in a format that suits you. In the plan you should organise the ideas that you would like to convey about the character into a suitable order. You can also note the sort of language that you will use in your response.

Organise your ideas

The structure of your empathic response will depend on you. Unlike an essay, there will not be an introduction, body paragraphs and a conclusion. However, it is possible that the first part of the response will set the scene and focus the reader's attention on the character's thoughts and feelings about what happened just before the specified moment. Thereafter, the emphasis might shift to the moment itself and reveal the character's thoughts and feelings about this.

Make appropriate language choices for the character

When you write an essay, you use textual references and comment on them. When you are writing your empathic response, you do not need to quote from the text. Quoting may well affect the flow of the character's thoughts. Instead, make language choices (words / sentence types) that are like those typically made by the character. This is challenging but it is worth the effort because it will help you to create an authentic voice for the character. You might use a word or phrase from the text to help you with this, but ensure that this only happens occasionally.

> **TIP**
>
> Be careful that you do not retell the story. The empathic response must show that you have developed your own detailed and personal understanding of the setting, character, themes and ideas.

> **TIP**
>
> Don't use vocabulary or refer to ideas that would be wrong for the character.

Exercise 9

In this exercise, you will write a plan for your empathic response.

a Choose the format that you would like to use for your plan: a mind map, a list or a table, for example.

b Add the ideas that you want to include about the character's thoughts and feelings.

c Add key examples of the language that you want to use.

Give yourself some time to reflect upon your plan before you write your first draft. Your plan will keep you focused and confident. If you start to struggle with your writing, take a break and check that you are still happy with the plan. If you have changed your mind, it is best to change the plan before you start writing again.

The information at the beginning of this unit includes the word limits for your empathic response. As a rough guide, if you are word-processing, your empathic response might be between just over a side and two sides long, depending on the font (Times New Roman or Arial in 12 point are good choices). Handwritten responses will vary. Be careful to stick to your plan and do not get carried away!

Redrafting

Once you have completed your first draft, you need to begin the process of reflection and improvement that will lead to your handing in work that you can be proud of. The first point to check is that you have answered the question that has been set within the word limit that applies – check the details given at the start of this unit. If you have gone over the word limit, check all your sentences to ensure that each one is helpful in responding to the assignment title.

You will have the opportunity to discuss your draft in a general way with your teacher. You can then refer to the notes that you have made during your study of this book to revise the relevant skills.

REFLECTING ON AND IMPROVING YOUR ESSAY

You might find the following prompts helpful before you redraft your essay:
» Does your assessment title make it possible to demonstrate your knowledge of the text and the way it is written and allow you to give an informed response?
» Have you written an essay that focuses on the task without being side-tracked into including irrelevant background information?
» Have you made a wide range of clear points?
» Have you connected your points to make a clear argument that explores ideas (rather than just retelling the story)?
» Have you supported your points with relevant textual references?
» Are your textual references brief?
» Have you included the textual references without breaking the flow of your sentences?
» Are the textual references thoughtfully chosen, and have you included a few less obvious references?
» Have you commented on the ways the writer's choice of language, structure and form shape meanings and effects?
» Have you used the correct terminology (key words) used in the study of literature?
» Have you based your essay on your own opinions about the text, rather than using ideas from your teacher or a study guide?

TIP

Take care with your spelling, punctuation and grammar. Before you submit your work, think about which words in your work might be misspelt. Check these words in a dictionary. Use full stops (rather than commas) to separate complete ideas into sentences. Use formal English throughout.

TIP

Part of making a personal response that shows a detailed knowledge of the text is sometimes selecting less obvious textual references to support the point that you are making. You might use such references by themselves or to supplement a more obvious textual reference.

REFLECTING ON AND IMPROVING YOUR EMPATHIC RESPONSE

You might find the following questions helpful before you redraft your empathic response:

» Does your assessment title make it possible to demonstrate your knowledge of the text and the way it is written and allow you to give an informed response?
» Have you stayed within the world of the text and not included new characters, places, events, and so on?
» Have you shown that you fully understand the character at the specified moment?
» Have you developed your own views about what the character is like?
» Have you used your personal understanding to create a completely believable voice and viewpoint for the character?
» Have you made appropriate language choices for the character by using similar words and phrases to the ones that they use?
» Have you based your empathic response on your own opinions about the text, rather than relying solely on ideas from your teacher or a study guide?

FINAL CHECKS ON YOUR PORTFOLIO

» Make sure that your work is on A4 paper.
» Make sure that the assignments are legible, if you have handwritten them.
» Make sure that you have chosen a clear font (Times New Roman or Arial) of an appropriate size (12 point is ideal).
» Put your name and candidate number on each assignment.
» Put the full title at the top of the first page of each assignment.
» Make sure the pages are in the correct order.
» Make sure that you have included your bibliography.
» Put a page number at the bottom of every page of each assignment.
» Do not staple your work together.

Unit summary

This unit has helped you to:
● Understand the approach required by coursework.
● Know what is expected of you in the coursework portfolio.
● Improve your study skills through a thorough note-taking, drafting and redrafting process.

Think about how you have demonstrated each of these skills in the exercises in this unit. Be sure to spend more time on the skills you feel you need to improve.

Glossary of key terms

Accent: How people in an area, country or social group pronounce words

Allegorical: Having a hidden meaning, because the characters and events represent particular qualities, ideas or real-life historical events

Allegory: A story that can be read as having a hidden meaning because the characters and events represent particular qualities, ideas or real-life historical events

Alliteration: The repetition of consonant sounds at the beginning of words or stressed syllables in adjacent words

Ambiguous: Not having one obvious meaning, or open to interpretation

Assertion: A strong statement of belief about something, often without evidence to support it

Assonance: The repetition of vowel sounds in adjacent words

Assuming a persona: Taking on the identity of another person

Bathos: A device used in literature; it is like an anti-climax and its effect is often humorous because it involves a mood change from something serious to something trivial

Bibliography: A list of references at the end of a piece of academic writing

Caesura: A pause or break in the middle of a line of poetry

Character arc: The inner journey of a character in a text in which they gradually change personality or perspective

Characterisation: The ways in which a writer presents a character to an audience

Chronological order: Events related in the sequence that they happened

Class: The way society can be divided into groups of people who have similar levels of wealth and status

Climax: The most exciting point in a text or performance when dramatic tension has increased to its highest point

Colloquialism: An informal, chatty or slang word or phrase, which we tend to use more in speech than in writing

Comedy: A text in which there is humour and a happy ending

Conflict: A situation in which there is an obstacle between a character and that character's goal; the conflict may be external or internal

Connotations: Feelings or ideas that are suggested by a word that are beyond its literal meaning

Consonance: The repetition of similar consonant sounds

Context: The circumstances around a text; for example, the writer's life or the historical background

Contraction: When a word is shortened in informal writing, for example it is / it's, or he is / he's

Conventions: Typical features found within a literary genre

Cross-referencing: Referring to another text or another part of the same text to draw attention to a similarity or difference

Dialect: A form of language that has some differences in vocabulary and grammar and that is spoken by people in a specific social group or from a specific place

Dialogue: A conversation between two or more people that is presented in a text; in prose texts, dialogue is often written as direct speech

Diction: The words and phrases chosen by a speaker or writer

Direct speech: A character's actual words, put inside speech marks

Dramatic function: The reason that an element, such as a character, is within a text

Dramatic irony: A situation in which the audience knows something that a character in the play does not know

Dramatic tension: The feeling of anticipation and excitement that builds within a text or a drama performance

Drawing room: A room with comfortable furniture, used for entertaining guests

Dynamic character: A character whose personality or perspective changes because of the action of the plot

Elevated language: Language that is formal and dignified; there is no use of slang or informal words – because of its heightened formality, elevated language can feel unfamiliar and difficult to relate to

Enjambment: A sentence that runs on beyond the end of a line in poetry

Epic style: A style of writing associated with long narrative poems set in ancient times about extraordinary characters who perform heroic deeds; it includes elevated language, with many metaphors and similes as well as rhetorical flourishes and old-fashioned word order

Epiphany: A moment when a character in the text has a sudden insight or realisation that changes their view or understanding for the rest of the text

Explicitly: In a way that is clear and precise, requiring little interpretation

External conflict: A conflict between a character and an outside force, such as another character, society, nature or fate

First-person narrative: A narrative in which the events of the novel are told through a character actually in the novel – we see events and other characters through their eyes; first-person narrators communicate what they themselves think, experience and witness, as well as what they have been told or heard

Flashback: When a writer describes an event from an earlier point in time than the main story; flashbacks may be used to present a character's memories

Flat character: A character who is uncomplicated and undeveloped

Folklore: The traditional beliefs, customs and stories within a community

Foreshadowing: Hinting at something to come in the future

Form: The text type a writer chooses to communicate in; the three main forms in English literature are poetry, prose and drama – within those main forms are other forms; for example, a sonnet is a poetic form and a short story is a prose form

Free verse: A form of poetry that takes no particular shape, rhythm, metre or rhyme

Genre: A category of literature

Hyperbole: Exaggerated claims or statements, not meant to be taken literally

Iambic pentameter: A line of poetry that contains five iambs

Iambs: Metrical feet made up of two syllables: an unstressed one followed by a stressed one

Image / Imagery: A word or phrase that prompts the reader to imagine the way that something looks, sounds, smells, feels or tastes

Implicitly: In a way that is not direct or obvious

Indirect reference: Using some of the same words as the writer but in a different form; quotation marks are not required for an indirect reference

Infer: Reading between the lines of a text to find clues to understand more than is said directly

Internal conflict: A conflict within a character's own mind, creating a psychological struggle

Interrogative sentence: A sentence that asks a question and ends in a question mark

Irony: The use of words that are the opposite of what you mean; a situation or an event that seems deliberately opposite from what people would expect

Juxtapose: Putting two images or ideas that are not similar close together to create a contrasting effect

Language choices: The specific words that a writer chooses to use to convey particular ideas

Literary aspect: An essential element within a text: the structure, the language, the themes and ideas, the character and perspective, the setting and the mood

Metaphor: A description of one thing as another thing that is mostly unrelated to make a comparison that highlights the similarity between the two things

Metre: The rhythmic structure of a line of poetry

Metrical feet: Groups or units of two or three stressed or unstressed syllables; they are repeated in lines of poetry to form the poem's rhythm

Middle class: Professional people, who are not poor but are not very rich

Monologue: A long speech by one of the characters in a play

Mood: In literature, the mood is the atmosphere or feeling created in the writing by the author through such features as setting, description or the attitudes of characters

Narrator: The person who tells the story in a text; what happens is told in their words

Non-chronological: When a narrative is chronological it relates events in the sequence that they happened; the narrative in the extract from 'The Sorrow of War' does not follow events in the order that they happened, so it is non-chronological

Non-verbal sounds: Sounds other than words that a person makes; for example: laughter, crying, groans or sighs

Onomatopoeia: Language that sounds like the idea it describes; 'crackle' is an example of onomatopoeia (make sure you can spell the term correctly)

Overlapping: Dialogue in which two or more characters speak at the same time

Oxymoron: Two opposing words put together for effect, for example 'bitter sweet'

Paralinguistic features: The methods of communication that accompany speech, such as facial expression, eye contact, gestures, pitch, laughter, intonation, volume and stress

Pathetic fallacy: A literary device by which human feelings and emotions are projected onto non-human things; for example, weather and the natural world are commonly used to reflect a poet or character's internal emotions or state of mind

Pathos: A feeling of sadness or pity created by a writer through their use of language or other devices

Patriarchal: A society ruled or controlled by men; the patriarch is the male head of the family

Pen name: A false name used by a writer instead of their real name

Personification: The description of an object or animal as if they have human characteristics

Perspective: Like a lens through which readers view characters and events in a text; the perspective of a text is created by the speaker: we interpret the characters and events based on what the speaker shows and tells us

Phonetics: The study of the sounds of human speech

Plagiarism: When somebody presents somebody else's ideas as their own

Plot: The main events in a play or other text that interrelate to make the story

Preposition: A word, often short, that uses direction, location or time to link together words in the sentence; examples include 'on', 'in', 'before' and 'after'

Problem play: A type of drama that developed in the 19th century; problem plays are staged in a realistic way to expose problems within society so that the audience will reflect on those issues

Prose-poem: A text that is half poem, half prose – as the name sounds; it lacks such features as rhyme, lines and traditional forms of poetry, as well as the narrative structure of conventional fiction

Protagonist: A main character in a literary text

Quotation marks: Punctuation that we use to show that the words we are writing down have been copied from the text (quotations); sometimes referred to as 'inverted commas' or 'speech marks'

Realism: A movement in theatre that started in about the 1870s; plays in this genre seek to imitate real life on the stage in the way that characters, events and settings are shown

Referencing: A convention used in academic writing to show an idea belongs to someone else

Refrain: A short part of a poem (or song) that is repeated between stanzas, like a chorus

Register: The style of language, grammar and words used in a particular situation

Resolution: The final part of a story, in which everything is explained or resolved; sometimes called the 'denouement'

Rhetorical question: A question that does not require an answer

Rhyme scheme: The pattern of rhymes at the end of each line in poetry

Rhythm: Patterns in long and short sounds, words and lines in poetry

Rounded character: A believable character with a complex personality

Sarcastic: Mocking somebody in an amusing but hurtful way

Secondary source: A document or recording that interprets, analyses or evaluates a literary text

Semantic field: A group of words connected by meaning

Senses: Sight, smell, hearing, touch and taste

Setting: The time, place and culture in which a text takes place

Sibilance: The repetition of sibilant consonants such as 's', 'z' or 'sh'

Simile: A comparison of one thing to another, using the word 'as' or 'like' – 'They are *like* pale hair' is an example of a simile; the comparison gives emphasis to a description or makes it more vivid, but similes are generally thought of as less powerful than metaphors

Simple sentence: A sentence that has a subject and a verb but no connectives (for example 'and' or 'but')

Slang: A type of language that is very informal and that is usually spoken rather than written; it is used by particular groups of people

Soliloquy: A type of speech in which a character in a play reveals their thoughts and feelings by speaking alone on the stage

Stage directions: Instructions in a play script that give details about where a character is and how they move and speak, as well as giving descriptions of set and sound and light effects

Staging: The process of designing the performance space in which a play takes place, taking into account the set, the lighting and the costumes

Stanza: A group of lines in a poem, similar to a paragraph in a prose text; common stanza lengths are two, three, four, six or eight lines – in popular music, we often call stanzas 'verses'

Static character: A character whose personality or perspective does not change as a result of the action of the plot

Stereotype: An idea or belief people have about an object or group that is based upon how they look on the outside; it may be completely untrue or only partly true

Storyboard: Resembling a cartoon strip in a magazine, it has a number of boxes (frames) in which a story is told through pictures; the skill in putting together a storyboard lies in picking the most important moments to represent – film-makers often use storyboards

Structural techniques: The ways in which an author structures their writing

Structure: The sequence of ideas in a text and how it is put together

Style: The way in which an author writes, determined by the sort of language they tend to use, the way they structure sentences and by any other writing patterns that commonly appear in their text

Subject (of a sentence): The person or thing doing the action described in a sentence; it can be a noun (for example, 'Thistles' in line 2 of the poem) or a pronoun (for example, 'it', 'they')

Subplot: A part of the story in a play or other text that develops separately from the main story

Subtext: A less obvious or unspoken meaning in a text

Superlative adjective: The form of an adjective used to show the noun described is at an upper or lower lower limit; for example, the bravest character or the most cowardly character

Syllables: The sound elements in a word; for example, the word car|rot has two syllables in it and the word pot|a|to has three syllables in it

Symbolism: The use of an idea, image or object to represent abstract ideas or qualities

Synonymous: Has the same meaning as another word

Syntax: The order of words in a sentence

Taboo: A topic that custom prohibits or restricts speaking about

Tercet: A three-line stanza; it is sometimes known as a 'triplet' – other stanza lengths are couplets (two lines), quatrains (four lines), quintains (five lines), sestets (6 lines), septets (7 lines) and octets (8 lines)

Theme: A key idea or subject that is repeated throughout a text

Third-person narrative: A narrative that is not told from the perspective of a character in the story

Third-person omniscient narrator: 'Omniscient' means 'knows everything'; this kind of narrator knows everything about the characters – what they think and what they do and why; the narrator is the third person, meaning that they tell the story, but they are not in the story

Tone (of voice): A character's personality conveyed by language choices for speech and thoughts; it can change over the course of a text

Turning point: A point in a literary text at which an idea or an attitude is changed or reversed

Turn-taking: The way dialogue is shared so that the people in it take turns speaking and listening

Upper class: The people with the highest status in society and who are usually rich

Upper-middle class: Wealthier, professional people with a higher status in Edwardian society

Viewpoint: The thoughts and feelings that a character has towards a situation

Volta: An Italian word that means 'turn'; it is a 'turn' in thought or ideas

Working class: Poorer people who have manual jobs with a lower status in Edwardian / Victorian society

Acknowledgements

The Publishers would like to thank the following for permission to reproduce copyright material. Every effort has been made to trace all copyright holders, but if any have been inadvertently overlooked the Publishers will be pleased to make the necessary arrangements at the first opportunity.

Author's acknowledgements

Geoff Case:
Dedication: For my parents, my wife Belle, and my children, Melissa, Alex and Eleanor.
Acknowledgements: My sincere thanks to everyone who worked so hard on this book. My special thanks to Rose for her invaluable support; Penny for her wisdom; Kelvin for his professionalism and Felicity and Debbie for their enthusiasm and kindness.

Photo credits

pp.7 & 8 © Dmitriisimakov/stock.adobe.com; **p.18 & 19** *left* © FrankBoston/stock.adobe.com; **pp.19 & 19** *right* © Studio Harmony/stock.adobe.com; **pp.24 & 25** *top left* © Rolf Vennenbernd/dpa picture alliance/Alamy Stock Photo; **pp.25 & 25** *top right* © Interfoto/Personalities/Alamy Stock Photo; **pp.25** *centre left* **& 26** © Roberto Contini/Alamy Stock Photo; **pp.25** *centre right* **& 27** © World History Archive/Alamy Stock Photo; **pp.25** *bottom left* **& 28** © Brigitte Friedrich/Sueddeutsche Zeitung Photo/Alamy Stock Photo; **pp.25** *bottom right* **& 29** © Photo Researchers/Science History Images/Alamy Stock Photo; **pp.30 & 31** *left* © Speedfighter/123 RF.com; **pp.31 & 31** *right* © Juulijs/stock.adobe.com; **p.35** © MS photos/Alamy Stock Photo; **pp.36 & 37** © Raisa Kanareva/stock.adobe.com; **pp.44–45** © Chizuko Kimura/Alamy Stock Photo; **pp.46 & 46** *left* © Goyoconde/stock.adobe.com; **pp.46** *right* **& 47** © William87/stock.adobe.com; **p.54** © Oliver/stock.adobe.com; **p.55** © M. Schuppich/stock.adobe.com; **p.56** *left* © Wrzesientomek/stock.adobe.com; **pp.56** *right* **& 56–57** © Patricia W./stock.adobe.com; **pp.64–65** © Belkin & Co/stock.adobe.com; **pp.67** *top left* **& 67** © Ksi/stock.adobe.com; **pp.67** *top centre* **& 68** © Pjirawat/stock.adobe.com; **pp.67** *top right* **& 69** © EKH-Pictures/stock.adobe.com; **pp.67** *bottom left* **& 70** © Puwasit Inyavileart/stock.adobe.com; **pp.67** *bottom right* **& 71** © S_E/stock.adobe.com; **pp.74–75** © Mark chaves/EyeEm/stock.adobe.com; **pp.76 & 78** *left* © Jenny Thompson/stock.adobe.com; **pp.77 & 78** *centre* © Anon/stock.adobe.com; **pp.78 & 78** *top right* © Le Do/stock.adobe.com; **p.78** *bottom right* © Monart Design/stock.adobe.com; **p.79** *top* © Ajr_images/stock.adobe.com; **p.79** *bottom* © Ranta Images/stock.adobe.com; **pp.84–85** © Walker Art Library/Alamy Stock Photo; **pp.86 & 86** *left* © Wayhome Studio/stock.adobe.com; **p.86** *centre* © Wayhome Studio/stock.adobe.com; **pp.86** *right* **& 87** © Drobot Dean/stock.adobe.com; **pp.88 & 88–89** © Oleksandr/stock.adobe.com; **pp.92–93** © Todd/stock.adobe.com; **pp.94** *top* **& 97** © Valerii Honcharuk/stock.adobe.com; **pp.94** *centre* **& 98** © Apinya/stock.adobe.com; **pp.94** *bottom*, **116, 118** *top & bottom*, **119** *centre* © Diversity Studio/stock.adobe.com; **pp.94–95 & 95** © Behindlens/stock.adobe.com; **p.101** © New Africa/stock.adobe.com; **pp.102–103** © Martin Shore, **p.104** *left* © Tatomm/stock.adobe.com; **pp.104** *right* **& 104–105** © Imageportal/stock.adobe.com; **pp.110–113** © R_tee/stock.adobe.com; **pp.117, 118** *centre* **& 119** *top & bottom* © Monet/stock.adobe.com; **pp.122–125** © Riccardo Niels Mayer/stock.adobe.com; **pp.130–133** © Cornfield/stock.adobe.com; **pp.138–139 & 142–143** © Zcy/stock.adobe.com; **pp.146–147** © Anton/stock.adobe.com; **p.148** *top* © Chokniti/stock.adobe.com; **pp.148, 148** *left* **& 152** © Rostovdriver/stock.adobe.com; **pp.148** *right* **& 149** © Bouybin/stock.adobe.com; **pp.154–157** © Kumpei/stock.adobe.com; **p.163** © Patrcia/stock.adobe.com; **pp.164–167** © Olga/stock.adobe.com; **pp.176–179** © Elizabeth Whiting & Associates/Alamy Stock Photo; **pp.180 & 180** *left* © Geraint Lewis/Alamy Stock Photo; **pp.180** *right* **& 181** © Geraint Lewis/Alamy Stock Photo; **pp.188–190 & 198** © Paul Giggle/Redbrickstock.com/Alamy Stock Photo; **p.191** © Syda Productions/stock.adobe.com; **pp.200–203** © Travelib history/Alamy Stock Photo; **pp.212–215** © New Africa/stock.adobe.com; **pp.224–227** © Seth Lazar/Alamy Stock Photo; **p.227** *left* © Thomas/stock.adobe.com; **pp.227** *right* **& 228–229** © Oneinchpunch/stock.adobe.com; **pp.236–239** © Dmitry Rukhlenko - Travel Photos/Alamy Stock Photo; **pp.236 & 244** © World History Archive/Alamy Stock Photo; **pp.247 & 248** © Laura Henao/stock.adobe.com; **p.249** © Pictures Now/Alamy Stock Photo; **p.264** © Nenetus/stock.adobe.com; **p.266** © Vectorfusionart/stock.adobe.com

Text credits

p.15 from *Wuthering Heights* by Emily Brontë; **p.17** from *Romeo and Juliet* by William Shakespeare; **p.18** from *The Old Man and the Sea* by Ernest Hemingway, 1952; **p.21** 'Sonnet 130' by William Shakespeare; **p.24** from *To Kill a Mockingbird* by Harper Lee; **Unit 4 & p.87** Maya Angelou, 'Phenomenal Woman' from *And Still I Rise*. Copyright © 1978 by Maya Angelou. Used by permission of Random House, an imprint and division of Penguin Random House LLC. All rights reserved & Maya Angelou, 'Phenomenal Woman' from *And Still I Rise* Little, Brown Book Group; **Unit 5 & p.87** 'Island Man' copyright © Grace Nichols reproduced with permissions from Curtis Brown Group Ltd on behalf of Grace Nichols; **Unit 6 & p.87** Ted Hughes (1967), Wodwo, Faber & Faber Ltd. 'Thistles' from *Collected Poems* by Ted Hughes. Copyright © 2003 by The Estate of Ted Hughes. Reprinted by permission of Farrar, Straus and Giroux; **Unit 7 & p.87** 'Search for My Tongue' Sujata Bhatt (2013). *Collected Poems*. Carcanet Press Ltd; **Unit 8 & p.88** 'Elegy For My Father's Father' with permission of the James K. Baxter Estate; **Unit 9** 'London's Summer Morning' by Mary Robinson, *The Star*, a London daily paper, 1812; **Unit 10** 'Dark August' from *Sea Grapes* by Derek Walcott. Copyright © 1976 by Derek Walcott. Reprinted by permission of Farrar, Straus and Giroux; **Unit 11** *The Secret River* by Kate Grenville, © Open Road + Grove / Atlantic 2007; **Unit 12** 'The Gold-Legged Frog' © Silkworm Books 2011; **Unit 13** *Nervous Conditions*, Tsitsi Dangarembga, Faber & Faber Ltd & Tsitsi Dangarembga, excerpts from *Nervous Conditions*. Copyright © 1988 by Tsitsi Dangarembga. Reprinted with the permission of The Permissions Company, LLC on behalf of Graywolf Press, Minneapolis, Minnesota, www.graywolfpress.org; **Unit 14** *Hard Times* by Charles Dickens, Odhams Press, 1854; **Unit 15** excerpt from 'The Red Girl' from *Annie John* by Jamaica Kincaid. Copyright © 1985 by Jamaica Kincaid. Reprinted by permission of Farrar, Straus and Giroux & From *Annie John Cure* published by Vintage. Reproduced by permission of The Random House Group Ltd. © 1997; **Unit 16** excerpt(s) from *The Sorrow of War: A Novel of North Vietnam* by Bao Ninh, copyright © 1995 by Bao Ninh. Used by permission of Pantheon Books, an imprint of the Knopf Doubleday Publishing Group, a division of Penguin Random House LLC. All rights reserved; **Unit 17** extract from *Villette* by Charlotte Brontë; **Unit 18** © Caryl Churchill, *Top Girls*, Methuen Drama, an imprint of Bloomsbury Publishing Plc; **Unit 19** extract from *A Doll's House* by Henrik Ibsen, 1879, © Outlook verlag; **Unit 20** *The Lion and the Jewel* by Wole Soyinka. Reproduced with permission of the Oxford University Press through PLSclear; **Unit 21** *Pygmalion* by George Bernard Shaw. 1912; **Unit 22** *The Merchant of Venice* by William Shakespeare; **Unit 23** extract from *The Dilemma of a Ghost* by Ama Ata Aidoo, © Pearson Education; **Unit 24** extract from *The Post Office* by Rabindranath Tagore, © The Macmillan Company 1914

Index